THE MYSTERY OF EXISTENCE

MILTON K. MUNITZ
New York University

The

Mystery of

Existence

AN ESSAY IN
PHILOSOPHICAL COSMOLOGY

APPLETON-CENTURY-CROFTS

Division of Meredith Publishing Company

NEW YORK

To
JUSTUS BUCHLER

PREFACE

LET US FORMULATE what the mystery of existence is, briefly, and for the moment, by means of the question "Why is there a world at all?" To clarify what it means to ask this sort of question, and to assess its philosophic significance, are the chief objectives of this book.

Part One, in what follows, is largely occupied in clearing the ground for the argument to be undertaken in the rest of the book, and in removing some obstacles in the way of a proper understanding of the scope of the inquiry. Parts Two, Three, and Four attempt to build up, step by step, the kinds of philosophic distinctions and arguments necessary to accomplish my principal task, namely, to show in what sense there is a genuine mystery of existence. While some sections traverse rather familiar ground, I felt it necessary for the sake of completeness to include them in the present account. Since I have addressed myself not only to students of philosophy, but to the general reader as well, not all parts of my argument will have the same interest or possible value. I have tried, however, to make the presentation as relatively self-contained and intelligible as possible, so that no special technical knowledge is presupposed. Also, here and there, the treatment of some topics ranges perhaps a bit more widely than is strictly necessary for my argument. It is hoped, however, that these sections will be found to be of sufficient intrinsic interest to merit the reader's attention.

It remains to express my grateful acknowledgment to those who have given me their assistance and support. I have benefited greatly by the detailed and searching criticisms of the manuscript made by a number of friends and colleagues, who read it in its entirety. These include Professors William Barrett and Raziel Abelson of New York University, Professor Justus Buchler of Columbia University, and Professor Richard Gale of the University of Pittsburgh. I wish to acknowledge, gratefully, the award of a fellowship from the John Simon Guggenheim Foundation in 1960-61, and an appointment as a Fulbright Research Scholar at Cambridge University for the same period. I am much indebted for the opportunities for study and writing these grants made possible. The Arts and Science Research Fund of New York University helped defray the cost of typing a draft of the manuscript; and I wish to thank, in this connection, Mr. Reed Straus for his secretarial assistance. I am indebted, finally, to my wife for her unfailing encouragement.

M.K.M.

CONTENTS

ix

PART FOUR

MYSTERY AND AGNOSTICISM

Part One

MYSTERIES, PROBLEMS, AND
UNANSWERABLE QUESTIONS

CHAPTER I

The Mystery of Existence

Statement of the Problem

PHILOSOPHY, or the love of wisdom, as Aristotle noted long ago, begins in wonder. "At first," he says, "men wondered about the more obvious problems that demanded explanation; gradually their inquiries spread farther afield, and they asked questions upon such larger topics as changes in the sun and moon and stars, and the origin of the world.[1]

Let us consider this last-mentioned topic, "the origin of the world." What kind of question does it raise? When the pre-Socratics asked this question—and it was their speculations that, apparently, Aristotle had in mind—they understood this to mean: "How did the world get to be the way it is at the present time? Through what processes of transformation and growth did it pass before it emerged as the ordered structure it is found to be now?" The entire subsequent history of science, including the recent development of scientific cosmology, may be thought of as continuing to ask (with some modifications, and along with a variety of other questions), roughly the same type of question initiated by the pre-Socratics. There has been, of course, a notable advance in the quality of the answers to which we, in our own day, can now turn. It would be naive to expect that the type of wonderment represented by scientific curiosity will someday find total satisfaction in the answers provided by a finished and per-

[1] Aristotle, *Metaphysics*, translated by J. Warrington, Everyman Library (London and New York, 1956), Book A, chapter 2.

fected science. Nevertheless, there cannot be any doubt of the enormous progress already made since the days of the pre-Socratics, or of the likely progress yet to come.

Meanwhile, there is another side to human wonderment, not considered by Aristotle, that finds expression in a different kind of question from that which he listed under the heading "the origin of the world" (as he understood this phrase). While one may continue to use even this same terminology to formulate this new question, it would no longer have the meaning previously mentioned. For, it would now be roughly equivalent to what is meant by speaking of "the mystery of existence." For those who are provoked by the mystery of existence, and so display another dimension of human wonderment, the root question is *why there should be a world at all*. To ask this latter type of question is not to ask a scientific question. If we are caught in the toils of this question, no amount of scientific explanation of how the world underwent various stages of development, on a cosmological or on a more restricted level, will serve, in any way, to allay the difficulty summed up by asking why there should even be a world in existence, whatever its stages of development or its patterns and qualities. It is with this side, or form, of human wonderment that the present book is concerned.

In asking the question I have labelled "the mystery of existence," we are at once struck by the differences from the type of question that the pre-Socratics first asked. Why is it that the scientific type of question is readily understandable, whereas it is by no means the case all would agree, in asking the type of question about the mystery of existence, we are asking something that is even meaningful? Why is it that whereas we can note steady progress in the development of our scientific understanding of the world, those who dwell on the mystery of existence are confined to reiterating the question, and cannot either claim any progress in its past study, or encourage us to believe that the prospects for answering it are likely to be better in the future, than they were when men first asked this question?

We are prompted, by these reflections, to ask whether the question about the mystery of existence illustrates what is sometimes the case with other "perennial" problems of philosophy.

May it not be that the asking of this question derives, at bottom, from certain confusions of thought, or from some radical misuse of language? Since the discussion of the mystery of existence does not depend on any settlement of an issue of fact, in the way ordinary scientific questions are commonly thought to be so dependent, should we not regard the mystery of existence as an intellectual knot into which we get ourselves in asking a meaningless, because unanswerable, question? We could then treat the mystery, not as a genuine intellectual problem, but as a puzzlement that needs disentangling through the patient analysis of language. If successful in such analysis, we should then find that the mental cramp will have disappeared—the question will have dissolved, and will no longer bother us.

In opposition to the foregoing suggestion, however, we need to consider the possible merits of another line of approach. Should we not say that while, admittedly, we are not dealing with a soluble problem, neither are we expressing something that is intellectually spurious and in need of being dissolved? May it not be that the mystery of existence is entirely genuine, that it is a *sui generis* question, and is neither a soluble scientific problem nor a dissoluble puzzle? Perhaps, then, the only way of dealing with it is to recognize it as an ineradicable feature of the human response to the world, and to understand it for what it is, rather than to seek to remove it, or to reduce it to something else? Instead of saying that the question expressing the mystery of existence is faulty or eliminable, because not a genuine problem, should we not declare that not all meaningful questions need be reducible to those that are answerable? Would not a more fruitful treatment of the question expressing the mystery of existence be found by undertaking a comparison of those respects in which it is similar to, and different from, other types of questions raised by the human mind? And might it not be found, through such an analysis, that it occupies a legitimate place in the manifold of the mind's question-raising propensities?

There is still another line of thought worth pursuing. We might ask whether the question "Why is there a world at all?" is indeed a universal question, the germs of which are to be found in all men, and, therefore, present to human consciousness in some degree, or form, throughout history, or whether, on the contrary, it is characteristic of only a very special and limited intellectual tradition in our own culture. Why is it that the Greeks, generally speaking, did not raise this question? May it not be that the question expressing the mystery of existence is linked with the creation myth of The Book of Genesis, and its subsequent elaboration by theology? Would, then, the mystery of existence be likely to occur to anyone not influenced by the entire body of doctrine of Hebraic-Christian theism, at the core of which is the belief in a creation *ex nihilo?* Should we not, therefore, treat the question "Why is there a world at all?" as an echo, ostensibly independent of the Hebraic-Christian tradition, as in fact originating primarily in that tradition?

On the other hand, if we say that the question expressing the mystery of existence is intimately related to the tradition of Hebraic-Christian theism, are we not overlooking, thereby, still another possibility? Should we not say, rather, that what is being expressed by the sense of the mystery of existence is independent of both the Greek and the Hebraic traditions? Why need we vacillate, or be under tension, between choosing either a "Greek" way of looking at the world, as something to be understood in itself, or a "Hebraic" way of looking at the world, as something made by a Power that transcends it? Both modes of thought are trying, each in its own way, to satisfy the human drive for rationality and intelligibility. Both operate with some form of a Principle of Sufficient Reason. Might we not say, instead, that the mystery of existence consists precisely in the fact that we do not know, nor do we have any reliable way of finding out, *whether* there is a reason for the existence of the world? If, however, we link a more acceptable treatment of the mystery of existence to a rejection of the presupposition that the demand for rationality *must* be satisfied by the very existence of the world, does this have any genuine philosophic merit? How could this view be developed, and by what arguments could it be supported?

As a final proposal, we need to consider whether use of the phrase "the mystery of existence" serves merely to express an emotional response to the awesome magnitude of the world.

People seem to vary in their capacity to make this response; some are more prone to it than others. In this case, are we not obliged to say that the phrase "the mystery of existence" does not have a genuine cognitive content at all?

These are some of the questions that need to be explored in any consideration of the theme summed up by the use of the phrase "the mystery of existence." As with other concepts that have philosophical interest, the essential task posed by the use of this phrase is primarily one of clarification. Such clarification can have, broadly speaking, two different types of outcome. In one, the concept, however meaningful it may appear at first glance, or by dint of repeated though uncritical usage, shows itself to be weak and indefensible. The concept and the position it sums up, therefore, presumably can be replaced by more adequate ones. Now, if this is the outcome of analysis, the process of philosophic discussion will have performed a valuable therapeutic service of exorcism. On the other hand, if the idea is at bottom sound and useful, analysis will have succeeded in giving us a firmer grip and deeper understanding of its conceptual ramifications and involvements. In the latter case, the concept in question can now be used with greater confidence and sophistication. In either case, the gain is indisputable. Thus, with respect to the present theme, we need to ask: Does the phrase "the mystery of existence" cloak a changeling, or does it, when clarified and disentangled, point to something that has a legitimate place in our efforts at arriving at a sound philosophy?

Contemporary Viewpoints

In current philosophy, those who consider the question "Why is there a world at all?" (or variants of this, such as "Why is there something, rather than nothing?") belong, generally speaking, to one or another of three groups.

(1) Some reject, outright, both the question and any attempt to find an "answer" to it, on the ground that the very asking of the question is itself a mistake and philosophically vacuous. Within this group are to be found those who appeal to some form of positivist or empiricist philosophy, as well as many who would be called "pragmatists" or "naturalists."

In an age such as ours, when science provides the unexcelled and acknowledged standard for achieving intellectual and technical control over Nature, it is readily understandable that many persons should hold the view that any reference to mystery smacks of obscurantism. Talk about "the mystery of existence," it is held, either tends to denigrate the powers of reason to exploit the sources of intelligibility *in* the world, or else it invites a non-rational and, therefore, irresponsible leap *beyond* the world. For those conscious of the former of these dangers, acknowledgement of mystery marks the abandonment of confidence in man's rational capacities, and a surrender of the belief in the world as an intelligible domain awaiting men's endless explorative probings. Representative of this viewpoint is the claim made by Moritz Schlick that "in principle there are no limits to our knowledge. The boundaries which must be acknowledged are of an empirical nature and therefore never ultimate; they can be pushed back further and further; there is no unfathomable mystery in the world."[2]

Those conscious of the other form of danger bound up with talk of "mystery" are of the opinion that this way of thinking induces an irresistible drive to transcend the world, and to account for the world's character and existence by reference to a God whose nature cannot be established or known in any genuinely rational way. Since this outcome represents a breakdown of thought, the source of this breakdown must be traced to the asking of a faulty and illegitimate question. This latter viewpoint has been summed up as follows:

> That anything exists at all seems a problem, in itself puzzling. There might have been nothing. Why should there be anything? There must always have been moods when people thought like this and wondered, when they stared at the mere fact of existence, as at a mystery requiring an explanation. If you think of the fact of existence itself as a mystery, then you will soon find yourself looking for an explanation of the universe outside of the universe itself; in other words, you will look for a transcendental explanation—for something beyond all existence which explains why any-

[2] M. Schlick, "Meaning and Verification," *The Philosophical Review*, 45 (1936), p. 352.

thing at all exists. Immanuel Kant gave reasons why it must be a mistake to look for something beyond, which would explain the the fact of existence.[3]

Not only the positivist or the neo-Kantian, but various other groups of contemporary thinkers, as well, would tend to reject the theme of "the mystery of existence" as a fruitful one for philosophy. The question is one that most naturalists, linguistic analysts, or empirically oriented thinkers have shunned. Insofar as they are at all concerned with ontological questions, these philosophers undertake to clarify such basic concepts as "time," "individual," "cause," "mind," and the like. But they do not find anything puzzling in the very existence of the world.

(2) Needless to say, there are many who remain unconvinced by the arguments of the positivist, neo-Kantian, naturalist, empiricist, or linguistic analyst. There have been several recent philosophic attempts at reviving the question classically posed by Leibniz in the form "Why is there something, rather than nothing?"[4] Those who find the question important and intriguing will be found to belong, for the most part, to one or another of two groups in contemporary thought.

One group comprises various types of theists, who use the concept of the mystery of existence as a stepping-stone to God. Belief in God serves to answer the question, or solve the mystery of the existence of the world. Jacques Maritain expresses the neo-Thomist strand of this position as follows:

> The Supreme "mystery" is the supernatural mystery which is the object of faith and theology. It is concerned with the Godhead Itself, the interior life of God, to which our intellect cannot rise by its unaided natural powers. But philosophy and science also are concerned with mystery, another mystery, the mystery of nature and the mystery of being. A philosophy unaware of mystery would not be a philosophy.[5]

The other group of writers who find the theme of the mystery of existence central, includes various "atheistic existentialists."

[3] S. Hampshire, "Metaphysical Systems" in *The Nature of Metaphysics*, edited by D. F. Pears (London, 1957), p. 23.

[4] G. Leibniz, *Principles of Nature and Grace*, 7.

[5] J. Maritain, *A Preface to Metaphysics* (New York, 1958), p. 5.

Prominent among these is Heidegger. For these philosophers, the very asking of the question is an important step in the search for metaphysical wisdom. Unfortunately, Heidegger's own treatment (as the chief example of this approach) takes the form of a reiterated insistence that this question is first in rank for us "because it is the most far-reaching, second, because it is the deepest, and finally because it is the most fundamental of all questions."[6] Absent from his discussion, however, is any clear analysis of what the question means. It is the need for such analysis, nevertheless, that must be met if the question is to be taken seriously.

(3) There are some philosophers, finally, who are uncommitted with respect to this question, though largely dissatisfied with the treatment given by the first two groups of writers. Within this category are to be found some who take their point of departure from the outlook and use of techniques associated with contemporary linguistic philosophy. J. J. C. Smart belongs to this group, and speaks for many, I suspect, when he writes:

> That anything should exist at all does seem to me a matter for the deepest awe. But whether other people feel this sort of awe, and whether they or I ought to is another question. I think we ought to. If so, the question arises: If 'Why should anything exist at all?' cannot be interpreted after the manner of the cosmological argument, that is, as an absurd request for the nonsensical postulation of a logically necessary being, what sort of question is it? What sort of question is this question, 'Why should anything exist at all?' All I can say is, that I do not yet know.[7]

The Program of the Present Work

The following pages represent a modest effort at satisfying this need for clarification. I propose to analyze the concept of the mystery of existence and thereby provide, among other things, what those who belong to the third group of writers, distinguished above, are looking for. As contrasted with the position of the first group, I shall argue that the concept of the mystery of existence does have a distinctive and important meaning. To the

---

[6] M. Heidegger, *An Introduction to Metaphysics,* translated by R. Mannheim (New Haven, 1959), p. 2.

[7] J. J. C. Smart, "The Existence of God" in A. Flew and A. McIntyre (editors), *New Essays in Philosophical Theology* (London, 1955), p. 46.

proposal that we reduce all alleged mysteries to problems, so that they can in principle be solved by science, I should reply by saying that this will not work for the question expressing the mystery of existence. It is this version of a naturalistic philosophy that I wish to challenge. I believe it fails on the ground of excess. While it is a justifiable goal to eliminate mystery-mongering where this can be done, and to replace it by the use of intelligence and a general reliance on the methods of science, I should maintain that the methods of science are incapable of being universalized to deal with all questions. The one type of question it cannot deal with at all, is precisely that which is conveyed by our statement of the mystery of existence.

At the same time, I should also want to differentiate my position from that of the theists, in the second of the above groups. I should agree that the sense of the mystery of existence is an important starting-point for philosophical inquiry. But I should reject the attempt to remove the mystery by trying to answer it. For the explanation in terms of a Creator is more difficult to accept than an admission of failure in trying to solve the mystery of existence.

I shall argue, accordingly, for the view that the mystery of existence has to be recognized for what it is. It is neither a problem nor a puzzle. It is meaningful as a philosophical question, though not as a scientific one. As a philosophical question, however, it is not capable of being removed, as is the case with some others, by being shown to stem from some radical confusion of thought or from some misuse of language. It persists because it is *sui generis*. It must be accepted for what it is, as an ineradicable feature of our human response to the world. To want to solve the mystery— this is the normal hope, and the inevitable mistake. That it cannot be solved, that indeed this is the very meaning and irremovable character of the mystery, is what the ensuing discussion will seek to establish.

In this sense alone, the analysis removes the puzzle and "dissolves the cramp" that comes upon us when we raise this question. But it is important to distinguish the sense of confusion that arises from not knowing how to treat the question, on the one hand, and, on the other, the feeling of frustration that is an essential and ineradicable component of the sense of mystery when the latter has been properly isolated and correctly identified for what it is. The latter feeling must always remain as long as we are at all sensitive to the mystery of existence; the mystery is never dispelled, and expressions of this mystery can only succeed in stating our feelings of frustration and awe. To have properly cornered and identified this matter, is itself the outcome of a philosophical analysis, and has, as its result, the dissolving of a puzzle. The puzzle is the statement, on the one hand, of the apparently sound claim that all our questions should be either soluble problems or dissoluble puzzles, and, on the other, the persistence of the question "Why is there a world at all?" in the face of all efforts to dispel it, and transform it away as either a badly conceived problem or a simple intellectual muddle. The question is recalcitrant simply because it points to a mystery, and is neither a soluble problem nor a dissoluble puzzle.

In saying there is a distinctive mystery in the existence of the world, I do not wish this to be understood as claiming that the awareness of this mystery requires a special form of mystical insight, and, therefore, that it cannot be adequately conveyed in language. The mystery of existence is not something that requires an appropriate silence on our part, on the ground that we are, supposedly, unable to say in what the mystery consists. On the contrary, it seems to me, one *can* state the basic character of the mystery of existence. And having done this, we are not called upon, further, to exercise a special faculty or mode of cognitive awareness to gain some deeper, or more hidden, insight into that mystery. The concept of mystery, to be developed here, has no connection whatever with mysticism.

In explicating the idea of the mystery of existence, I shall adopt the working hypothesis that this idea contains the following main elements:

(1) the awareness that the world exists.

(2) the asking of the question "Is there a reason-for-the-existence-of-the-world?"

(3) the reasoned conviction that the preceding question, though meaningful, has neither been satisfactorily answered by any known rational method, nor can be. This conviction amounts to

the realization that the existence of the world is incomprehensible, and cannot be adequately explained in any way.

(4) the feelings of astonishment, awe, and perplexity that arise from, and accompany the awareness of the incomprehensibility of the world's existence. These feelings persist and cannot be removed.

To assess the soundness of this way of analyzing the idea of the mystery of existence, it will be necessary to examine these several components, and to consider the arguments that may be raised in connection with their proper formulation. It is only insofar as the view, thus laid bare, can be defended against attack, that it can be said the idea of the mystery of existence ought to be retained and incorporated in any sound philosophy.

Part Two (Chapters IV and V) will be devoted to the analysis of (1)—to the analysis, that is, of our awareness that the world exists, as summed up by the statement "The world exists." As for (2), I shall consider, throughout this book, a variety of ways of expressing, by means of a question, the mystery of existence. These include: "Why is there something, rather than nothing?", "Why does the world exist?", "Is there a reason for the world's existence?", and, finally, "Is there a reason-for-the-world's-existence?" In Chapter III (pages 45-47), I consider the first of these formulations ("Why is there something, rather than nothing?"). Part Three (Chapters VI, VII, VIII, and IX) deals with various ways of replying to the question "Why does the world exist?". In Part Four, I examine the two remaining formulations ("Is there a reason for the world's existence?", and "Is there a reason-for-the-world's-existence?"), and show the role they play in expressing the mystery of existence. In Chapter XI (pages 211-219), I give my reasons for selecting the question "Is there a reason-for-the-world's-existence?" to express that which is unanswerable about the mystery of existence. The arguments to uphold (3) above, that is, to support the claim that there are no rational answers possible to the question just mentioned, are explored in Chapter XII. Finally, item (4) in the list (the factor of feelings of awe, astonishment, and perplexity that belong to the sense of mystery), is touched on at various places throughout the book, for example, in Chapters III, VIII, and XIII.

CHAPTER II

The Meanings of "Mystery"

BEFORE TURNING to the fulfillment of the tasks indicated at the end of the preceding chapter, I shall undertake, in the present chapter, an analysis of the uses of the term "mystery." Although it does not suffice for the analysis of the expression "the mystery of existence," it is, nevertheless, helpful to consider something of the way in which the term "mystery," when taken by itself, is used in ordinary language, as well as the meanings it has when used to refer to certain historical practices and doctrines. For we should then be in a better position to appreciate the sense which the term "mystery" has in the phrase "the mystery of existence."

Ordinary Usages

One of the chief uses of the term "mystery" in ordinary language, is to stand for what is taken to be *inexplicable*. We use the term most often to represent that which is unexplained, though not as excluding the possibility that a solution might be found. In other cases, the term "mystery" may be reserved for what is thought to be beyond human comprehension altogether. In its generalized and popular meaning, we frequently use the term "mystery" to indicate the fact that there is some item of information which, being unavailable, shields us from knowing something we should like to know. In this sense, a mystery is any unanswered question; and the question may be formulated not simply by the use of the term "Why," but by means of other interrogatives, such as "Which," "Who," "When," and so on.

According to this use, we speak of "the mystery" of what causes something to happen, for which some persons, though not necessarily all, do not have an answer. For example: "I've searched to see what causes the squeak in my automobile, but it's still a mystery to me." Or, an insurance policy may refer to "the mysterious disappearance" of an object as the ground for making a claim. Or, again, in mystery-stories, the reader is kept in suspense until the detective makes everything clear. When we do not have access to certain areas, for example, we may speak of what lies in those areas as a matter of mystery: "When China finally conquered Mongolia in 1691, she locked it up and closed the frontiers to foreigners. In the long intervening centuries, Mongolia became a land of mystery." To one uninstructed in Go, that game is a mystery; the spectator does not understand the moves made by the players, or what they are trying to accomplish. We thus sometimes speak of a mystery where the mystery exists for some people, but not for all: the automobile mechanic may not consider the body-squeak a mystery; the Go players know what they're doing; those in Mongolia do not consider their land, a land of mystery.

In other cases, we use the term "mystery" to designate an unanswered question for *anybody* at a given time. Thus, at one stage of scientific inquiry, there are (or were) many "mysteries," in the sense of unanswered questions, for which even the experts are (or were) at a loss to provide satisfactory answers. For example, "What is the surface of Venus like?", or, "What causes multiple sclerosis?" One group of meanings of the term "mystery," as used colloquially and informally, then, as in the foregoing examples, has to do with that which is unexplained, lacking in relevant information or comprehension, for some or all individuals who are interested in having such information or understanding.

A second meaning of the term "mystery" appears in those cases in which we say that someone *keeps* something a mystery, in the sense of keeping something *secret*. In this connection, for example, one might refer to "trade-mysteries," meaning thereby, the particular techniques by which something is accomplished. For example, the magician guards the mystery how he made it appear that he sawed the woman in half. Or, the chef keeps it a mystery how he prepared the sauce.

The foregoing uses of the term "mystery," in popular speech, are themselves best understood against a wider historical background in which earlier usages of the term had a more technical and sharply defined set of meanings. When looked at historically, the word "mystery" is connected with two principal contexts of use: (1) as a name for certain secret rites, and (2) as a term referring to supernaturally revealed truths, essentially unintelligible to human intellect. Having surveyed these, we shall then consider to what extent, if any, any of these ordinary or technical meanings of the term are relevant to "the mystery of existence."

Secret Rites: Eleusinian Mysteries

The term "mysteries," as used by historians and anthropologists, denotes a type of cultural phenomenon found in various primitive societies, as well as among the peoples of ancient Greece, Anatolia, Syria, Mesopotamia, and Egypt. This consists in certain practices associated with annual or periodic ceremonies of initiation. These ceremonies were conducted in a general setting of great solemnity and secrecy. Already in the fifth century B.C., Herodotus, for example, had used the term "mysteries" in this broad sense to include the secret cults of Egypt as well as those more familiar from Greek history.[1]

The specific cult built around the festivals known as *Mysteria* in ancient Greece, serves as a prototype for the rest, and is, in fact, the source from which the term "mysteries" is derived. Later, the term was extended to other, similar ceremonial cults of initiation. The term *Mysteria* was the name given to certain festivals in ancient Athens associated with the Goddesses Persephone and Demeter. The *Greater Mysteria* were celebrated at Eleusis in the autumn, the *Lesser Mysteria* were conducted in the spring at Agrae (both towns being within relatively short distances of Athens). The collective name *Mysteria* refers to the festivals performed at these specific times of the calendar, and at these particular places. The chief benefit that came to the initiate in the rites that were an

---

[1] Herodotus, *The Persian Wars*, II, 171; cf. *The Mysteries*, papers from the Eranos Yearbooks, Bollingen Series (New York, 1955); M. Eliade, *Myths, Dreams, and Mysteries* (London, 1960), chapter 8.

essential part of these festivals, was the hope of securing to himself a happier lot after death.[2]

But from what does the term *Mysteria* itself derive? Whereas the goddesses Demeter and Persephone were the chief divinities involved, the festivals were not named after them, but after the human participants in the initiatory ceremonies. The human participants were the *mystai*, individuals undergoing the initiation ceremonies. They were enforced by vows of secrecy not to disclose the contents of the rites. The term *mystes* derives from the Greek verb *mouein* (μνεῖν), meaning "to initiate," and this, in turn, is derived from the verb *muein* (μύειν), "to close the eyes or mouth." The latter term has a double appropriateness in this context; first, because at a crucial stage in the ceremonies, the initiate was asked to close his eyes, so that upon opening them he might experience the "revelation" or display of the sacred objects that were shown to him in the bright light that accompanied the final, culminating stage of the ceremony. Secondly, the closing of the initiate's eyes represents a going into darkness, just as was his being led, at one stage of the ceremonies, through cavernous, underground passages. Also, of course, the closing of the mouth is appropriately descriptive of the fact that the initiate was obliged to hold in secret, and was not, under any circumstances, to disclose the contents of what he had seen.[3]

Such details as are known of the contents of the Eleusinian rites are few. It is known, for example, that there were several degrees of initiation, the highest being known as *epopteia*, a ceremony held a year after the initiates had attended the Greater Mysteries. The ceremony of the main initiation contained three elements. These were, first, *dromena:* enacted pageants, dramas, or plays. These

---

[2] "Happy is he among men upon Earth who has seen these mysteries; but he who is uninitiate and who has no part in them, never has lot of like good things once he is dead, down in the darkness and gloom." Homer, *Hymn to Demeter*, 480 ff.

[3] One recent authority comments: "It is amazing indeed that the basic and important substance of the secret rites was never disclosed, when these mysteries were held at Eleusis annually for some two thousand years, when a multitude of people from all over the civilized world was initiated, and when their content was transmitted orally from Hierophant to Hierophant over so many generations." G. Mylonas, *Eleusis and the Eleusinian Mysteries* (Princeton, 1961), p. 226.

undoubtedly consisted in representations of the wanderings of Demeter, the search for her lost daughter, and their final reunion. Secondly, there were *legomena:* the words spoken to accompany several stages of the rites. Finally, there were *deiknymena:* the sacred objects taken from the chests or containers in which they were kept, and displayed to the initiates. The High Priest at Eleusis was called the "Hierophant" because it was he who showed the *hiera,* or sacred objects, to the initiates. What the sacred objects were, has been a matter of conjecture, some believing that it was an ear of corn, others, various sexual symbols—the phallus or the womb. Whether these objects were actually handled or merely looked at, is, of course, completely unknown. In any case, what is of primary importance for our present interest, is that the whole ceremony, including its various parts or stages, were matters about which the participants kept a vow of secrecy, not reporting, divulging, or showing what they had seen, done, or handled. (The celebrations that formed part of the rites of the *Mysteria* were not all held in secret; some were public, and were held in the open air, so that they could be observed both by the initiated and the un-initiated. These public parts were, for example, the various processions, the taking of the *hiera* or sacred objects from Eleusis to Athens, the public proclamations announcing the ceremonies, the descent to the sea for rites of purification, the sacrifice of pigs, and so on.)

An essential element of the mystery cults was the matter of *keeping* secret what the initiates had witnessed, rather than the having of an experience that *could not* be reported. To be sure, there may have been emotional experiences of an overpowering sort: Aristotle tells us that the *mystai* were not meant to learn anything, but to suffer an experience and to be moved. For all his emotional involvement, however, the fact remains that the initiate witnessed certain things, and it was the injunction against reporting anything of this, that is the essential ingredient (as far as our present analysis of the meaning of "mystery" is concerned) in this entire phenomenon.

It is clear that the sense of the term "mystery" we have been examining, has nothing to do with "the mystery of existence." There is, in the mystery-rites, no primary interest in the cosmic scene of all life. The kind of existence that these mysteries circle about, is human existence. And here, too, it is not a matter of raising certain speculative *questions*. It is rather a *doing* of what is necessary and effective: performing a magical act, participating in an appropriate rite, and, by mimetic means, becoming identified with the life of those divinities who symbolize and preside over all birth and regeneration in Nature. The mysteries are rituals to be shared in, and emotionally focussed in the responsive concentration of the initiate.

Plato's Use of Mystery-Terminology

A second major stage in the development of the concept of mystery is that in which mystery is associated, not with the performance of *ritual*, but with the adoption of certain items of *doctrine* of a metaphysical and theological sort. The magical interest in the renewal of life that the mystery-rites served, that of securing the salvation of the individual, is by no means lost even in this next stage. However, what now comes into prominence is the emphasis upon the acceptance of metaphysical beliefs whose truth is essentially mysterious, in the sense that their full meaning and warrant lie hidden from the understanding of men. This new concept of mystery is illustrated by the development of various doctrines in the Hebraic-Christian tradition.

Some features of that tradition were foreshadowed in a number of things that Plato says about the way in which the mind comes to know the Forms. Plato himself avoids any appeal to a supernatural revelation; unaided reason, for him, is the sole source or method by which man can come to have knowledge and wisdom. Nevertheless, Plato's use of the language of mystery, taken from the context of the mystery-rites, prepares the way for the use of similar language by the later religious tradition, in connection with its teachings on divine revelation. From an earlier emphasis on the performance of acts held in secret, we are now introduced by Plato to a conception of mystery having an essentially *cognitive* significance.

Just as other ancient philosophers, for example Diogenes and Heraclitus, turned with scorn upon the practices and beliefs of the mystery-religions, so, too, Plato expresses the same general contempt for the magical superstitions inherent in these rites. Nevertheless, Plato found the language and symbolism belonging to the process of initiation, congenial. Since he makes frequent use of myth and metaphor, Plato is able to turn the language of initiation into a means for conveying the basic convictions of his own philosophy.[4]

Plato uses the language of the mystery-rites to describe the intellectual experience of becoming aware of the Forms. The beholding of the Forms is an experience the soul enjoyed once, before its incarnation, and might enjoy again. Thus in the *Symposium*, what is described as the path to Beauty through an undergoing of "the lesser and greater mysteries of love," is, in the *Republic*, paralleled by the account of the stages of education, culminating in the vision of the Form of the Good, to which the study of Dialectic leads. And in the *Phaedrus*, Plato tells us:

> There was a time when with the rest of the happy band . . . we philosophers . . . beheld the beatific vision and were initiated into a mystery which may be truly called most blessed . . . which we beheld shining in pure light, pure ourselves and not yet enshrined in that living tomb which we carry about, now that we are imprisoned in the body, like an oyster in his shell.[5]

It is the memory of a perfect grasp of the Forms, while in a disembodied state, that the soul appeals to for its inspiration in trying to simulate that experience, here and now, in this world. When successful, the stages of intellectual initiation culminate in a vision of the Forms in their purity and clarity—particularly, in a grasping of the Form of the Good.

Participation in the life of philosophy and initiation into the realm of Forms, however, demand special training and preparation. Initiates into the intellectual life are required to have special intellectual qualifications. Unlike the mystery-rites, candidates for initiation could not be drawn, indiscriminately, from all segments of the population. The content of the revelation of "mysteries," not being sacred objects, pictorial representations, or carven images that can be beheld with ordinary eyesight, are matters of refined insight, trained understanding, and sophisticated intellectual vision.

---

[4] Cf. *Theaetetus*, 156 a; *Phaedrus*, 248-50; *Symposium*, 210-212; *Phaedo*, 67c.
[5] *Phaedrus*, 250.

Mystery and Theology; Philo Judaeus

The concept of mystery associated with the doctrines and practices of the Hebraic-Christian tradition is an enormously complex matter; it is no part of my present purpose to undertake any detailed review of its development. It is sufficient, however, to recall the central idea. The chief meaning of "mystery" that belongs to this tradition is bound up with the conception of God as the ultimate source of all being, the creator of the world and of man. God reveals something of his purposes in a sacred text whose study and interpretation is required of all the faithful. Unlike heathen mysteries, the sharing of mystery now requires acceptance of a revelation deriving from God. Also, unlike Plato's conception of mystery as involving philosophic understanding, mystery is now grounded in *faith*. Certain beliefs about God, the world, and man, are taken to be true, because they are revealed by God, not because they are arrived at by unaided human reason. These ideas are developed by Philo Judaeus of Alexandria and are subsequently elaborated and transformed by various Christian writers.[6]

Jews had a traditional abhorrence of idolatry and polytheism, and in line with this attitude, the practice of mystery-rites as they were known in Palestine (for example, the rites of Tammuz) or the extensive, widely-practiced mystery-rites of Greek religion in Hellenistic culture, came under their severe condemnation. Philo shares this traditional Jewish view of the nature of mysteries. Though Philo condemns the acceptance and practice of heathen mysteries, he, like Plato before him, nevertheless finds the language deriving from the mystery-cults a highly congenial and appropriate one for expressing his own religious convictions and metaphysical beliefs. Just as the translation of the Pentateuch into the Greek language resulted in the Septuagint, so Philo uses the language and thought of Greek religion and philosophy, in order to support the doctrines and practices of traditional Judaism. In the light of this aim, we are to understand his choice of the vocabulary of the mystery-religions as no more than a useful device.

[6] Materials for the present summary are to be found in H. A. Wolfson, *Philo* (Cambridge, Mass., 1947), 2 vols., and the same author's *The Philosophy of the Church Fathers* (Cambridge, Mass., 1956), vol. I.

Just as Plato had transformed the term "mystery" from one that referred simply to an initiation rite, into one that represented a mode of obtaining knowledge and insight, so too, Philo adapts the language of "mystery" to philosophic purposes. However, Philo, unlike Plato, does not use the language of "mystery" to describe what unaided reason can accomplish. On the contrary, mystery is a form of initiation into a body of knowledge to be obtained from study of the sacred text of the Old Testament. This text contains the revealed word of God, and is the chief evidence of the covenant into which the children of Israel entered with God. Whereas Plato does not speak of any supernatural Being or Divine Mind as deliberately holding *secrets* from man, it is precisely this sense of the term "mystery" which is crucial for Philo.

Moreover, Philo gives a new meaning to the idea of secrecy as compared to what it signified in earlier mystery-rites. In those rites, the secrets were kept by the *participants*, namely, the Hierophant and the initiate. These were human beings who, having seen, done, or displayed certain things, were prohibited by tradition and law from disclosing their contents. For Philo, however, the secrets are *kept by God himself*. They are not objects; rather, they are purposes and plans. God's plans are never divulged completely to any finite mind. In this sense, the secret is fully and eternally kept in the mind of God. Man, as a finite creature, could never aspire to know the full truth. However, God does divulge *something* of his plans. God is the principal Hierophant and also operates through subsidiary Hierophants, for example, Moses, Jeremiah, and other prophets. He conveys to the Israelites some hints of his purposes. This knowledge is contained in the revealed Law. What the text says, however—what its deeper and hidden meaning is—needs to be extracted and made more evident. And this calls for interpretation. Thus, the term "mystery" has a two-fold meaning in Philo—it signifies not only *a divine secret kept*, but also a *hidden meaning* to be disclosed after inquiry and suitable interpretation. What the mysteries of the Law are, consequently, needs to be developed by those properly equipped and trained. Philo, of course, as many others since, undertakes to make clear to us what that hidden meaning is.

Mystery in Christianity

The use of mystery-terminology is a characteristic and pervasive feature of the development of Christian thought and ritual, from its very beginnings up to the present time. It is, indeed, difficult to imagine how one might undertake to characterize the nature of Christian thought and ritual, unless one were able to fall back on the use of this terminology. Already in the New Testament, particularly in the Pauline Epistles, the use of mystery-terminology is a central and outstanding fact. The Church Fathers, among them Clement of Alexandria and Origen, make use of this terminology in their first efforts at constructing a system of consistent theological doctrine. Similarly, the writings of the Scholastics and their later followers, as well as many writers in the Protestant tradition down to the present time, find the concept of mystery (especially as bound up with the meaning of *revelation*) fundamental in their interpretation of the essence of the Christian religion.

A random selection of the phrases in which the term "mystery" is used in Christian literature displays at first, a bewildering variety of seemingly unrelated meanings. One reads of "the mystery of the Cross," "the mystery of Baptism," "the mystery of the Eucharist," "the mystery of the Trinity," "the mystery of the Incarnation," "the mystery of the Kingdom," and so on. Behind this apparent chaos of usages, however, there is a central and unifying meaning that can readily be extracted, and in terms of which this apparent chaos can be reduced to some order. The principal point is that *mysterion*, in the Christian sense, relates to a divine plan for human salvation. Once more, unlike the original sense of the term "mystery" deriving from the cultic practices of the mystery-religions, and unlike the Platonic adaptation that applies to a mode of knowledge to be achieved by the philosophically sophisticated rational mind, the Christian sense develops the meaning already present in Philo's adaptation of the same language. In Philo, the term "mystery" relates to the will and purpose of a transcendent creator who discloses something of that will and purpose in the revealed Law, to serve as a guide for man. In carrying forward this latter conception, the Christian sense of "mystery" introduces a further element not present in the thought of Philo. For the divine plan includes the saving of men's souls through the agency of Jesus. "Mystery" stands for the total drama of human redemption issuing from God and revealing itself, in its crucial phases, not simply through a revelation of words—the supplying of a law or a creed—but through a series of acts, chief of which is the death and resurrection of Christ. The plan of God becomes revealed through the person of Christ to all those who have faith in that revelation and come to accept its meaning and efficacy. The offering of divine love and the sharing in divinity are its rewards, both in this life and in the hereafter.

With these facts as a general background, we can now place, for example, "the mystery of Baptism" or "the mystery of the Eucharist" as ceremonial instruments through which the faithful come to share in this total drama of human redemption. One aspect of Christian mystery is bound up with the use of these sacraments, that which relates to the initiation of the individual into a transformed mode of existence. This sacramental side of Christianity may be regarded as a continuation, in principle, of the magical interest of the mystery-religions in securing to the individual a means for his rebirth or salvation through identification with divinity.

There is, however, another aspect to the concept of mystery in Christianity of equal importance to the sacramental; it has to do with the cognitive status of certain theological beliefs. In its efforts at constructing a general picture of the world, Christian theology, from the very beginning, relied heavily on the notion of mystery as revelation. It thereby can be distinguished from any purely rational exercise of thought. A mystery, in this special theological, doctrinal sense, is a belief whose truth is initially established by revelation. It is a truth that could not be arrived at by human reason alone, and is, therefore, ultimately unintelligible to human understanding. While all sorts of analogies or linkages with established systems of thought may be attempted in order to confer a certain amount of meaning on these truths of revelation, these efforts are ultimately unsuccessful. What is given to us by revelation remains, according to those who elaborated the system of Christian theology, strictly speaking, incomprehensible. That these revelations are true, cannot be denied, they would say, but what their full meaning is, eludes human competence.

There are three characteristic instances of such mysteries, that have come down to us from the earliest attempts by the Church Fathers to order Christian thought within a coherent theological system. These three mysteries, to be singled out for brief illustration here, concern "the mystery of the Generation," "the mystery of the Trinity," and "the mystery of Incarnation."[7]

The mystery of the Generation has to do with the relation between God and the heavenly or pre-existent Christ. According to the Jewish tradition, God is a creator, a cosmic artisan who creates a world out of nothing (and, according to Philo's version, creates a plan, logos, or wisdom as an incorporeal structure even before the latter is embodied in the materially created world). This view of God as creator is not wholly consistent with the view of God that emerges in the Christian tradition. For how can God, in his special relation to Christ, also be thought of as a *creator?* While wishing to dissociate itself from the pagan polytheism that took seriously (or half-seriously) the model, or analogy, of animal generation in constructing a theogony, Christianity needed to reconcile the combination of its own adherence to the image of a *father-son* relation, on the one hand, and the incorporation of a Jewish and Platonic reliance upon the image of God as an artisan or creator, on the other. When, in John, the pre-existent Christ is identified with Philo's conception of the pre-existent logos, it becomes necessary to think of the relation of this pre-existent logos to God, in wholly different terms from what was interpreted under the earlier model of "making" or "creation." The mystery of the Generation consists in the fact that, whereas all things are created by God, only Christ is begotten of God. The uniqueness of God's relation to Christ, as compared to the relation that God bears to the rest of his handiwork, makes of that relation a special mystery. Although various efforts are made by the Church Fathers to interpret this "fact," it remains, ultimately, recalcitrant.

The second mystery whose truth is grounded in revelation and

---

[7] Cf. H. A. Wolfson, *Philosophy of the Church Fathers*, Vol. I, pp. 387-493; R. Garrigou-Lagrange, *God, His Existence and His Nature* (St. Louis, 1934), Vol. II, pp. 170 ff.

incomprehensible to human reason is that of the Trinity. The problem is this. Jewish religion had insisted on, and retained throughout its history, a belief in the uniqueness of God. With the emergence of the Christian doctrine that, in addition to God (as conceived in the Jewish tradition), the pre-existent Christ and the Holy Spirit are themselves God, the problem arose how to reconcile the Christian belief in three Gods, with the inherited Jewish monotheistic belief. Once more, for all the skillful and ingenious efforts at trying to express the possibility of such tri-unity, the fact remains that belief in the Trinity is an unfathomable mystery, incomprehensible to human reason.

There is, finally, the mystery of the Incarnation. As in the two previous instances, the problem arises from trying to adapt and reconcile ingredients derived from New Testament revelation, Jewish antecedents, and Greek philosophy. The problem centers around the fact of the birth of Jesus—that Jesus became manifest in flesh. How can the pre-existent logos (now identified with the pre-existent Christ) take on the form and likeness of a man? The problem becomes acute for philosophic interpretation, for it consists in trying to understand a conjunction of two natures in one person: a thoroughly divine nature and a material, human one. Again, this problem is insoluble and remains, therefore, in the present technical sense, a mystery.

Colloquial Adaptations and Philosophic Uses

The term "mystery" as it has passed into ordinary language, represents a trivialization and transformation of the meanings which the term bore in traditional systems of theology. Cut off from its association with earlier theological meanings, the term has, nevertheless, continued to preserve, in ordinary discourse, two basic meanings that remind us of its earlier affiliations. The first is brought out when we use the term to refer to some *secret* kept by men from other men. The other meaning of "mystery" is that in which it is used, in a very general way, to refer to any matter for which we do not have any requisite knowledge or information, and more particularly, for something for which we do not have an *explanation*. Here, ordinary usage does not invariably carry the meaning that the unavailable knowledge is forever beyond the possibility of achievement. The term, rather, tends to be used loosely, both for a question whose answer is unknown, as well as for a question for which it is held an answer is altogether unattainable.

Clearly, the rehabilitation of the term as having a *philosophically warrantable use* in this last mentioned sense, namely, as standing for an *in-principle unanswerable question*, is one that needs to be critically supported by argument. It is this use of the term, as borrowed from colloquial and nontechnical usages, that occurs in the phrase "the mystery of existence." That there is a mystery of existence, in the sense of there being a question about existence that cannot in-principle be answered—because that question is incapable of yielding to a satisfactory method of solution by any rational means, *this* is what calls for detailed and critical examination.

Is there such a mystery? Once we surrender any commitment to having to accept some extra–rational revelation, what need is there to admit any element of mystery in our philosophic interpretation of the world? We shall have to face the challenge, in the first place, of those who argue that to speak of a mystery as an inherently unanswerable question, unanswerable by any rational method, is meaningless. This challenge will be taken up and discussed in Chapter III (pages 33-44). Having met this challenge, I shall then turn, beginning with Chapter IV, to an examination of the way in which the concept of mystery can be provided with a philosophically defensible meaning. I shall attempt to show why, without appealing to some antecedent source of revelation or faith, reason must admit to its own limitations; these consist in the fact that it is powerless to provide an answer to the question whether there is a reason-for-the-existence-of-the-world.[8]

"Problem" and "Mystery"; Marcel

Among those in contemporary thought who have urged the importance of the concept of mystery for philosophy, Gabriel Marcel occupies a central position. In his well-known essay "On the Ontological Mystery," and in his book *The Mystery of Being*,

---

[8] The justification for the use of this hyphenated expression, and an analysis of what it signifies, will be given in Chapter XI, pp. 211-219.

he develops the contrast between "problem" and "mystery," as he understands these terms, in a way that not only plays a major role in his own philosophy, but that has influenced others who find the distinction an illuminating one.[9] It might be thought, therefore, that since the view I am engaged in developing myself in this book also gives emphasis to the idea of mystery, it must be in evident sympathy with Marcel's position. This, however, would be incorrect. For the conception of mystery here being analyzed is at such variance with the sort of thing that Marcel and the other writers alluded to, undertake to defend, that it would be well, at the outset, to indicate the points of divergence.

The distinction that Marcel seeks to draw between "problem" and "mystery" is one that he arrives at in the course of giving an account of what he takes to be the status of modern man. His primary interest is, as he puts it, to give a global and intuitive characterization of what man has become in the modern world under the influence of science and technology, and what, as a result, in his opinion, has been lost in the process of this spread of the influence of science upon our culture and upon human experience. What has been lost, in Marcel's opinion, is a cultivation of what he calls "man's ontological need." It is a need that has become stifled and repressed in the engulfing onrush of modern civilization. To point to what this ontological need is, to what he thinks of as "the order" in which mystery makes its appearance, is then, one of the primary purposes of his analysis.

From a scientific point of view, according to Marcel, man, as any other natural phenomenon, becomes simply an object whose functions and interactions with his environment are carefully dissected, measured, and predicted. Man, in short, is treated as a mechanism with an intelligible structure. The individual man becomes depersonalized into a set of functions. Breakdowns in those functions are *problems* that call for dispassionate engineering-analysis. Such analysis has, as its goal, the restoring of smooth

---

[9] G. Marcel, *The Philosophy of Existence* (New York, 1949), *The Mystery of Being* (London, 1950); cf. J. Maritain, *A Preface to Metaphysics* (New York, 1939), First Lecture, section 2; A. M. Farrer, *The Glass of Vision* (Westminster, 1948), Chapters IV, V; E. L. Mascall, *Words and Images* (London, 1957), pp. 76-87; M. B. Foster, *Mystery and Philosophy* (London, 1957), pp. 18 ff.

functioning. To treat man—or any other natural occurrence—in this way, is to treat him as part of the order of the natural. This natural order Marcel also describes as "the order of first reflection." A problem, thus, is a question that arises with respect to the order of the natural in which the questioner, the scientist, must, first of all, keep his subject matter at a distance and treat it objectively. The interest of the investigator, the value he places on the solution, play no role in the statement of the problem or in the finding of a solution. The paradigm of the problem is the kind of question that could be solved, in principle, by a machine. And the inquirer himself, in his handling of a problem, need be no more, in fact, than an efficient machine. He is simply one object dealing with another object. Thus the engineer, physiologist, astronomer, or psychologist is each dealing with problems in a manner that involves the complete rejection and neglect of what Marcel cals "the ontological need."

But what is this ontological need? It is in the satisfaction of this need that Marcel identifies the coming-into prominence of a sense of mystery. It occurs as part of the exercise of what he calls "the order of second reflection." The ontological need is a need for being. Being, however, is something that cannot be adequately described as a natural order, an order of objects to be approached by dispassionate rational analysis. Being, in Marcel's treatment of it, is constituted of a center of value. It can only be approached and "understood" by a subject that is itself enmeshed and interacting with it in an order of appreciation, love, and fidelity. To satisfy an ontological need, therefore, is to find an appropriate target for awareness in something that could be a *presence*, a radiating source of concern and love, and to which we can respond in an appropriate way.

The prototype for this type of experience is found in the case of two individuals in love. For the lover to stand back, objectify, dissect, and understand love, is no longer to *be* in love. It is to treat the beloved as an object at a distance. To understand love on the first order of reflection, is to treat it as a problem. But to be in love, to participate in the experience, and to undergo the presence of the beloved, is of an altogether different order from the merely problematical and objective. It is to be in the presence of what Marcel calls "a mystery." When men treat one another as tools or objects, that is, when they regard the other person as an "it" rather than a "thou," there is, in Marcel's way of thinking, absence rather than presence; life is empty rather than full, the spirit of man is not engaged. It is only when men undergo the experience of love, fidelity, and "*disponibilité*" (being available as a person for another), that one can hope to escape the dehumanization of man that arises from the dominance of the scientific and problem-solving attitude.

Up to this point, we may claim to understand the distinction Marcel is driving at, without necessarily agreeing with the weight of disapproval he gives to the scientific attitude and to the influence of the scientific mentality upon modern culture. But why does Marcel refer to the kind of experience he calls "presence" by the use of the term "mystery"? Surely, the distinctions between objective understanding and undergoing, or between knowing that something is the case, on the one hand, and experiencing it directly in some non-conceptual way, on the other, are familiar enough. However, the way these distinctions are normally drawn do not involve the terms "problem" and "mystery." Why, in particular, does Marcel identify the second half of this set of contrasts by the use of the term "mystery"?

The answer to this question is readily available by considering the broader framework for Marcel's analysis of presence. For we can then see the hidden lines of connection between Marcel's thought and the traditional theological treatment of revelation. By making explicit these lines of connection, the reasons will appear why my own analysis of the mystery of existence, in this book, diverges from Marcel's account of "ontological mystery." The clue we are seeking is to be found in the fact that Marcel, despite his coming to Catholicism late in life, had been adumbrating, all along, a religious point of view. It eventually came to full flower, and found a suitable home in the religious doctrines to which he confessed his allegiance.

For, according to Marcel's account, presence, as the locus within which mystery is experienced, is at best only partially satisfied by human experiences of love, fidelity, and *disponibilité*, when these have as their targets other human beings. The ontological need for being is only partially satisfied in finite centers of response. According to Marcel, however, they cannot completely satisfy the hunger or ontological need that men have. That need can only be satisfied by turning to a Being who is infinite and un-conditioned, and who provides a source of love, hope, and faith that transcends all human limitations. It is this encounter with sanctity and divinity that constitutes total presence, and the true source of mystery. Accordingly, Marcel does not look for proofs of the existence of God after the manner of the Thomists. He finds it in the immediacy of revelation. Marcel's concept of "presence" is thus closely related to the traditional theological concept of revelation. His stress, however, is not upon truths re-vealed in some sacred text. It is, rather, an emphasis upon com-munion with Christ. It is in this communion and presence that man experiences a mystery that lends purpose and meaning to his own existence.

When we see Marcel's account of the distinction between "problem" and "mystery" in the light of this half-hidden religious orientation, we can understand why he should have chosen the term "mystery" to describe that type of experience which, for him, is already foreshadowed on the level of love of one person for another human being. For what he is describing by the use of the term "mystery," is not the counterpart of a problem, in the sense in which a problem poses a question. It is not a *question* at all. The contrast between "problem" and "mystery" is not a con-trast between two kinds of questions that the human mind can raise. It is a contrast between what can be expressed, on the one hand, as a question, and what, on the other, has the form of faith in divine or human presence.

Marcel, in discussing mystery, nowhere raises a question about the existence of the world. For him, the ontological mystery is not a cosmological mystery. Ontological mystery is always rooted in some person, whether human or divine. It has, as its locus, some center of value, affection, and concern. The world does not pro-voke mystery, since the world is not a person.

Marcel's account of mystery is thus best understood as an off-shoot of the traditional doctrine of revelation. His use of "mys-tery," accordingly, needs to be contrasted not only with a problem, but with the sense of mystery that I am, myself, in the present discussion, concerned to isolate, namely, as a special type of un-answerable question about the existence of the world.

This point is confirmed for us by the fact that those who have followed Marcel in his distinction between problem and mystery, view mystery as a form of revelation. They would agree with Marcel that the best way of appreciating mystery is in terms of a concept of divine presence, the revelation to man of the spirit of Christ with whom the individual experiencing the mystery is identified.

The notion of mystery, as it figures in the discussion of the mystery of existence, however, does not involve any type of revelation. It has nothing to do with the presence of a center of value, or a source of personal support and encouragement for the pursuit of value. It has nothing whatever to do with rescuing life from futility; nor does it involve falling back on centers of love, whether human or divine. The sense of mystery is brought into focus through the confrontation of the mind with the fact of the existence of the world about us. This confrontation takes the form of the mind's struggle with a *question*, namely, "Why does the world exist?" The mystery consists in the mind's inability to find an answer to that question.

CHAPTER III

Are There
Unanswerable Questions?

THE PRINCIPLE OF ANSWERABILITY

It will be said by many empirically oriented philosophers that the asking of a question such as "Why does the world exist?" is a good example of what they should identify as a wholly futile form of rhapsodical metaphysical discourse, and stands in need, therefore, of being eliminated from any serious philosophic discussion. The specific charge is that in setting up our question as admittedly unanswerable, we are using language in a way which, strictly speaking, has no literal cognitive meaning. Far from pointing to a difficulty that cannot be resolved because of the inherent limitations of the human intellect, our critic would say, we are, instead, using words with only the apparent form of a question, though actually not expressing a genuine question at all. At best, he would conclude, the "question" serves to convey certain feelings of astonishment and awe, but these feelings do not derive from, or accompany, a question that in itself can be understood literally as significant.

It is commonly recognized that the positivist "ban on metaphysics" has been seriously weakened, if not universally abandoned in recent years. Nevertheless, the charge of "meaninglessness" against our question that I have briefly summarized above, is one that not only old-guard positivists would defend, but finds many other adherents as well. The charge of "meaninglessness" is here being made on behalf of what I shall call the *Principle of*

Answerability. This principle expresses the requirement that every meaningful question must have a *possible* answer. It is a view about the nature of questions that was given much prominence in the philosophy of positivism and that continues to be widely held, even by those who no longer have any stake in a narrowly-conceived positivist philosophy. Here, then, is a familiar, though serious challenge that must be met at once, if our inquiry is to proceed at all. Unless this obstacle can be shown to be removable, our whole enterprise of trying to identify what can be meant by "the mystery of existence" collapses from lack of inner substance. Are there some genuine questions that are unanswerable?

Types of Unanswerability

I propose to distinguish three principal types of unanswerable questions: (1) these violating accepted rules of linguistic use, (2) those resting on false presuppositions, (3) those for which no answer is obtainable by a known rational method.

(1) Suppose someone with whom we were talking were to say suddenly: "Does it fly?", where nothing in the preceding discussion, either by way of explicit mention or tacit understanding, could be taken as antecedent for the "it" in the above question. We should undoubtedly be baffled by this use of language. If the person with whom we were talking were to persist in asking his question without clarifying what he means by "it," that is, by supplying a name or definite description which could be substituted for this pronoun, or by pointing to some object, we should say, rightly, his question is unanswerable. Although there has been an interrogatory expression used, it is a question we cannot answer, simply because we do not understand *what* is being asked. There has been a breakdown in communication because of a simple failure to adhere to certain rules connected with the proper use of the word "it."

Cases of wholly degenerate unanswerable questions occur where some term in the question is altogether lacking in any accepted or proposed rule of use that would specify its meaning. Thus, if one were to ask "Does a rahjumbix fly?", again the question would be unanswerable, since we do not know what a "rahjumbix" is. Such unanswerable questions, being genuinely meaningless,

need to be differentiated from those illustrated by "Does it fly?".
In the latter question, at least all the terms have standard uses,
though one of them ("it") is being misapplied in the present
instance, since the rule for its proper use is being violated.

Consider now the question "Does aeronautics fly?". Again
we should have to say this question is unanswerable, this time,
because the way in which the term "aeronautics" is usually understood, wholly excludes, or makes inappropriate, the term
"fly" as applied to what it designates. The term "aeronautics,"
we should say, refers to a science or branch of study that has
flying as its subject matter, but it, itself, is not the kind of thing
that can possibly fly. The rules of use connected with the terms
"fly" and "aeronautics" forbid our applying the term "fly" to
aeronautics. These rules no doubt reflect an accepted scheme
of knowledge and category distinctions. For example, on the basis
of our accepted category distinctions, we allow that we could ask:
"Does this machine fly?", just as we ask without any hesitancy,
"Can this (hurt) bird fly?". However, on the basis of these
same category distinctions, we do not have any rules of use that
permit us to speak of a study, or science, or indeed of any abstract
term, as something that can fly. It is this scheme of knowledge or
category distinctions, whether embedded in common sense, scientific knowledge, or in some explicitly elaborated philosophy, that
supplies the warrant for our rules of use.

We may distinguish, finally, another subtype of unanswerable
question under the general heading "violation of linguistic rules of
use," namely, one that is excessively vague, and where such vagueness arises from the failure to make explicit in the asking of the
question, some of the minimal, relevant conditions required for
any attempt to answer the question. As an example of this kind of
unanswerable question, consider the following: "When it is 2 A.M.
in New York, what time is it on the Moon?"[1] The question cannot be answered under the rules of the language of astronomical
time-keeping, until one first selects some particular place on the
Moon whose position can be specified by means of some common
framework of spatial coordinates in relation to that of New York.

---

[1] Cf. L. Wittgenstein, *Philosophical Investigations* (Oxford, 1953), I, sec.
350.

Further, it is necessary to be prepared to indicate the conventions or procedures by which time-assignments can be carried out to the selected place on the Moon, procedures and conventions also applicable to giving time-assignments to local events in New York, and that permit the comparison within a common time-map (or coordinate system) of events at these spatially separated places.

(2) Consider, now, the following question: "At what time did Lindbergh's plane, *The Spirit of St. Louis*, fly over the North Pole on its historic flight to Paris?" We should say this question, too, is unanswerable. This time, the unanswerability stems from the fact that there is a *false presupposition* in the asking of the question, such that no possibly true answer can be given. This is the familiar "fallacy of complex question." We should say that no answer can be given since Lindbergh's plane did not fly over the North Pole at all. Our original question, then, can be treated as made up of at least two questions: (1) "Did Lindbergh's plane fly over the North Pole?", and (2) "At what time did it fly over the North Pole?" The original question presupposes that the answer to the first question (1) is "yes." By showing this to be unwarranted (that is, the statement "Lindbergh's plane flew over the North Pole" is false), the rest of the question, stated in (2), *dissolves*. It no longer has any possible answer, since the presupposed basis of fact on which it rests, does not exist.

Let us call a question *properly framed*, if it meets the following conditions: (1) The entire interrogatory sentence does not violate any rules of use. (These rules are explicitly and rigorously stated for formal calculi, or highly systematized bodies of knowledge, less rigorously formulated for natural languages. Yet in the latter case, too, there is, normally, sufficient exactitude to permit the identification of a certain number of non-controversial cases of violation of these rules.) (2) The presuppositions on which a question rests can be accepted as true, or warrantable.

Each of the types of unanswerable question we have considered thus far, suffers from one or another fault in the framing of the question. It is the presence of these faults that prevents the question from having any possible answer. The proper way of handling these questions is not to try to find answers to them, but to point out the relevant flaw in the framing of the question. It is the flawed use of language, or the making of false presuppositions, that makes it futile to look for an answer. In this sense, therefore, the proper "answer" is not *an answer to the question*, so much as it is *a response or reply to the person* asking the question. This response takes the form of making the kind of critical remarks I, myself, have made in connection with the foregoing examples. Only properly-framed questions *might* be answered; but if a question is not properly-framed, it is unanswerable.

(3) I come, now, to a third type of unanswerable question which, though properly-framed, is unanswerable, because there is *no known rational method* by which it is possible to reach an answer.[2] It is against the very meaningfulness of this type of unanswerable question that the positivist argued, and against which all those who share an adherence to the Principle of Answerability would protest. We must, therefore, turn to consider these objections. The matter is of central importance for our present theme, since, if we can speak at all of there being a mystery of existence, it will be as an example of an unanswerable question of this type.

The Positivist Criterion of Verifiability

The view that a question to be meaningful must be answerable *in principle*, was formulated as a central thesis in Wittgenstein's early writings. In the *Tractatus* he wrote: "For an answer which cannot be expressed the question too cannot be expressed. *The riddle* does not exist. If a question can be put at all, then it *can* also be answered."[3] This thesis subsequently received elaborate defense in the writings of other positivists, particularly in Schlick's essays "Meaning and Verification" and "Unanswerable Questions."[4] Schlick's views on the meaningfulness of *questions* is guided by his analysis of what constitutes the criterion for determining the meaningfulness of *assertions* or *declarative sentences*.

[2] An analysis of the term "rational method" will be given below, in Chapter X, pp. 189-193.
[3] L. Wittgenstein, *Tractatus Logico-Philosophicus* (London, 1922), 6.5.
[4] M. Schlick, *Gesammelte Aufsatze*, (Vienna, 1938); reprinted in W. Barrett and H. Aiken, *Philosophy in the Twentieth Century*, (New York, 1962), Vol. II, pp. 23-51.

Schlick argues that whenever there is any question raised about the meaning of a declarative sentence or assertion, the only way of removing the doubt is to specify the circumstances under which we could go about determining the truth or falsity of that sentence. To clarify the meaning of a sentence, then, is not to restate the sentence in slightly different words; it is, rather, to specify the rules in accordance with which we use the various terms or words in the sentence. To state those rules is to state what, in effect, would be the kinds of situations, or circumstances, that would have to be identified in order for us to be able to say that the sentence, as a whole, is true or false. To specify the meaning of a sentence is thus not to say, in fact, that it *is* true, or that it *is* false, since meaningfulness is a prior condition for truth or falsity, and relates to the *logical possibility* of its being either true or false.

The requirement that a meaningful sentence must be capable of verification, constitutes the *Principle of Verifiability*. It is this criterion that determines whether or not a sentence is meaningful. For Schlick, the reasons for setting up the Principle of Verifiability, so that it can be applied to assertions, are precisely the same ones that need to be considered in determining whether an interrogatory expression formulates a genuine question or not. The theory of the meaningfulness of *assertions*, as summed up by the Principle of Verifiability, is extended without modification to the analysis of *questions*. For, just as not all combinations of words that have the apparent grammatical form of an assertion are, in fact, genuine assertions, so, not all interrogatory forms of expression necessarily express genuine questions. Interrogatory expressions may fail of interrogatory meaningfulness, just as declarative combinations of words may fail of assertion-meaningfulness. The importance of this analysis is best seen in connection with the question whether there are unanswerable questions.

Schlick, in treating this theme, insists that we cannot answer this question by a simple "yes" or "no." He suggests that we make a distinction between different senses of the word "impossibility," that would clarify what is meant by saying it is impossible to find an answer to some particular question. There may be certain questions that are indeed unanswerable, but only because one cannot find an answer to them for practical or technical reasons.

There are, admittedly, such technically, or practically, unanswerable questions. These are of a kind, however, where the unanswerability can be traced to some deficiency in human knowledge, or limitation in technical competence. Schlick illustrates unanswerable questions of this type, by the following: "What did Plato do at eight o'clock in the morning of his fiftieth birthday?"; "How much did Homer weigh when he wrote the first line of the Iliad?"; "Is there a piece of silver to be found on the other side of the Moon three inches long and shaped like a fish?"[5] Whether or not these questions will ever be answered, will be determined solely by the availability of the evidence, or the equipment, sufficient to provide answers. But this availability is not a matter of principle. It is a matter of the accidents of human existence and experience. Such questions are not insoluble in principle, or absolutely insoluble. While we may never know, in fact, the answers to these questions, they are not meaningless questions. The impossibility that underlies their unanswerability is of an empirical or technical sort, not of a logical sort. Indeed, what may be assigned to the category of unanswerable questions at one time, because of technical or empirical limitations, may be removed from that category altogether, at a later time, and be answered, when the conditions or instruments become available for providing the answer.

But what about those questions that are absolutely insoluble, or insoluble in principle, and such that, no matter what the advances in human experience and technical competence, men will never be able to discover their answers? Schlick characterizes a question as being "absolutely insoluble" when it is logically impossible to find an answer. By "logical impossibility" he means the failure or inability to provide a description of the *method* to be used in finding an answer to the question. For Schlick, however, this impossibility is tantamount to saying that the question itself has no meaning. For every meaningful question has connected with it a method of finding answers. And an answer, moreover, being an assertion, must itself be meaningful, that is to say, be either true or false. It follows that an interrogatory

[5] M. Schlick, "Unanswerable Questions?" (in Barrett and Aiken, *loc. cit.,* p. 24).

expression that purports to state an in-principle unanswerable question, fails to state a genuine question. It lacks meaningfulness. Rather than confess a human *ignorabimus*, a fateful inability of men to find an answer to their questions, we ought to treat all such questions as "nonsensical series of words with a question mark after them. As it is logically impossible to give an answer where there is no question, this cannot be a cause of wonder, dissatisfaction or despair."[6]

Schlick argues that, whereas all questions of a genuine scientific sort satisfy the requirement of being answerable in principle, those questions commonly called "metaphysical" (unless they actually cloak scientific ones) are, in fact, meaningless because insoluble in principle. For him, accordingly, to ask, for example, "Can we know the Absolute?" is as meaningless as to ask, "How much does philosophy weigh?" Similarly to speak of a "Riddle of the Universe" or to despair of such problems as the "cognition of things in themselves," is to be concerned with meaningless, because unanswerable, questions. The proper treatment for these questions is to show them to be nonsensical, and, hence, to eliminate them altogether. The questions that can be properly put to the human mind are, in principle, answerable; it is for this reason, he maintains, there are no limits to human knowledge, and there is no unfathomable mystery in the world.

The set of conditions which Schlick and his followers offer as a criterion for the meaningfulness of *assertions*, has come to be known as *The Principle of Verifiability*. As far as I know, there is no similar locution to identify the parallel criterion for the meaningfulness of *questions*. I propose, as a suitable designation, *The Principle of Answerability*. This principle names the criterion to be used for determining whether a question is meaningful. The criterion is summed up by two conditions: (1) It must be possible to specify the methods by which an answer can be found to a proposed question, and (2) given a proposed answer to a question, it should be possible to determine, in principle, whether the statement is true or false.

What we have now to consider is whether, or to what extent, *The Principle of Answerability* is an acceptable principle for

[6] M. Schlick, *loc. cit.*, (Barrett and Aiken, p. 26).

determining the meaningfulness of all questions, and the bearing this has on the question used to express the mystery of the existence of the world.

The Irrelevancy of the Positivist Criterion to the Mystery of Existence

There is a major objection to the attempt of positivism to find a *general* criterion for the meaningfulness of questions in terms of *The Principle of Answerability*. I shall argue that, given this objection as sound, it follows that *The Principle of Answerability* in no way challenges the meaningfulness of the question "Why does the world exist?" or closely related ones. The objection is this: at best the criterion consisting of *The Principle of Answerability* accomplishes the formulation of a *definition* of a scientific (or, more generally, an empirical) question, but nothing more. Science, in particular, is an activity of raising questions of various kinds for which, it is hoped, answers may be found. It is essentially a method for appraising answers offered to its questions. To say a question is asked for which there is no hope of finding an answer, or for which there is no way of judging the adequacy of any proposed or possible answers, is tantamount to admitting that it is not the kind of question in which a scientist is interested. In short, a question to be *called* "scientific" *must be* answerable—which is not to say, of course, that it *will* be answered. The method of empirical science (however the details of this method may be characterized by some particular philosophy of science) offers a set of criteria for the appraisal of statements that might serve as possible answers to scientific questions. The method of science is a set of *decision-procedures* for the evaluation of answers proposed to scientific questions. For example, consider typical scientific inquiries involved in: (1) giving descriptions of actually observed individual events, or reports of the outcome of particular experiments; (2) finding law-statements to sum up the form of observed regularities; and (3) finding theories to systematically relate, and explain, law-statements. Insofar as the terms "true" and "false" (with suitable qualifications appropriate to each type) can be predicated of each of the above kinds of statements, the method of science provides a set of operative rules for judging proposed answers to its inquiries, and reaching a decision as to their truth or falsity. A scientific question is a question that is answerable by the method of science. Clearly, what has been accomplished by this analysis is to give a definition of what we shall understand by a scientific question. Yet this definition cannot rule out the possibility of asking other types of meaningful questions.

Just as *The Principle of Verifiability* only serves, at best, to indicate, in a general way, the conditions to be met in expressing an empirical sentence, while leaving other types of sentence quite untouched, so *The Principle of Answerability* that purports to distinguish, in some absolute way, meaningful questions from meaningless ones, at best only serves to identify the requirements for a scientific or, more generally, an empirical question. If a properly framed interrogatory expression does not state a question to which an answer may be found, we should say it does not state a scientific, or empirical, question, not that it does not state a question *at all*. For the matter is still open to consideration whether there are genuine interrogatory expressions of a kind that, though they cannot receive any scientific answer, indeed, any answer at all, are, nevertheless, perfectly genuine questions. That there are questions of this sort, and, in particular, that the question expressing the mystery of existence is such a question, is, of course, what is here being argued.

Admittedly, this question is not a scientific question. Indeed, it cannot be a scientific question because it *is* unanswerable. Despite the fact that it is unanswerable, however, it is not meaningless. The fact that it does not fulfill the requirements of being a meaningful scientific question, simply warns us that it is not to be included among the kinds of questions to be found in a scientific discourse. From the fact that we do not find this question discussed in science, it does not follow, however, that it cannot be appropriately discussed in philosophy. On the contrary, it *is* appropriate for philosophy to investigate this question without having the road blocked to its inquiry, at the very outset, by the imposition of a criterion relevant to science. This does not, by itself, of course, insure that the question "Why does the world exist?" (or closely related ones) can be given, on purely philosophic grounds, a satisfactorily clear meaning. But, at least, it leaves the matter open for further investigation.

Emotive Meaning and Cognitive Meaning

There is one further matter to be discussed in this connection. It is sometimes said, in defense of the positivist view, that we need to distinguish *cognitive meaning* from *emotive meaning*. While metaphysical statements or questions may have emotive meaning, it would be said, they do not have cognitive meaning.

I should grant, by way of reply, that if "cognitive" means "that which can be treated by the method of science" or, as applied to questions, "that which can receive a possible scientific answer," then this definition would rule out the metaphysical question "Why does the world exist?" as not having cognitive meaning. The use of the term "cognitive," as synonymous with "scientific," makes it impossible to allow any question for which there may not be a possible empirical or scientific answer, to have cognitive meaning. To say that it has cognitive meaning, on this use, means that, in principle, there could be a true answer to a question. And since the question "Why does the world exist?", as it is here being argued, is unanswerable, it would not have cognitive meaning.

Clearly, however, the restriction of the use of the term "cognitive" as synonymous with "scientific," reflects a classification wholly inappropriate for identifying the principal use of language in raising a question of the type "Why does the world exist?" For why should we accept a classification that restricts all "cognitive" uses of language to scientific or empirical ones? Such use of "cognitive" is too narrow. The principal use of language in the question "Why does the world exist?" is to express a *philosophic* question. This question does not have any possible answer. We need, nevertheless, to recognize in this question a use of language that, even if non-scientific (i.e., non-cognitive in the positivist sense) is not simply emotive. I am not denying, of course, that there is an emotive component (connected with the feelings of awe and cosmological astonishment) in the statement of the mystery of existence. But I deny that this is *all* there is to it, or even its principal feature. These are feelings derivative from the realization of the unanswerability of the question "Why does the world exist?", when this question is considered philosophically. In a sufficiently broad use of the term "cognitive," even a philosophic question of the kind we are examining, would be classed as being "cognitive" in character.

The Type of Unanswerability Belonging to the Mystery of Existence

I have now enumerated three different senses in which one may use the phrase "unanswerable questions," namely, to refer to (1) those involving violations of linguistic rules of use, (2) those resting on false presuppositions, and (3) those due to the unavailability of a rational method for finding answers. When confronted with the question "Why does the world exist?", as allegedly unanswerable, it still remains to be discussed under which of these headings we are to place our question. It is the hypothesis of the following investigation that the question belongs to the third group. The question "Why does the world exist?" (or, more accurately, as I shall argue later, "Is there a reason-for-the-existence-of-the-world?") is a properly-framed question, though unanswerable, because of the unavailability of a rational method for finding an answer to it. To show that it is properly-framed, we must undertake to make clear the meanings of the key terms in the question, and we must also show that we are not falling back on any presuppositions whose truth might not be reasonably sustained. To fulfill this task, I shall first devote some attention to the use of the term "the world" (in Chapter IV). Next, I shall investigate two chief presuppositions involved in the asking of the question, namely, (1) the presupposition that the world exists (to be examined in Chapter V), and (2) that it makes sense to speak of a "reason" in connection with the world's existence (to be examined in Part Three, Chapters VI and IX, and in Part Four). The arguments to support the claim that there is no rational method available to answer the question "Is there a reason-for-the-existence-of-the-world?" will be presented in Chapter XII.

"WHY IS THERE SOMETHING RATHER THAN NOTHING?"

Before turning to these matters, however, let me indicate briefly, why I have chosen for consideration the question "Why does the world exist?" (or as a later transformation, "Is there a reason-for-the-world's-existence?") rather than the question made familiar by Leibniz and Heidegger, viz., "Why is there anything at all, or something, rather than nothing?" The reason is that the latter question suffers from a number of faults.

It is, to begin with, not properly framed, since the words "something" or "anything" are wholly indeterminate in their reference. Just as we should say the interrogatory expression "Does it fly?" is unanswerable without some clue as to what name or descriptive phrase may be substituted for "it," so too, unless we know, even if only roughly, what is the range of values for "something" or "anything," we cannot consider this a properly framed question. Would the term "anything," for example, include the number "three," or the possibility that my chair might collapse in the next five minutes, or the smile of the Cheshire cat? If we answer negatively, on what grounds do we do so? If, on the other hand, we say that these, too, in some way have existence, does this not merely shift the difficulty to how we shall construe "existence"? For, clearly, there is ground here for reasonable doubt as to whether these can be said to exist in the same way, or, indeed, what it would mean to say that any of them "have" existence. And even if we should waive this difficulty, would it make sense to ask *why* any one of these exists? Is the question "Why?" relevant, and appropriate, in the same way—does it have the same meaning when applied to numbers, fictional objects, possibilities, or natural occurrences? Are we provoked in the same way to express our sense of the mystery of existence by the existence of the number "three," or the smile of the Cheshire cat, as by the spectacle of the starry heavens above? I should be inclined to answer the latter question by saying that we are not. The spectacle of the starry heavens has a certain pre-eminence, here, that the others do not have. In any case, the question "Why does anything at all exist?" gives us no clue about all of this, and does not even suggest any order of priorities among existences with respect to their capacity to arouse our sense of the mystery of existence.

There is a second difficulty with the question "Why does anything exist, rather than nothing?" Even if we restrict the range of values that the variable-term "anything" has, to natural occurrences (including human activities and products), it does not follow, upon substituting a reference to some particular entity, or occurrence, for "anything," that the question is then unanswerable. For example, let us substitute for "anything" the term "this chair." Then our question becomes "Why does this chair exist?" (We leave out for the moment, the other part of the question, ". . . . rather than nothing," since the alternative to "this chair existing" is not absolute nothing). And to *this* question, viz., "Why does this chair exist?", the answer is simply the same as to the question "Why was this chair made?": to which a ready explanation is available. Similarly, if we substitute for "anything," reference to some individual occurrence of a natural phenomenon, or the statement of some regularity, the occurrence of the event or class of events in question is open to satisfactory explanations of a scientific sort. Questions about the existence of thunderstorms, eclipses, and the like, become standard scientific problems about the space-time location, or other characteristics, of these phenomena, and in no way arouse for us the sense of mystery in existence.

A final combination of difficulties in the posing of the question "Why does anything exist at all, rather than nothing?" is connected with the use of the term "nothing." If, as is normally the case, one intends to refer to absolute nothing, and not merely to the relative absence, or nonexistence, of some particular object or entity, then it is highly doubtful whether this idea can be given a sufficiently clear meaning. I shall return to this matter later (Chapter VIII), since we shall have to consider whether even the formulation of the question "Why does the world exist?" does not, itself, tacitly involve reference to the idea of absolute nothing. I shall argue that it does not.

There is a further objection to couching the fundamental question about the mystery of existence so that it depends essentially on making use of the concept of "absolute nothing." The objection is that, in so doing, many writers tacitly appeal to a formulation of the question that leans especially heavily on a particular metaphysical view, namely, that of theism. This view undertakes to solve the mystery of existence by reference to a transcendent ground for all existence; God, it is said, brings the world into existence *out of nothing*. However, in trying to find a way of stating initially the mystery of existence, it would be desirable to do so without committing oneself to a particular conceptual frame that already presupposes a certain way of handling the question.

The foregoing difficulties that attend the use of the question "Why is there anything at all rather than nothing?", are avoided in the question I shall consider as a more adequate first-approximation to stating the mystery of existence, viz., "Why does the world exist?" To be sure, there will be special difficulties that crop up in the use of *this* formula, as well, and we shall have to be on our guard to note these, and to see to what extent they can be met, or a better formulation offered. But instead of referring in some wholly indeterminate way to "anything" or "something," we shall be dealing, in the substituted question, with a more determinate subject matter, that is to say, with "the world." Moreover, in this formulation, we shall deliberately avoid any reference to "nothing," as that with which the existence of the world is to be contrasted, for, what the mystery of the existence of the world is, can be articulated without making use of this term.

Part Two

THE WORLD EXISTS

CHAPTER IV

The World

THE STATEMENT "The world exists," as a presupposition of the question "Why does the world exist?", at first sight appears to be so incontrovertibly true, that we might be tempted to think there is no need to stop to explore the grounds for its acceptance. Yet in this we should be deceived, of course, since reflection about the way in which we are to understand the terms "the world," and "exists," and the assertion "The world exists," reveals that, far from these expressions being clear, precise, non-controversial, and univocal, indeed the very opposite is the case. Some attention to how these ideas are to be understood is, accordingly, necessary.

One of the important and underlying difficulties in any treatment of statements about the world (for example, "The world exists"), is that we naturally wish to apply to them, those rules and standards of logical analysis that have been worked out, and successfully applied, to other subject matters. Thus we ask: "Is a statement about the world, about an individual? Or is it about a class of objects?" It is natural to want to assimilate the logic of world-statements to other types of statements. For example, Aristotle regarded the world as "a particular, material thing," and Leibniz spoke of *this* world as contrasted with other, possible worlds. Nevertheless, there is at least a reasonable doubt about this application of ordinary distinctions to the world, without first examining their appropriateness and value. Our ordinary rules of logic, whether crude or sophisticated, are fashioned to deal with the kinds of subject matters to which they find most ready application; they are of the kind encountered in ordinary, commonsense experience, or in the inquiries of the specialized sciences. It may be, nevertheless, that such widely useful rules of logic are unsuitable for dealing with the world. For example, it might be the case that the term "the world" stands neither for a singular object (an individual), nor for a class, since the world cannot be said to be either (in an unqualified way), although we might wish, for certain purposes, to think of it *as if* it were one or the other. Similarly, it may be the case that the ordinary analysis of existence-statements does not apply to the analysis of the statement "The world exists." (Indeed, we shall see in the next chapter, where the latter statement is analyzed, that this analysis does not altogether apply.)

Let us begin by considering the use of the term "the world." As a first crude approximation, this phrase can be understood as being a name for "the earth, the heavens, and all that in them is." The merit of this brief formula is that it calls attention to the fact that we find it useful to have a term to serve, at once, for the astronomical expanse or inclusive spatio-temporal frame for the great variety of natural objects, events, and processes disclosed in human experience, as well as for this variety itself. The latter includes purely physical phenomena, manifested both terrestrially and throughout the astronomical universe, as well as those of life, mind, and human culture.

We may ask: Does the use of the word "the" in "the world" imply we are dealing with some type of individual object, or is the world an absolute whole or unique class? If the latter, what kind of class or whole is it, and in what sense is it unique or absolute? In what way, if at all, does it have features comparable to other objects, classes, or wholes? Such questions serve to remind us of the considerable vagueness that accompanies any uncritical use of the phrase "the world." Rather than pointing to the wisdom of abandoning the term altogether, however (as some have suggested), we must do what we can to reduce its penumbra of vagueness. I say "reduce" rather than "eliminate," since, as I shall argue, there is a residual and uneliminable vagueness, or indeterminateness, both in the reference of the term "the world," and in its connotation, that are essential to it.

THE UNIVERSE FOR SCIENTIFIC
COSMOLOGY

In order to get some help in the analysis of the expression "the world," it will prove useful to turn to a cognate term, namely, "the universe." "But," it will surely be asked, "are these not like Tweedledee and Tweedledum? If the use of 'the world' is surrounded by unclarity, is the case really any better with 'the universe'?" By way of reply, I must say at once, therefore, that I do not intend to consider the term "the universe" as simply a synonym for "the world." Rather, my suggestion is that we consider the way in which the term "the universe" functions in the specialized context of physical, or scientific, cosmology. There are a number of advantages in making this move. For whatever else the world is, it is, at least, a physical universe. And if we should discover certain limitations in the way in which we can describe the universe, then, *a fortiori*, these will also apply to our attempt to characterize the world. Moreover, it is the physical universe that provides the environment and the physical conditions necessary to the emergence, and sustenance, of biological and psychological phenomena; it thus has a certain primacy in our study of the character of the world. Any tolerably adequate account we can give of the physical universe will, thereby, give us an understanding of the most fundamental physical environmental conditions for the existence of living and conscious creatures. Now, while it must be admitted that even by restricting ourselves to this aspect of the world, namely, to the physical universe, we shall encounter a nest of difficulties, nevertheless, these difficulties, and the ways we might try to resolve them, will offer some helpful clues in our attempts to structure the use of the phrase "the world." It is for these reasons that the following brief excursion into the use of the term "the universe" in cosmology, is undertaken.

The Scope of Scientific Cosmology; Some Philosophical Questions

A common characterization of scientific cosmology is to say that it is a study of the universe as a whole, or of the large-scale properties of the universe. A major problem in the clarification of the conceptual foundations of this discipline is connected with the use of the terms "the universe" or "the universe-as-a-whole." Is the universe the same as the observed, or observable, universe, or should a distinction be drawn between what is open to observation, and what (for various reasons) might, in some sense, be said to lie beyond what is observable? What are the roles played by both observation and theory in describing, or construing, what the universe is? Are models of the universe to be thought of as, in some way, articulating the structure of the universe itself? But what is "the universe itself"? Is it a unique whole? Does it have some particular structure? Are we justified in making use of such a concept at all? These are notoriously difficult questions, surrounded by much controversy. And it would clearly be foolhardy to pretend to be able to give completely satisfying answers to all these questions. Nevertheless, we must attempt to deal with some of these, however briefly, insofar as they bear on our present interest in defining "the universe."

The Observed Universe

The starting point for any empirically oriented study of cosmology is to be found in the disclosures of the astronomer concerning the astronomical entities of relevance to a large-scale survey. What these entities are, and how much is observationally known about them, reflects both the nature of the astronomical classificatory schemes accepted at a given epoch, and the type and sensitivity of the instrumental resources available to the observer. Regarded in this way, the data obtained from observational astronomy, of interest to cosmology, exhibit marked changes, and reflect steadily improving schemes and resources, as we trace the history of man's efforts at constructing an astronomically grounded cosmology. The history of these efforts had its crudest beginnings in a cosmology whose basic divisions consisted of "earth and sky," and for which reliance was had simply on unaided eyesight. It is a history that emerges, in our own day, with a cosmology that is dependent on the use of powerful, earthbound, optical and radio telescopes (and, hopefully, even satellite-based instruments), to yield information about a region billions of light-years in spatial extent, and populated by an enormously large collection of galaxies and clusters of galaxies.

Let us use the term "observed universe" to refer to what, at a given stage of astronomical research, is the widest domain that has been, to some extent, already explored by available instruments. At the present time, the observed universe is defined by the population of galaxies whose remote members have been emitting electromagnetic radiation that is finally received, here, on earth, after having travelled over distances of billions of light-years, and over periods of billions of years. The limits of this observed region are not precisely drawn. For one thing, astronomers are constantly improving their equipment and obtaining fresh data, so that any attempt at fixing these limits is constantly being revised. Again, understandably, because of the character of the subject matter, considerable differences exist, even among the experts, as to how the data are to be reduced and interpreted. What the observed universe is, for present knowledge, cloaks, therefore, a considerable zone of uncertainty and disagreement. Despite these reservations, the term "observed universe" does have a useful function to perform. It reminds us of the fact that the observed-universe is not necessarily the same as the universe observed. For it is clear that the observed universe is, at best, a fragment, or incomplete segment, of some wider domain.

Also, however one might come to describe the universe, on the basis of some particular cosmological model, and whether or not it is taken to be observable in its entirety, we can assert that any attempt to base an account of the universe on experience, must not only start with the data obtained from the observed universe, but also must submit its claims in behalf of some model to the verification of observational data. Cosmology, in its efforts at determining the structure of the universe as a whole by means of various models of the universe, must *test* these models by the empirical data obtained from study of the observed universe.

In using the phrase "the observed universe," it is worth remembering, we need not construe "observation" so narrowly that it excludes the use of all conceptual tools of interpretation. For any watertight separation of "observation" and "interpretation" would be, of course, wholly indefensible and unreal. Justification for using the term "observed universe" is, nevertheless, to be found in the fact that it is primarily by means of observational clues— through optical images and radio signals—that we become aware of the existence of these remote objects. The pulses of energy these objects emit, register their radiations upon the plates and antennae of the astronomer's instruments. The observed universe, in short, consists of the most inclusive region, or collection, of physically existent objects and processes observationally detected at a given stage of inquiry.

Nevertheless, the observed universe, however extensive its scope, is essentially incomplete. There is no reason to believe that the region actually observed at the present time, coincides with what is, in principle, observable, and whose makeup would be disclosed to more adequate instrumentation. This raises the further question whether the region accessible to improved, or even "ideal," instrumentation, would necessarily coincide with the universe as this can be defined by means of theory.

Cosmological Models

Cosmological models play a fundamental role in all cosmological inquiry. It is by means of theoretic models of the universe that the conceptual means are given for discussing such questions as: whether the observed universe is to be regarded as a fair sample of the universe as a whole, or, whether the region of objects and events accessible to an observer equipped with even ideal instruments can be identified with the universe as a whole.

Variously different treatments are given to these questions by models under current discussion. The majority of models, for example, impose a condition of spatial uniformity upon the distribution of matter throughout the universe, and so adhere to what is known as the *Ordinary* (or *Narrow*) *Cosmological Principle*.[1] In addition, other models (for example, the steady-state model of Bondi and Gold) rely on a *Perfect Cosmological Principle*, that defines a temporal uniformity, as well as a spatial one,

---

[1] The whole class of models employing the Robertson-Walker line element, those involving homogeneity and isotropy of spatial distribution, and a uniquely defined "cosmic time" embody the Cosmological Principle.

for the universe. For these models, there is no secular variation in the density-distribution of matter throughout the universe over very long stretches of time. Further differences among models can be specified with respect to the presence, or absence, of horizons for observers situated within the model. These horizons (differentiated into "event-horizons" and "particle-horizons"), define different types of limits of what is observable to observers situated on fundamental particles (galaxies) belonging to the universe. Thus, not only will different cosmological models assign different space-time properties to the universe, they will also differ in the way they conceive of the range of what is accessible to observational study by differently situated observers within the model.[2]

The Cognitive Worth of Cosmological Models

These first-order differences among various cosmological models pose, in turn, a number of second-order philosophical questions. Chief among these is the question as to the cognitive worth of models, in general, with respect to the subject matter they purport to describe. The question is this: Are there any good reasons for believing that the universe as defined by some preferred cosmological model corresponds to, or in some way approximates to, the structure of the real universe? How we are going to answer this question will depend on a number of things: (1) What meaning are we going to give to the phrase "the real universe"? If, in attempting to explicate the latter concept, we introduce the notion of the universe as an absolute whole, how is this to be understood, and what warrant, if any, do we have for positing the existence of such a whole? Is there any way in which the position of the sceptic, who rejects any claim to know of the existence of an absolute whole, can be effectively overcome? (2) Are we to think of cosmological models, with the

---

[2] For a general survey see H. Bondi, *Cosmology* (Cambridge, 1960); G. J. Whitrow, *The Structure and Evolution of the Universe* (New York, 1959); H. Bondi *et al.*, *Rival Theories of Cosmology* (Oxford, 1960); G. C. McVittie, *Fact and Theory in Cosmology* (London, 1961); M. K. Munitz, *Space, Time and Creation* (New York, 1957). For a discussion of horizons, cf. W. Rindler, "Visual Horizons in World-Models" *Monthly Notices, Royal Astr. Soc., 116* (1956), 662-77.

realist, as giving us an account of the structure of some independently existing entity? Or, are we, rather, with the conceptualist and the instrumentalist, to think of these models as
offering us, simply, useful representational devices for the interpretation of observational data, but not as having any ontological
significance?

Insofar as these questions call for philosophical analysis, it is
well to remember that not only are cosmologists, themselves, at
loggerheads as to how to answer them, but that it would be vain
to look to them for answers to be obtained from a further ac-
cumulation of observational data, from refinements in mathematical
analysis and computation, or even from some fresh spurt of
creativity in devising new mathematico-physical principles of interpretation for use in cosmological models. The character of
these questions is philosophical, and they need to be treated by
the philosophical analyst.

Two Principal Meanings of "The Universe"

The term "the universe" (without the qualifying adjectives
"observed" or "observable") can be used in at least two basically
different senses. According to one sense (I shall label this "U_1"
or "the universe$_1$"), it will mean "that to which the observed
universe belongs"; according to the second sense ("U_2" or "the
universe$_2$"), it will mean "that which is implicitly defined by the
traits assigned to it by some cosmological model." Those who
take cosmological models in a realistic way, intend that the
universe as defined by some cosmological model (i.e., U_2), is
the same universe that is characterized by the fact that it is
that to which the observed universe belongs (U_1). But there
is no antecedent guarantee that this realistic way of regarding
cosmological models is the only defensible one; the distinction
here being proposed allows us to keep this question open. If a
realistic philosophy is adopted, the necessary modifications can
then be made. In any event, short of begging the question, it is
by no means the case that we are required to say of the universe$_1$
("that to which the observed universe belongs"), everything that
we can properly say of the universe$_2$ ("that which is implicitly
characterized by the use of some cosmological model"). In par-

ticular, the character of being a whole, or an absolute totality, might perfectly well be predicated of the universe in the latter sense (U_2), though not necessarily of the former (U_1). By way of justification of this last point, let us consider the concept "whole" and the sense this term bears in the construction and use of cosmological models.

The Meaning of "Whole"

The term "whole" enjoys a wide variety of uses. In esthetics we speak of a constructed, or created, individual *work of art*, as a "whole." Biology takes the individual *organism* to be a "whole." Again, in mathematics, reference to "wholes" is made in connection with finite or infinite *classes* of numbers or of points. Finally, in ordinary physics one may speak of a "whole" in the sense of a *system* of bodies or processes as structured by a set of physical laws.

While in the past history of cosmology, cosmogonic myths and some metaphysical cosmologies made extensive use of the meanings of "whole" borrowed from its paradigm uses in craftsmanship or biology, modern scientific cosmologies rely almost exclusively on the mathematical or physical meanings of "whole." It is the task of scientific cosmology, through the construction of cosmological models, to determine: (1) the spatial and temporal metric of the basic collection of particles and events thought to constitute the universe; (2) the distribution of matter and energy throughout the system; and (3) whatever systematic motions belong to the major constituent particles.

By the very nature of its construction, a cosmological model presupposes that the universe can be theoretically described as a whole. Since "whole" carries meanings derived from analogy with the use of totality-concepts in mathematics and the physical sciences, the use of "whole" as applied to the universe reflects these meanings. Thus, the universe is said to be a whole, in the sense that it is a *class* of bodies, events, and processes. In this way, the language of mathematical set-theory is used, for example, to describe the number of bodies (galaxies) as finite or infinite. Similarly, the language of geometry is introduced in order to describe the spatial metric of the universe; the bodies making up the universe are thought to belong to a field whose structure can be specified by a Euclidean, or one of the non-Euclidean, geometries. Again, the fundamental bodies and processes constituting the universe are presumed to form a *physical system*; the laws or principles defining the character of the system (whether taken from "ordinary" physics, or specially devised) bind the various units and segments in a single interrelated framework.

Is the Universe a Whole?

To the extent that cosmology seeks to articulate the character of the universe *as* a whole, it may be said to rest upon the methodological postulate that the universe *is* a whole. The specific traits assigned to the whole will vary from model to model; but the assumption that the goal is to characterize the universe *as* a whole, remains unchanged. In this sense, therefore, it is perfectly true to say that the statement "the universe is a whole" is a matter of definition, an analytic statement. It should be noted, however, that the term "the universe," as used in this definition, is "universe$_2$" ("that which is the object of characterization by a cosmological model").

In addition to requiring, as a matter of definition, that the universe$_2$ be thought of as "a whole," that is to say, as being intelligible in the way in which mathematical classes, geometric relations, or physical systems are, cosmology also posits that the universe as a whole is *unique* or *absolute*. By this is meant that there is at least one such class, pattern, or system, and not more than one, and that all other physical objects, processes, or systems of lesser scope (i.e., duration, spatial extent, or systematic interrelationship) are to be regarded as only parts of this all-inclusive whole. Again, therefore, each model of the universe will so define the universe$_2$ that it is unique; to speak of a "plurality of universes" would be a contradiction, or a misuse of language.

Can we say, however, that the statement "the universe is an absolute, unique whole" is also analytic, if "the universe" means "that to which the observed universe belongs" (U_1)? Here, the answer must be that we are *not* committed, by the very nature of the underlying methodological postulate of cosmology, to saying that the universe$_1$ *is* a whole, as we were in the case of the just-considered conception of the universe$_2$. We are dealing now with an ontological matter, not a methodological one. While it may be necessary for the setting-up of the *science* of cosmology to presuppose there is a definite and pervasive structure to be investigated and articulated, this need not be binding on what the universe$_1$ itself is existentially. If by "the universe" we mean "that to which the observed universe belongs" (U_1), there is nothing in *this* meaning that analytically contains the idea that it is a whole or an absolute whole. It is not required, as a matter of definition, that we include the notion of being an absolute, unique totality in the meaning given to "the universe$_1$." For even if we allow that the observed universe is structured in some way, it does not necessarily follow that the wider universe$_1$ to which it belongs, is itself pervasively structured.

Nor can we say that the very characterization of the observed universe as being a "segment" or "part" of some "wider domain," necesssarily commits us to the view that the universe$_1$, as this "wider domain" is a unique or absolute whole, in some literal sense. For the use of terms like "part," "whole," "belong," and so on, that we invariably fall back on, reveals the mind's need to employ analogies, in reaching into the unfamiliar, as it relates the latter to what it already knows. That the universe$_1$, as the "wider domain to which the observed universe belongs," is literally a complete, unique, and intelligibly structured whole, is a claim to which we need not commit ourselves. It should be left open as an unresolvable question, for it is something on which, properly speaking, we do not have any knowledge. To stipulate that it *is* so, by definition, is, of course, no way of establishing this knowledge.

It cannot be established by any appeal to *direct* experience that the universe$_1$ is a unique and absolute whole. The only domain of which it can be said more or less direct observational experience is to be had, is the observed universe. But this, of course, cannot be identified with the universe$_1$. Nor can we resort to the use of induction, as a form of argument-by-experience, in the way this argument would normally be employed in connection with inferring to something not already within the range of observational experience, on the basis of what is within the range of observational experience. Inductive reasoning is employed whenever an accumulated body of information about a certain number of instances of A, within our present or past experience (say that they have the property B), is used as a basis to generalize about all A's, including future instances of A. Inductive reasoning is employed to support the statement "All A's are B's." Insofar as inductive reasoning is the attempt to provide good reasons for inferring something about unobserved instances, on the basis of observed instances, it has to do with the inference to further *instances* of some regularity or *law*. However, the problem faced in cosmology is not that of finding a warrant in experience for establishing *laws*. This is the task of ordinary physics. The task of cosmology, rather, is to say something about the universe₁; for this purpose, a *model* of the universe needs to be employed. And a model is not a law.

However, in the use of cosmological models, one cannot find any empirical warrant of the type that is obtained by directly examining the object of which it may be thought to articulate the structure. One cannot use, or verify, cosmological models in the way ordinary physical scale-models are employed for objects already in existence. In the case, for example, of a scale-model of the Empire State Building, it is possible to examine, independently, the original in order to note the points of similarity between it and the model. The cosmologist, however, cannot inspect the universe₁ directly, in the way in which one might examine the Empire State Building, to see how faithfully his model corresponds to the original.[3] At best, some cosmological model yields predictions that can be observationally confirmed, or disconfirmed, by appeal to what is found in the observed universe. There is no way, however, of directly experiencing the universe₁, that is to say, that to which the observed universe belongs. The only way of having any cognitive access to the universe₁, is *through* models, not independently of them. The claim to knowledge about the universe₁ rests upon the use of cosmological models. In these models, the universe is defined as some kind of intelligible whole (U_2), and is used to describe U_1.

The realist maintains that an empirically confirmed cosmo-

---

[3] Cf. M. K. Munitz, "The Logic of Cosmology," *British Journal for the Philosophy of Science*, May, *1962*, pp. 34-50.

logical model articulates the structure of the real universe (U_1). He believes the structure of the whole, as defined by the model, coincides with the presumed structure of the universe$_1$. He believes the universe$_1$ to be an absolute, unique totality with its *own* inherent intelligible structure. This view, however, expresses a metaphysical faith, and cannot be empirically tested. The sceptic's challenge to the realist—that the latter cannot show the real universe (U_1) *is* a whole, or that it has a pervasive structure, or that it can be adequately articulated by some cosmological model, would seem to be an effective challenge.

Such scepticism, however, need not be damaging to a more modest conceptualist, or instrumentalist, view of what cosmological models can accomplish. For insofar as cosmology, as a scientific discipline, can fruitfully carry on its inquiries both as a guide to the observational astronomer (suggesting the direction for obtaining observational data), and as a search for convenient pictures of what it chooses to think of as "the whole," its results need not be thought to give us any more than heuristically valuable devices of representation or tools of inquiry.

THE WORLD AS KNOWN AND UNKNOWN

Now that we have had a glimpse of some of the problems connected with the use of the term "the universe" in cosmology, let us return to our initial and principal interest in trying to clarify the way in which the term "the world" is to be understood. What clues for the analysis of "the world" can be found in the discussion of "the universe"? We have found that in referring to the universe it is necessary to try to do justice to two features: (1) its relative or partial determinateness, insofar as attention is confined to the observed universe, and (2) our ineradicable ignorance, insofar as any question concerning the real existence of a unique and ordered totality is concerned. One can point with some assurance to the existence and discernible structure of the observed universe (although its precise makeup and boundaries are not fixed with precision). But the universe, in the sense of "that to which the observed universe belongs"

(U_1), is a matter about which no genuine knowledge can be claimed. Whether the universe$_1$ itself conforms to some one cosmological model, or to none, or whether it is a unique and absolute whole with a determinate structure, is something on which philosophical scepticism can always be legitimately maintained. This type of philosophical scepticism is justified, however much the presupposition that the universe is an ordered totality, is essential for building cosmological models in the science of cosmology. In short, beyond the somewhat vague boundaries of the observed universe, as well as beyond the region to which one may reasonably extrapolate—as accessible to foreseeably improved instruments, the amount of uncertainty as to what is in that "beyond" becomes so large, that a reasonable view must take the form of a suspension of judgment.

Now, something of the same type of result, I should maintain, is what we are finally forced to acknowledge in any sufficiently clear and acceptable use of the term "the world." Rather than discard this term altogether, I believe it can be made to serve a useful function. I should agree it does not have this useful function when it is taken to mean, simply, "the totality of whatever exists." The term "the world," however, can be usefully construed to mean something that at once possesses a zone of relative determinateness and intelligible specificity, and also a possibly existent dimension of indeterminateness that is, and will remain, wholly unknown and incomprehensible to us.

Can the World Be Identified Demonstratively?

As a preliminary step to a further elucidation of this point, and by way of staking out, in a rough way, what can usefully be said about "the world," let us ask whether that to which the term ostensibly refers, might be identified by means of a demonstrative expression, such as "this" or "that."[4] Consider someone who claims not to have any comprehension, at all, of what the term means. Could we, by way of clarification, use the phrase "*this* world," as we point to what we intend? It is clear that we could not, at least in the straightforward and non-controversial

---

[4] Cf. P. F. Strawson, *Individuals* (London, 1959), pp. 19 ff.

way in which we customarily use these demonstratives in their paradigm cases. In these cases, we single out some particular object, as noticed by means of one, or a combination, of our senses, and, by an accompanying gesture of pointing, identify it. Thus, in a bakery shop, we say to the salesperson—as we point to the selected object—"I'll have *this* cake." Obviously, we can't identify the world in this way. Anything I might point to, would be come particular object, individual happening, or quite restricted group of objects, discriminated against a background of other objects and events. But what is the background against which to discriminate the world? There is no background of objects or events left out, or not to be considered. If there were such, these should have been included in any successful demonstrative identification of the world.

Nor can this difficulty in giving a demonstrative meaning to "the world" be overcome by using a sweeping gesture—as when standing below the starlit sky, I encompass everything in sight, and say: "I mean *all this*." Again, it would be proper to ask whether some things or events not literally within one's sight, might not also be intended. And it would seem that, in some way, there are objects or events that, not being within our sight, ought to have been included in any acceptable reference of "the world."

On Describing the World

If, then, the term "the world" is not of a type that can be successfully elucidated by making use of a demonstrative such as "this," is it, instead, a name for something we can describe? And how is this to be done? A name, to be useful, must permit us to identify the object or entity being named, by means of a definite description, in those cases where we cannot resort to demonstrative identification. Where we are able to give a satisfactory description of this sort, we can then use the name in place of the description. Is this the situation we face in trying to give meaning to the term "the world"? Can we identify what the name "the world" refers to, by means of a suitable description? In what would such a description consist? This is the question we must now examine.

The World as an Absolute Totality

We might, of course, undertake to provide the required description by saying, for example, "the world is everything that is the case," or, "the world is the absolute totality of whatever exists in any way." However, there are two types of difficulty in the use of these formulae. In the first place, it is exceedingly doubtful that a formula of the above type can be made sufficiently clear. Have we been given a description that serves the purpose of conceptual discrimination? Does one know what, if anything, is being denied? A second difficulty is that in thinking of the world as an absolute totality, we are thereby construing it as an all-inclusive order of some sort. But what warrant is there for the view that what exists is, in fact, pervasively ordered? If what exists were not pervasively ordered, how could it possibly be known? Let us consider, briefly, each of these difficulites.

(1) The term "absolute totality" does not already have a sufficiently clear use. In the case of other terms with tolerably clear meanings, the kinds of problems we face are either ones of deciding whether a given object or experience is to be described by the use of terms already possessing established meanings, or whether the object or experience can only be described by using analogies. In the latter case, one points out similarities and differences by means of terms already in use. Consider the situation faced in using a term to describe some color sensation. We already have a vocabulary of color terms, embodying a particular scheme of classification, and allowing for the making of discriminations up to some degree. "Is the color of this object before me blue?" Assuming we already know how to use the term "blue," our problem in answering this question is one of decision as to whether to apply this, or some other, term to it. If our color vocabulary consisted simply of "blue," "red," "yellow," "white," and "green," we should have to decide which of these terms to apply. If the object does not fall clearly within one or the other, we may resort to saying: "It is something like blue, but also, it is something like green; it is not quite one or the other." Finally, we may find it convenient to introduce a new color term into our vocabulary, for example, "teal," to take care of cases not adequately described

by terms already in use. However, the problem connected with the use of the term "absolute totality" is of a different character from that which attends the use of terms already possessed of fairly definite meanings. The problem is precisely that this term does not already possess a sufficiently clear meaning.

We might suppose that this deficiency can be remedied by supplying a rule that would tell us how to operate. Thus if I make some assertion about the totality of positive integers, I can give meaning to the use of the term "totality," in this context, by specifying a rule by which to construct, or enumerate, the members of this class; the rule tells me that, by starting with zero and making use of the concept of the successor of a number, it is possible to reach any positive integer. But once more, the difficulty with saying that the world is the absolute totality of whatever exists in any way, is that of knowing what falls under this "rule," and what, if anything, does not. Thus, to speak of "whatever exists in any way" only shifts the difficulty, rather than solves it. For we should have to ask questions such as: "Does $5 + 7 = 12$ belong to the world?"; "If God, or the Devil, exist, do they belong to the world?"; "Is the breakfast I might have eaten yesterday, but didn't, part of the world?"; and so on. The disentangling of these questions is notoriously difficult and highly controversial. Hence, we have not really gained much by a formula such as "the world is the totality of whatever exists." In order to be effectively usable, the formula should allow itself to be used as a rule for settling issues of the type raised in the above questions; however, it doesn't.

(2) There are two principal components in the notion of absolute totality: one, that it includes everything, the other, that there is an intelligible structure that binds all things together. We have seen some of the difficulties inherent in any attempt to specify what the all-inclusive content of an absolute totality might be. However, the notion of a unifying, all-embracing intelligible structure is just as difficult to accept as the notion of a universal content.

There is no problem, of course, in understanding how conceptions of a unifying intelligible structure come to be developed. Man reads into the world as already there, a completely unified structure that would fill out all those partial successes, and incomplete fragments of intelligibility, he has already managed to establish in patches of his experience. Analogy, vision, and faith come to support the projection of what is a human need into an allegedly antecedent ontologic fact. The variety of these drives to total intelligibility, and of belief in a unifying structure, are as wide as the history of human culture itself. Myths, metaphysics, theology, and science furnish countless illustrations. One finds examples of these drives to intelligibility in primitive mythical cosmologies and cosmogonies: in them the development, or the coming-into-existence, of the world is analogized to a work of craftsmanship; or to the obedient outcome of an authoritative command; or to the product of a process of growth from a seed; or to the fruit of the mating of a primeval pair. Indeed, the very notion of a *cosmos*—as an ordered totality that binds all phenomena in a universal scheme, and whose details are accessible to patient rational inquiry—is the chief contribution of Greek thought to Western civilization. Its outlines were already present in the work of the pre-Socratic cosmologists, for example, in Anaximander and Democritus. Seventeenth-century science and its philosophic commentators (particularly the Continental rationalists), simply continued this tradition, and gave it voice in terms of the materials of that day. Spinoza, in rejecting—as a myth— the medieval penchant for reading the world in terms of final causes and anthropomorphic imagery, is not at all aware he is substituting another myth, viz., his own conception of "Nature (or God) to be conceived through itself." In projecting a rationalistically completed science as defining the essence of reality, he does not think of this as being simply another *human ideal*. Kant, however, showed convincingly, that all these notions of a unified system of thought express, at best, a *regulative ideal* of inquiry.

Yet, despite the criticisms of Kant, the general Greek conception of the world as a cosmos, or the Spinozistic conception of a completely intelligible Nature continues to inspire and guide many minds, down to our own day. A prominent recent example is Einstein's life-long search for a unified-field theory, and his view that the world is a "puzzle to be solved." While there is no need to impugn the importance of these conceptions of unifying intelligible structure as marking legitimate programs for inquiry, the danger is always the same as that inherent in any form of idolatry. It is the tendency to treat as existent in its own right, and as, therefore, independent of human will or consciousness, what is only a product of man's own creative imagination.

In saying all this, and in tracing, in this wholesale fashion, the genesis of unified visions of a universal, and all-encompassing, order, to the human need for believing in such an order, it would be equally indefensible and dogmatic to *deny* that there is some ontological warrant for that belief. After all, the world *may be* a cosmos. There *may be* a *scientia intuitiva* to ultimately, and completely, satisfy man's craving for intelligibility. All that a proper scepticism can affirm is that there is no evidence this is the case; nor can we ever have sufficient evidence it is the case. For, the intelligibilities man finds are always incomplete, no matter how far the process of unification may have proceeded, or how convincing the ideal of total success may appear to be. There is no assurance that what the mind hankers after, it will asymptotically approach, or even completely realize, in the final disclosure of a unifying order in the world. For the world may contain elements of disorder, or refractory indeterminateness, that would frustrate any drive to all-encompassing intelligibility. If there were such elements of "chaos" or indeterminateness in the world, they could never be known or understood, since to know them would imply they are intelligible, and so would be contradictory of our assumption.

The Meaning of "The World"

However, if we deny to the term "the world" the meaning of being an absolute and pervasively ordered totality, can we give it a more acceptable meaning? The answer, though perhaps meager and unexciting, would be that we can. It might run something like this. "The world" refers to the "entity" that includes, first of all, the vast, though raggedly defined, observed universe—the spatially and temporally extended expanse of astronomical bodies, and systems of bodies. Making up these vast agglomerations of matter and energy, and forming the physical basis of not only all astronomical entities, but the more-subtly organized bodies of living things and of man, are those physical processes and structures whose existence the physicist has succeeded, to some extent already, in identifying. In addition to the foregoing, here on earth, and possibly, too, in various other habitable places in the universe, there are not only living creatures that crawl, fly, and swim, but conscious and intelligent beings as well, who love, pray, dream, talk, make wars, and laugh. These things we know belong to the world. How many other creatures, or entities, there are, having a space-time locus, and that carry on activities, or perform functions, quite different from those we already are familiar with, we do not know. We have no way of writing a complete list of the world's contents, or of giving a rule by which such a list could be drawn up; nor do we have a way of assuring ourselves that there is a complete list that could, in principle, be drawn up. Beyond the well-established core of things and processes we know about—and even allowing for a substantial zone of indecision, reasonable guesswork, or the gradual shifting of what is on the frontier of the unknown and controversial into the zone of the established and known—no secure knowledge about the rest can be claimed. What we know about the world, as far as its *contents* are concerned, belongs to what, in analogy with the observed universe, we may call "the observed world."

Further, to the extent that our experience (whether commonsensical or scientific) has succeeded in rendering these contents and their comings-and-goings intelligible—to the extent that science, in particular, has succeeded progressively in achieving unifications of otherwise disparate and unrelated domains within the scope of a single theory—to *that* extent one may assert the observed world is a unified cosmos. But what of the wider world to which the observed world belongs? Once more, the growing frontier of discovery will undoubtedly enlarge the list of contents of the observed world, and find ways of unifying and integrating ever-more inclusive regions of fact within the scope of more and more powerful theories. Whereas some ambitious science might think it is steadily approximating to the formulation of a single, all-encompassing theory that would finally render all natural existences intelligible in terms of some selected set of principles, this claim, if taken as having an ontologic warrant in the nature of the world, must be challenged as unsubstantiated. The philosophic sceptic can point to the fact that this claim represents, at best, an ideal of reflective inquiry. However, there is no way in which we can establish that the world is at all like *that*. Even our using the phrase "the world" is misleading, if it presupposes a single unity or order, an all-inclusive totality. Still, when used critically, this term serves as a perfectly adequate name for that "entity," such as it is— whether it is wholly determinate or partly indeterminate, whether it is wholly comprehensible or only partly so—to which the observed world, and such contents and such order in it as we have already succeeded in identifying, belong.

CHAPTER V

The World Exists

OUR NEXT PROBLEM is to analyze the assertion "The world exists," as one of the major presuppositions of the question "Why does the world exist?" One way of focussing on the kind of question we need to consider with respect to this assertion, may be put in terms of the familiar and much-debated topic: whether "existence" is a predicate (or, more accurately, whether "exists" is a predicate). When the sentence "The world exists" is asserted, is "exists," in this sentence, being used to tell us something about the world? Or, on the contrary, is it the case that the entire assertion, unlike genuinely predicative assertions, can be treated so that the word "exists" drops out as a predicate telling us something about the world, and assumes a different logical role? If we take the latter view then "the world exists" may be analyzed after the manner of other existential statements, i.e., as saying "there is something to which the term 'the world' applies"; no more is said by the sentence "The world exists" than is already said by giving (as in the previous chapter) an analysis of the expression "the world," and by showing that this expression can be used referentially.

There are a number of variants, in contemporary philosophy, of these two basic positions. Each of them has its own philosophical lineage in the writings of the past. Confronted with these conflicting views, I propose to argue (1) the statement "The world exists" *does* say something about the world. However, (2) the statement "The world exists" does not commit one to the view that the world is contingent; nor, at the same time, does it follow, by this denial, that one has to say that the existence of the world is, in any way, necessary. My concern, in what follows, is neither to argue the general merit of the view that "exists" is not a predicate, nor, on the other hand, to challenge this position by pointing to some possibly fruitful uses of the word in which it is informative of either contingency or necessity. My sole purpose is to try to show that, in the case of the assertion "The world exists," the term "exists" is uniquely descriptive of the world; at the same time, this predication does not warrant us in claiming either contingency or necessity for the world. The rest of the present chapter will be devoted to the first of these matters, namely, to showing how "exists" can be used predicatively of the world. The analysis of the claim that the existence of the world cannot be characterized as either "contingent" or "necessary" will be taken up in subsequent chapters; Chapters VI, VII, and VIII discuss the question of the contingency of the world, and Chapter IX examines the question of its necessity.

" 'EXISTS' IS NOT A PREDICATE"

The slogan " 'Exists' is not a predicate" is one for which philosophers have offered different kinds of reasons, associated with different contexts of analysis and types of problems with which they have been concerned. It is not, therefore, a single doctrine so much as it is a statement that sums up the results of a variety of types of inquiry, although there is some overlapping among these. Since the statement " 'Exists' is not a predicate" does not have a single philosophic source, I shall first briefly review two principal strands that make it up. We shall find, however, that even if one is prepared to admit the cogency of the types of consideration and philosophic motivation in each of these lines of argument, these do not apply to the statement "The world exists."

The Kantian Treatment of the Question

The first type of problem in modern philosophy that led some philosophers to the view that "exists" is not a predicate, is connected with the analysis of what is involved in stating the *meaning* of a concept, and in specifying the *logical relations* among concepts in ordinary subject-predicate statements. The claim that "exists" is not a predicate that, like other predicates, can be used to define a concept, forms a characteristic element of the philosophy of British empiricism, particularly as elaborated by Berkeley and Hume. *In this respect*, Kant took over the empiricist view of concepts, and used this doctrine in mounting his attack on the Ontological Argument for the existence of God. He thereby gave the doctrine " 'Exists' is not a predicate" the prominence it has since retained in philosophy.

Though Kant discusses this point in connection with the Ontological Argument, and so makes it particularly relevant to this issue in theology, the doctrine " 'Exists' is not a predicate" has a wider validity and bearing. Whether or not, therefore, it is thought to be especially damaging to the Ontological Argument, it would be defended by all thinkers who share, in some way, the type of analysis of concept-formation first given by the British empiricists. Indeed, the concepts treated by way of example would not normally be theological at all, but empirical in character. Kant's famous example of the concept of one hundred dollars, is precisely of this kind. He called attention to the fact that "A hundred real dollars do not contain the least coin more than a hundred possible dollars." What, then, is the argument? Kant expressed it as follows:

> *"Being"* is obviously not a real predicate; that is, it is not a concept of something which could be added to the concept of a thing . . . By whatever and by however many predicates we may think a thing—even if we completely determine it—we do not make the least addition to the thing when we further declare that this thing *is*. Otherwise, it would not be exactly the same thing that exists, but something more than we had thought in the concept; and we could not, therefore, say that the exact object of my concept exists.[1]

Kant, of course, allows that "exists" is a grammatical or—as he calls it—a "logical" predicate. What he is challenging is the

[1] I. Kant, *Critique of Pure Reason*, translated by N. K. Smith (London and New York, 1933), B 627.

view that "exists" is (in his terminology) a "real" or a "determining" predicate. His argument is that "exists" cannot be a real predicate since, if it were, whenever we asserted that something exists, we should be enlarging or changing our concept of whatever that something is, and we should then have a *different* concept from the one with which we began. In that case, we should not have said anything about the existence of the subject of which we formed our original concept. Since, however, we can and do constantly make assertions about the existence of entities of which we already have definite conceptions, without changing or enlarging these concepts, the fact that we can do so, shows, according to him, that "existence" is not part of the string of real predicates that had formed the "original" meaning of those concepts.

Now, in order to make this argument plausible, it is necessary for Kant to establish that *no* concept has, as part of its "original" string of predicates that define it, the predicate "existence." Here, Kant falls back on the empiricist view of how we come to construct *empirical* concepts out of the component qualities identified by one or another of the senses. These qualities of sensation, being conjoined in experience, serve to mark out one *kind* of entity from another, or one *individual* from another. The string of predicates that define "dog," for example, are different from those that define "cat." And, similarly, the sensory experiences that we use to distinctively characterize some particular object, say, my dog "Lassie" from other individual collies, are found to be conjoined in experience in a fairly regular and constant way—and thereby warrant us in using a proper name to refer to this object.

However, while we have sensory impressions corresponding to "brown," "smooth," "loud," "round," "large," and so on, Kant would say we do not have a sensible experience of any quality of existence, to be employed in defining an empirical concept. This much had already been insisted on by Berkeley, who pointed out that we neither have an abstract idea of existence, nor a particular idea, since it is not a color, smell, taste, sound, or feeling.[2] Hume, too, had argued that "the idea of existence is not derived from any particular impression," and, therefore, "that idea, when

[2] G. Berkeley, *Philosophical Commentaries*, 671, *Principles of Human Knowledge*, 81; cf. G. J. Warnock, *Berkeley* (Pelican Books, 1953), p. 198.

conjoined with the idea of any object, makes no addition to it."[3] Whenever, then, we are concerned with giving a list of qualities (each of which is derived from some sensed feature of an object) that tells us *what* that object is, or (what comes to the same thing), what the meaning is of the concept that designates that type of object, we do not find "exists" among the qualities listed. Existence, in short, is irrelevant to the specification of the meaning of empirical concepts. Where, therefore, there is a statement in which "exists" occurs as the logical or grammatical predicate of the statement, this predicate is not part of the analyzable meaning of the concept. In Kant's terminology, the statement in which "exists" occurs as a logical predicate, is to be classified as "synthetic" rather than as "analytic." (It is worth remarking at this point that, if one does not accept Kant's narrowly empiricist view of the range of qualities accessible to experience, and which excludes "existence" from any list of such qualities, then there need be no objection to considering some statements as analytic that included "existence" among the defining characteristics of a term. I shall return to this matter, below.)

It should be noticed Kant is not denying that "exists"*can* serve as the predicate of a *synthetic* statement, and that we have, in this case, a genuine subject-predicate statement. All he is denying is that it is an analytic or a definitional statement, one in which the predicate explicates the meaning of the subject term. The criticism that "exists" is not a predicate at all, and cannot serve as a predicate in *any* statement, whether analytic or synthetic, is a criticism associated with the treatment of existential statements in modern logic (to be discussed below). It is not present in Kant's doctrine, which, if summed up by the slogan " 'Exists' is not a predicate," applies only to analytic statements, as he conceives them.

Of course, if the foregoing interpretation is correct—that Kant intends to restrict the claim that "exists" is not a predicate, to analytic statements—then a difficulty can be raised about how Kant proposes, as in fact he does, to treat a judgment that ascribes existence to something, as a *synthetic* judgment. For, let us assume, there is a true synthetic judgment in which the predicate is "exists." Then this judgment can be said to add to our *knowledge*,

---

[3] D. Hume, *A Treatise of Human Nature*, Bk. I, Part 2, sec. 6.

if not to our understanding of the *meaning* of the term represented by the subject. In this event, the warrant for the judgment will have to be found in experience; in Kant's terminology, the judgment is *a posteriori*. But how, on the empiricist view of the kinds of qualities of which we can have experience, can this predication of existence have meaning, since existence will not, at any time, be the object of any sensory experience? Kant nowhere satisfactorily answers this question; he nowhere reconciles his adoption of the empiricist criterion of the meaning of concepts, as based on sensory qualities, with his evident belief that, nevertheless, we do predicate existence of some objects, in true synthetic judgments.[4]

We have, now, to ask what bearing all this has on the analysis of the statement "The world exists." I have no desire to consider, here, the general question whether the empiricist view of the meaning of empirical terms (as definable completely and adequately by supplying a list of sensory impression terms) is a sound thesis. My purpose is not to explore this broad theme, but simply to ask, first, what merit it has when applied to the statement "The world exists." Nor do I wish to explore the quite tangled web of Kant's doctrine of the classification of judgments, or the overall merit of his distinctions. Yet the question, secondly, needs to be faced, how to classify the statement "The world exists" within the terms of Kant's own distinctions, and insofar as we can make some sense of them.

In considering these matters, I propose to show: (1) "The world" includes "existence" as one of its defining characteristics. Moreover, the fact that the world exists, is discovered in experience, though not in a narrowly conceived sense-experience. (2) If we adopt Kant's classification of judgments, then also, if what is said in (1) is valid, it would be best to classify the judgment "The world exists" as *analytic a posteriori*.

The Concept of "The World" and the Awareness of Existence

"The world" (if our earlier analysis has any merit) cannot be classified as an empirical term, in the sense in which this is understood in the empiricist tradition. For, as we have seen, while it has

[4] Cf. J. Shaffer, "Existence, Predication, and the Ontological Argument," *Mind*, LXXI (1962), 307-325.

a component that refers to what is, more or less, directly observed through sense-experience, namely, in including what I have called "the observed world," the term "the world" refers to whatever it is to which the observed world belongs. And that to which the observed world belongs, may not be wholly observable. Indeed, it may not be wholly determinate. Such being the case, the concept "the world" cannot be analyzed into those characteristics, and only those characteristics, that are sensorily identifiable. Nor is it the case, unless we show all components of the world to be identifiable as qualities sensed by one, or a combination of, the five senses, that the term is then meaningless. I have no wish to consider what the situation may be with other terms employed in philosophy, or in the theoretical sciences, that is, whether they, too, have, as part of their meaning, some components that are not reducible to some sensorily identified quality. It is sufficient for my present purpose to show this to be the case with the term "the world." And in order to show this, all I wish to insist on, as relevant to my present argument—and, indeed, as an example of a component of the meaning of the concept "the world" that is not reduced to a sensorily identified quality—is precisely that the quality, or trait, of existing is not so identifiable by sensory means.

Existence is a trait of the world that is not given to us by a mode of sensory observation, although it is established for us in experience, in a sufficiently broad use of that term. If someone were to ask, "How do you know of the world's existence, or, that the statement "The world exists" is true? Is it by sense-experience or by conceptual analysis?", I should have to reply that it is neither. The knowledge of the existence of the world is nevertheless part of ordinary experience. We have no common name for it; one might call it "cosmic consciousness." Some people have spoken of this experience as a mystical experience, but I think this is a mistake, since mysticism is frequently linked with all sorts of special metaphysical claims not relevant to the experience to which I am here referring. They have meant, for example, by the mystical experience something described as "a union of the alone with the alone," or "becoming one with God," and so on. However, the awareness of the existence of the world is not the prerogative of some few, relatively isolated, mystics. Far from being the outcome of some highly specialized concentration or exercise of the spiritual life, it is the most primordial, commonplace, and universally shared experience. We are likely to overlook it, only because it is so trivial and omnipresent.

At any rate, the awareness of the existence of the world is primary and not reducible to any other type of experience. It is uniquely directed to its own object, namely, to the world as existing. If it should be retorted, "You are begging the question" or "To appeal to some special experience is always the mark of a last measure of desperation, where all argument or analysis fails. It is wholly unworthy of serious philosophical use!", I should challenge this attack, since I believe it *is* worthy of philosophy to acknowledge what cannot be argued. Moreover, I should admit that I cannot *argue* the matter. For the sense of the existence of the world, to which I am here appealing, is not the outcome of a process of reflection or inference. One can only try to give pointers or clues to those who claim they do not have it. If a man is congenitally blind, you cannot tell him what a seen color is. If one has never seen a color, nothing else—not even language at its clearest and most aseptic—will take the place of the experience. One must either see, or have seen, the color, in order to understand a term used to refer to this experience. Similarly, one has to be aware of the world's existence, in order to know that it is true to predicate existence of the world. And, I submit, all men normally do have this experience, although they may not either have given it a special name, or brought it within the special focus of their attention. It has been reported that "Wittgenstein once read a paper on Ethics . . . in which he said that he sometimes had a certain experience which could best be described by saying that 'when I have it I *wonder at the existence of the world*. And I am then inclined to use such phrases as "How extraordinary that anything should exist!" or "How extraordinary that the world should exist!" ' "5 Neither Wittgenstein's experience of *wonderment* at the existence of the world (nor anybody else's),

5 N. Malcolm, *Ludwig Wittgenstein: A Memoir*, (London, 1958), p. 70; cf. L. Wittgenstein, *Tractatus*, 6.45; Ingvar Hargby, "The Double Awareness in Heidegger and Wittgenstein," *Inquiry*, 2 (1959), pp. 235-264.

however, could be aroused unless it were in response, in the first place, to an awareness of the *existence* of the world.

The Classification of the Statement "The World Exists"

A second point to be considered now, has to do with the question of logical classification of the statement "The world exists." Much of the traditional discussion of the classification of statements follows Kant's well-known (though, unfortunately, not rigorously formulated) distinctions between "analytic" and "synthetic" and between "a priori" and "a posteriori" types. Let us consider, first, how, according to Kant, a statement in which existence is predicated of something, is to be classified in terms of the first distinction, that is, as either synthetic or analytic. He writes:

> Is the proposition that *this or that thing* (which, whatever it may be, is allowed as possible) *exists,* an analytic or a synthetic proposition? If it is analytic, the assertion of the existence of the thing adds nothing to the thought of the thing; but in that case either the thought, which is in us, is the thing itself, or we have presupposed an existence as belonging to the realm of the possible, and have then, on that pretext, inferred its existence from its internal possibility—which is nothing but a miserable tautology . . . But if, on the other hand, we admit, as every reasonable person must, that all existential propositions are synthetic, how can we profess to maintain that the predicate of existence cannot be rejected without contradiction? This is a feature which is found only in analytic propositions, and is indeed precisely what constitutes their analytic character.[6]

Let us assume, for purposes of our discussion, that we may speak of the world as some kind of "thing." (It is true that Kant, himself, would disavow any attempt to make valid cognitive judgments about the world, *if we think of the world as an absolute totality*. But, as my previous discussion has shown, there is no need to characterize the world as an absolute totality. To this extent, therefore, my own analysis is in broad agreement with Kant's position in the *Critique of Pure Reason*.) The question is whether the alternatives posed by Kant, in the above quotation, are exhaustive of the possibilities, and whether what he says, of the

[6] *Critique of Pure Reason*, B 625.

alternatives he does consider, is relevant and valid with respect to the judgment "The world exists."

Kant rejects the possibility that a judgment asserting the existence of something is analytic. He claims that, in general, the assertion of the existence of the thing *adds nothing* to the thought (or concept) of the thing. But what if the "thought" of the thing already contains, as part of its very meaning, that its object exists? This, I have argued, is the case with the concept "the world." It makes no sense to say that the world, as identified in our experience, does not exist. For the very reference to the world already presupposes that we have identified it *as existing*, and to actually deny (or even entertain the possibility that one might deny) the existence of the world is, therefore, contradictory of the meaning of the term. Whatever, then, may be the case with concepts of other "things," the concept of the world includes the trait of existing as one of its essential features. It would be gratuitous to *add* the trait of existing to what we mean by "the world," since it already contains it. Kant, however, does not, in the present context, consider the concept "the world"; instead, he bases his arguments, in the above quotation, on other concepts, and argues that, since existence does not add to the thought (concept) of a thing, nor forms part of its definition, a judgment of existence could not be analytic.

If we were to suggest that a judgment asserting existence could be analytic, Kant would say this could be the case in only two possible situations: (1) if, instead of the normal case (where we draw a distinction between a thought of a thing, and the thing to which the thought refers), we regard the thought and the thing as identical, then we can say (as I interpret him), that if existence belongs to the thing, this means it also belongs to the thought. In this case, however, we have not employed the thought in its normal role of being a sign, enabling us to refer to something beyond itself. Insofar as we predicate existence of the thought, it is only as a mental act and not as a sign; in any case, not of any "thing" as distinct from the thought. Since we should not be using our thought as a means of representation for what is not a thought, it could not give us any knowledge of the thing. On the other hand (this is the second alternative he considers), if we regard the construction of a concept as the stipulation of the traits necessary to define some *possible* thing, and we choose to list among the traits of such a possible thing, that it exists, we can, to be sure, treat the judgment that this possible-thing exists, as analytic. However, as Kant rightly insists, this would be "a miserable tautology," since we should then make explicit in the predicate only the postulated, but not necessarily genuine, trait of existing. He concludes, therefore—since we are interested in knowing of the genuine existence of something, and not of a postulated existence—that this kind of analytic judgment of existence would be of no value in giving us knowledge.

Now, one possibility Kant has not considered at all, is precisely that which obtains in the case of the statement "The world exists." Here we can say, correctly, it seems to me, that the statement is analytic. However, neither of the alternatives that Kant mentions, in which there are analytic statements containing "existence" as a predicate, applies to this case. For: (1) the thought-of-the-world and the world are not the same; the thought-of-the-world refers *to* the world. Yet the world itself has an independence and extensiveness that are surely not confined to the pullulations of my brain, nor to the products of my mind. Therefore, when existence is said to be a trait of the world, it is not the existence of some mental act or thought. (2) At the same time, in asserting existence of the world we are not, as in the second alternative considered by Kant, merely attaching the *postulated* trait of existing to an object. For the world is not merely possible, or merely conceived; it is an *actual* entity. And the warrant for saying that it is actual, is found in experience. The warrant is not, as in the case of wholly constructed concepts (for example, in fiction, mathematics, or speculative metaphysics), the result of the mind's own creative conceptual powers.

However, if the judgment "The world exists" is analytic, then, as in the case of all other analytic judgments, one could not deny existence to the world without contradiction. Kant maintains that the characteristic of non-contradiction (as a necessary and sufficient criterion for its truth) is to be found, for analytic judgments, only among those that are a priori. And an a priori judgment is one whose truth is known independently of experience. But if, as I have been arguing, the statement "The world exists" is known by experience, then we are obliged to reject the suggestion that the statement "The world exists" is to be classified as analytic a priori. It must be classed, consequently, as analytic a posteriori. While the predicate "exists" explicates the meaning of "the world," the warrant for assigning existence to the world is found in experience; it is, therefore, a posteriori.

In Kant's writings, the term "analytic" can only be conjoined with "a priori"; there is, for Kant, nothing that corresponds to an analytic a posteriori judgment. However, within the category of "analytic a priori judgments," Kant recognizes two separate types of subject-concepts: those that are empirical in character, and those that are "pure a priori." An example of the former would be "cow"; of the latter, "substance." Those analytic a priori judgments whose subject-concept itself is pure a priori, are of primary interest for Kant. However, for the purpose of the present analysis, it is the other type of analytic a priori (whose subject-concept is empirical) that is of greater interest. That Kant uses the same term ("analytic a priori") to cover judgments in which both types of subject-concepts occur, tends to obscure the point that there is an empirical "source" for some analytic judgments, and that not all judgments in which an empirical "source" is involved, are to be regarded as synthetic. In the analytic a priori judgment "Gold is yellow," the predicate "yellow" belongs to the subject "gold" as something contained in the subject-concept; this shows the analytic character of the judgment. It is a priori as well, because no *further* appeal to experience, beyond the initial empirical observation that the character of being yellow is regularly conjoined (for this object) to other observed traits, is required; moreover, the regular conjunction of yellow with these other traits is then given the class name "gold," by stipulation. Now if "yellow" can be joined to other qualities to yield the concept "gold," even though the warrant for affirming this conjunction is empirical, so, too, "existence" can be joined to other traits to yield the concept "the world" by a similar empirical warrant. Thus the judgment "The world exists" might well be an example of this less-important (for Kant) type of analytic a priori judgment. Or (in the interest of making explicit the empirical reference involved), it can be classified as analytic a posteriori.

The Approach to "Existence" in Modern Logic

The second major source of support for the thesis that "exists" is not a predicate, is derived from the logician's analysis of existential statements. This analysis was given its most influential formulation, in contemporary philosophy, in the writings of Bertrand Russell. Although Russell's views themselves later came under attack, for example at the hands of P. F. Strawson, the latter (as do many other philosophical logicians) continues to adhere to the claim that "exists" is not a predicate, and offers a more refined version of the same broad thesis. I shall, first, briefly summarize the Russellian formulation of this thesis, and then its more recent version. My purpose will not be to reject this type of analysis altogether, since it does clarify some uses of "exist"; rather, I shall try to show that this analysis does not suffice for explicating the meaning to be given to "exists" in the statement "The world exists." As it appears in this statement, the word "exists" functions as a genuine predicate, and cannot be eliminated altogether as performing this role. My only protest, therefore, against the theory we are about to consider would be that if it purports to clarify every possible legitimate use of "exists" (as in fact some defenders of it have urged), then this extreme claim is to be rejected; it does not do justice, for example, to what is meant by saying "The world exists."

In his lectures on "The Philosophy of Logical Atomism," Russell proposed the theory that "existence is essentially a property of a propositional function."[7] By a propositional function is meant "any expression containing an undetermined constituent, or several undetermined constituents, and becoming a proposition as soon as the undetermined constituents are determined."[8] An example of a propositional function would be "x is a man," or "n is a number," since by substituting for "x" in the first expression, say, the name "Socrates," we obtain a proposition, and similarly,

---

[7] B. Russell, "The Philosophy of Logical Atomism" (1918) in *Logic and Knowledge*, ed. R. C. Marsh (London, 1956), p. 232.
[8] *Ibid.*

by substituting for "*n*" in the second, say the term "3," again a proposition results. According to Russell:

> When you take any propositional function and assert of it that it is possible, that it is sometimes true, that gives you the fundamental meaning of 'existence.' You may express it by saying that there is at least one value of *x* for which that propositional function is true. Take '*x* is a man,' there is at least one value of *x* for which it is true. That is what one means by saying that 'There are men,' or that 'Men exist.'[9]

In line with this analysis, Russell claims, it makes no sense to affirm, or deny, that things exist in the world. With regard to actual things in the world "it is a sheer mistake to say that there is anything analogous to existence that you can say about them."[10] Statements that seem to contain "exists" as a genuine predicate (and not merely as a grammatical one), that is, that might be taken as giving us (through the use of the term "exists") some descriptive information about the subject to which it is applied, need to be treated, therefore, in such a way that this mistake is avoided. This is done by rewriting the original sentence so that "exists" does not appear as a predicate at all. Whatever is accomplished by the use of the word "exists" as a predicate, is now performed, more satisfactorily from a logical point of view, by the use of the phrase: "*there is* (or, *is not*) . . . something that has the property *p*." A statement that makes use of the phrase "there is . . . ," in the manner indicated, is known as an *existential statement*.

As a further clarification of Russell's treatment of the use of "exists," it needs to be stressed that for him the idea of existence can be replaced by a use of the concept of *truth*. He says:

> The fundamental form [of the notion of existence] is that which is derived immediately from the notion of "sometimes true." We say that an argument *a* "satisfies" a function ϕx if ϕa is true; this is the same sense in which the roots of an equation are said to satisfy the equation. Now if ϕx is sometimes true, we may say that there are *x*'s for which it is true, or we may say "arguments satisfying

[9] *Ibid.*
[10] *Ibid.*, p. 241.

φx exist." This is the fundamental meaning of the word 'existence.' Other meanings are either derived from this, or embody mere confusion of thought.[11]

Since, for Russell, "existence" can be assimilated to "truth," and since for him, too, "truth" is bound up with the use of language and the exercise of thought, it makes no sense to say that an object (e.g., this man) exists. G. E. Moore, in analyzing Russell's position, has brought out, clearly, this feature, by the contrast he draws between the analysis one would give to the statement "Some tame tigers growl" and to "Some tame tigers exist." There is, first of all, the difference that whereas the statement "Some tame tigers growl" can be analyzed into "There are some values of x for which it is true that x is a tame tiger *and* growls," the statement "Some tame tigers exist" means "There are some values of x for which it is true that x is a tame tiger." There is a second and more important difference: In saying "Some tame tigers exist," we do *not* mean "It is true for some value of x that x is a tame tiger and x exists." For while we can point to a particular tiger and say "This is a tame tiger," we cannot say, meaningfully, in pointing to the same tiger, "This *exists*." On the other hand, we could meaningfully say, in pointing to a particular tiger, not only "This is a tame tiger," but "This tiger growls."[12] The reason we cannot claim the statement "This tiger exists" to be meaningful, on Russell's view, is that "exists" has to do with *truth* (or true values of propositional functions) and cannot be asserted of entities such as tigers.

Russell's original investigations in the logic of propositional functions and existential statements have been absorbed in the more refined versions of the predicative or functional calculus of contemporary logic. As a standard treatment of this subject, use is made of quantification-expressions for the analysis of existential statements. Examples of quantification-expressions are: "there is at least one . . ."; "there are some . . ."; "there are no . . ."; "for every . . .". It is unnecessary for our present purpose to go

[11] B. Russell, *An Introduction to Mathematical Philosophy* (London, 1919), p. 164.
[12] Cf. G. E. Moore, "Is Existence a Predicate?" in *Philosophical Papers* (London, 1959), p. 124.

into the details of this development. Yet one advance in clarification, due to the work of P. F. Strawson, may be singled
out for summary, and as helpful in this connection. Strawson
points out that in the analysis of predicative formulae of the
subject-predicate type, we can make a broad, yet important, distinction between those terms that serve in a referring-role (marking out the subjects of our statement), and those terms that
function in an ascriptive, descriptive, or predicative way (thus
occupying the position of predicates).[13] We can call these, respectively, "individual variables" and "predicative variables." The
resources of modern logic are equipped to deal with all manner
of complexities of predicative formulae, in ways that the older
Aristotelian subject-predicate logic hardly sufficed. The use of
this logic also makes clear that a special treatment needs to be
given to what looks like a subject-predicate formula, but isn't,
namely, "such-and-such exists."

When given a statement of this form, Strawson points out, we
cannot regard the "such-and-such" as performing a genuine referring use. It does not occupy the role of a subject, nor does
"exists" perform the role of a normal predicate. One way of treating this expression is as a *presupposition* for a genuine subject-
predicate statement, rather than as itself a subject-predicate statement. (A statement S' is said to be a "presupposition" for another
statement S, when the truth of the first (S') is to be accepted as
a precondition for determining the truth or falsity of the second
(S).) Thus, the statement "All the books on Heraldry in my library
are leather-bound" presupposes that "There are books in my
library on Heraldry." Unless this latter statement were true, it
would not make sense to say that the first statement is either true
or false. I could not, so to speak, even get started referring to "the
books in my library on Heraldry" (as a potential subject of my
sentence, and to which I might then add the predicate "are leather-
bound"), unless, in fact, I do have such books in my library;
unless, that is, the presupposition is true. The question of the
truth or falsity of the statement "All the books in my library
on Heraldry are leather-bound" does not arise unless there *are*

13 P. F. Strawson, *Introduction to Logical Theory* (London, 1952), p. 129,
145; cf. the same author's *Individuals* (London, 1959), Chaps. 5, 6.

things referred to by the subject term. "Consequently," as Strawson says

> if we tried to assimilate a statement of the pattern "*x*'s *exist*" to any of the four forms [of traditional Aristotelian logic], or to regard it as a subject-predicate statement at all, we should be faced with the absurd result that the question of whether it was true or false could only arise if it were true; or, that, if it were false, the question of whether it was true or false did not arise. This gives a new edge to the familiar philosophical observation that 'exists' is not a predicate. When we declare or deny that 'there are' things of such-and-such a description, or that things of such-and-such a description 'exist,' the use of the quoted phrases is not to be assimilated either to the predicative or to the referrring use of expressions.[14]

For Strawson, as for Russell, the word "exists" has to do primarily with *the use of language*. Whereas Russell maintains that the "fundamental meaning" of existence is derived from one of the uses to which we put, specifically, the phrase "is true," Strawson prefers to approach the matter by way of an analysis of the different logical uses to which we put terms, generally, in our language. He accordingly points out that if we start by making a basic distinction between referring-uses and ascribing-uses, then, as a precondition for the exercise of the referring-uses of some term, we have already committed ourselves, by way of presupposition, to its existence. A statement affirming such existence is what he calls "an existence (or existential) statement," yet it is not itself a subject-predicate statement. Strawson's proposal consists, then, in breaking up an ordinary subject-predicate statement into two statements: (1) an existential statement that serves as a presupposition for (2), the subject-predicate statement proper; (1), the existential presupposition, certifies that the subject expression in (2), used referringly, is properly used.

This way of regarding the matter surely has many advantages. Yet it also has a special feature worth noting: it would be relevant to ask with respect to the existential statement that serves as the presupposition of the subject-predicate statement, how one can

---

[14] *Introduction to Logical Theory*, p. 191; cf. *Individuals*, p. 239.

determine *its* truth. In creating a separate category of presuppositional existence-statements, Strawson has not eliminated the difficulties he supposes occur where existence-statements are treated as subject-predicate statements. He merely pushes the main issue into the background. If a subject-predicate statement requires that a related presuppositional statement be true, we must still face the question: To what does a presuppositional statement have reference? and how can it be confirmed? If a presuppositional statement, when taken as a whole (rather than in terms of a subject and predicate taken separately, and as conjoined), refers to a situation in which some subject matter exists, then the ground for the truth of this presuppositional statement must be the actual existence of that subject matter. A presuppositional statement of the form "there are *x*'s," if true, refers to a situation in which *x*'s exist. In this event, even on Strawson's analysis, it would be necessary to recognize another use of the term "exists," namely, in connection with that to which the presupposition-statement of existence (on which subject-predicate statement rests), itself refers. And if we did recognize this other meaning of the term "exists," would it not in some way *characterize something?*

The logician is undoubtedly justified in pointing out that there are some uses of "exist" in which it is not logically proper to speak of "exists" as a predicate. Within the context of his system of discourse, he can so choose to define "exists" that it has, indeed, the meaning he assigns to it. The relevant question for our present concern, however, is whether this restriction does not do violence to other ordinary uses of the same word. Now to say that "exists" has other uses than the logician's, is not to suggest the wisdom of abandoning his use; it is simply to recognize that the term may also be used to refer to other matters. And, as I am arguing here, there is at least one other further and normal use of the word "exists" in which it does make sense to say that it *characterizes something,* namely, the world. To say that existence characterizes the world is not to say anything about the use of a referring-expression. In fact, it is not to say something about language at all (except indirectly and incidentally insofar as language, and language-users, are themselves part of the world.) It is to say something about *the world*: existence may be predicated

of the world. That the world exists, holds of the world whether
or not there are any terms in our language by which we could
refer to the world, or to its existence.

Existence and Status-Claims

We have thus far considered one use of the word "exists"—that
in which, as Strawson points out, it marks a pre-condition for the
referring-use of some term in the subject position of a sentence.
Others prefer to say this meaning is conveyed by the use of the
expression "there is . . .". In either case, we may agree,
"exists" is shown not to be a predicate. However, while this
analysis of "exists" is valuable, I am suggesting it does not exhaust
all possible meanings of the term, and, therefore, leaves open the
possibility it may also be found to serve as a legitimate predicate
for the world. Before turning to a statement of what this other
meaning of "exists" is, and in what sense it can be said to be informative or predicative of the world, I wish to take note, briefly,
of still another use of "exists." This use is different both from
the one already considered (the meaning given in quantificational
logic) and the meaning yet to be isolated as applicable to the
world. This other meaning of "exists" appears whenever we use
it to emphasize the contrast with that which is fictitious or
imaginary.

According to this use, we say that so-and-so *does* exist, when
we wish to challenge the claim that so-and-so is "only imaginary."
"Those stories you read, about what took place in a concentration camp," we say, "they're not just made up, the conditions
they describe really *existed*." Let us call this use of "exist," *making
a status-claim.*[15] This use of "exist" may be interpreted to assert
that, instead of being assigned the status of being imaginary,
that to which it refers is to be accorded the status of something
taking place in the world—of belonging to the same context and
environment as those of other real objects and events. One way,
then, of explicating the difference in status between that which

---

[15] Cf. K. E. M. Baier, "Existence," *Proceedings of the Aristotelian Society,*
lxi (1960-61), pp. 20 ff; also G. E. Moore, *Some Main Problems of Philosophy* (London, 1953), pp. 292-295.

is existent and that which is non-existent (imaginary) is this: whereas the former can be found in the world, the latter cannot. (In saying that so-and-so is non-existent, there is no need to deny that the mental act of imagining, or the telling of fictional stories, are—as acts or as activities—themselves in the world, and have, therefore, the status of being genuinely existent (in the present sense). What is being denied is that the *subjects* of these stories or the *referents* of these mental acts of imagining, have the status of being genuinely existent.)

Given this use of "exists," the question can now be put, whether it can be applied to the world. If we adopt our previous analysis of "the world," the answer must be that it cannot. For while "exists," as a status-term, might be a relevant term to use even in connection with the world, in a hypothetical discussion with a solipsist (in which we might wish to disabuse him of the view that the world is merely an idea in his mind), this use would be a highly special one. However, aside from this fancied and self-defeating colloquy with a solipsist, the term "exists" as meaning "having the status of belonging to the world" cannot be used to describe the world. For, whereas "exists" could apply to this or that particular object or event *within* the world, it could not be predicated *of* the world. The world could not, meaningfully, be said "to belong to the world." Therefore, if it does make sense to say that *the world exists*, there will have to be still another meaning of "exists" to be used for this purpose. And it is to this distinctive and important meaning of the term that I now, finally, turn.

"EXISTS" AS DESCRIPTIVE OF THE WORLD

Our argument, thus far, has been that the assertion "The world exists" cannot be analyzed after the manner of existential statements (e.g., as "*There is* an x, such that x has such-and-such a property"), nor on the pattern of those statements that, in affirming existence, are concerned to deny to something the status of being imaginary or fictitious. How then is "exists" being used when we say "The world exists"? One clue to the answer we are seeking is to be found in the fact that the word "exists" is a verb.

Now while it is possible to eliminate the verb altogether, and to replace it by some other grammatical expression, for example, by a noun or adjective (by saying: "The world has existence" or, "The world is existent"), these expressions will be found to derive *their* meaning from "exists" as a verb. The latter, accordingly, may be taken as containing the meaning we are seeking, if it has it at all.

Generally speaking, a verb suggests some form of activity; it describes what things or persons *do*. Is there any way in which "exists," as a verb, genuinely describes some *activity* of the world? Some philosophers would reject this suggestion as not having any merit at all. For example, the late John Austin remarked: "The word ["exist"] is a verb, but it does not describe something that things do all the time, like breathing, only quieter—ticking over, as it were, in a metaphysical sort of way."[16] Austin's comment is a perfectly sound one to make with respect to the word "exist," should we be tempted to use it as a verb in connection with ordinary things (including persons) *within* the world. He does not elaborate on this remark, himself, and perhaps he had no thought of the world as something that can be said to exist in contradistinction to ordinary things. In any case, that it can be so used—as a verb denoting the special and unique form of "activity" the world exhibits—is what I am proposing, and wish now to examine.

Let us begin by not only acknowledging, but underscoring, the point that as a verb, "exists" does not represent a mode of *activity* that can be applied to describe what some person or thing does. It makes no sense to say of some ordinary thing or person, that it or he *just exists*, or *just goes on existing* in the sense of engaging in some activity. For to speak in this way is, at best, an elliptical or foreshortened way of saying that the thing or person persists in carrying on some *particular* activity, or group of activities. Thus, when I say "Socrates existed" or "The moon exists" (and I do *not* mean to use "exist" here in the sense either of the logician's analysis of existential statements, or as denying fictitious status to these entities), the terms "existed" or "exists" serve as loose and general surrogates for other terms that can be substituted for them. To say that Socrates existed, is to say that Socrates *lived*, or that he per-

[16] J. L. Austin, *Sense and Sensibilia* (Oxford, 1962), p. 68, footnote.

sisted in some particular state, and to say that the moon exists, is to say that the moon occupies space and endures in time, that it behaves as a physical object. Whenever, in short, "exists" is used as a putative descriptive term for some activity—or group of activities—of something, we can get rid of the term "exists" altogether, and replace it, more informatively and fruitfully, by specifying the particular activity or kinds of activities that the object in question engages in.

Where "exists" is used in this way (as a substitute for some other, more successfully descriptive, term that designates some activity, function, or mode of behavior), it is desirable to replace the term "exists" by these activity-terms. For then the terms, thus substituted, will help to distinguish one type of entity from another, or one individual from another. The manner in which a body (for example, a satellite) "exists" (functions) will be different in certain important ways from the way in which a man "exists" (functions). Similarly, the whole complex of functions, processes, and activities that make up the "existing" of Socrates, differs in certain respects from the complex that identifies the "existing" of Bertrand Russell. Whatever can be said, informatively or descriptively, of the bundles of functions that distinguish one individual from another, or one type of object from another, can be said without using the term "exists" at all. It can be said through the use of verbs other than the verb "to exist."

But what of the world? In saying that the world exists, the term "exists," as I am using it, does have a distinctive and unique role to perform: it designates *what the world does*. Whereas we can say that the man lives, the satellite occupies space and time, and interacts physically with other bodies, none of these other verbs describe that the world does. They all describe what specific individuals *in* the world, do. Except for purposes of poetic or mythologic description, we should not say that the world lives, or moves, or grows, or breathes, or oscillates, or anything else of this sort. It does not even occupy space or endure in time. (Objects or entities *in* the world occupy space and have a history.)

What then does the world do? Well, the world does what the world does. It cannot be assimilated or literally compared to anything else. All other terms of description would be, at best, analogical, or only partially enlightening. But how can we describe what the world does, distinctively? The term used to describe its mode of "activity" should be irreducible to any other; it should not be replaceable by some other term. It is to serve as such a distinctive and unique term to describe what the world does, and nothing else does, for which we may use the term "exists." The mode of functioning that is appropriate to the world is—to exist. Instead of saying "The world worlds" or "The world carries on as a world," we say "The world exists." To exist is all that the world can do; this is what it is "fit" to do; or—to use traditional terminology—the essence of the world is its existence.

It has been reported that in the course of his lectures on existence, John Austin remarked that when God called out to Moses from the burning bush "I am," Moses (according to Austin) should have asked God: "You are what?" Now while it is not my intention to defend traditional conceptions of God, it would seem to me that Austin here missed the point about the uniqueness of God; for it is appropriate to God, though not to anything else, to be able to say "I am that I am," or, "I exist, for that is my essence." Whatever be the case with traditional conceptions of God, however (and without going so far as identifying God and the world, as Spinoza did), in this respect, we can say of the world exactly what Austin thought was an incomplete predication, namely, "it exists." If the world could speak, it, too, would say "I am," "I exist," and this would be a complete statement coming from the world, though not if made for, or by, anything else *in* the world.

If, on the other hand, "exists" has the force, simply, of expressing the claim that we can identify something to which we refer by the use of the name "the world," then in using the expression "The world exists," we should not be saying anything about the world. We should be saying, instead, that the expression "the world" can be applied. It can serve as a name for something we can undertake to describe. However, in saying that the world exists, I should not be adding to, or contributing to that description. On this analysis, then, I would not be predicating anything of the world in saying "The world exists." Instead, I should only be setting up the world as a subject, so that I might proceed (in the predicate of the sentence) to say something about that subject. For example, one might say "The world contains objects that have three spatial dimensions," or, "The world contains conscious creatures," and so on. If this were the type of analysis of "exists" we were to follow, then, of course, this would serve to cut the ground from under any claim that there is a *mystery* to the existence of the world. Since, if one follows the standard analysis of existential statements, existence is not anything that can be predicated of the world, but at best tells us something about the use of the *term* "the world" (that it can be used referringly as the subject of a sentence), we should then not be able to ask "Why does the world exist?" For, when we pose the question expressing the mystery of existence, we do not intend to ask "Why does the term 'the world' have a successful use as a referring expression?" If there is a genuine mystery of the existence of the world, in some way it must be connected with the fact that we *can* meaningfully predicate existence of the world. In posing the question about the mystery of existence, we are raising a question about this feature of the world, namely, that it exists; we wish to ask, "Why does the world have this feature, that it exists?"

But here we face a fresh difficulty. For if we claim that "exists," in the statement "The world exists," describes something about the world (indeed, that it describes the world uniquely, that it is part of the *meaning* of the term "the world,"), then it would appear, by this analysis, we place ourselves in a position that makes impossible the raising of a question about the mystery of existence. For, if "to exist" is what the world does, then where, in this, is there an unanswerable question?

To utter the statement "The world exists" is, on the foregoing analysis, to affirm a tautology, and to deny it would be self-contradictory. Thereby, we appear to have rendered the question "Why does the world exist?" futile and beside the point. We do not ask "Why does a triangle have three sides?" If anyone were to ask this question, our reply would take the form of rejecting the question as bogus. The question looks for a reason—but it is unwarranted to ask for a reason here. We should say "A triangle has three sides because that is how we define 'triangle'." Should we not, therefore, in response to the question "Why does the world exist?" have to reject this, too, if it purports to look for a reason, whereas, at bottom, there is only a question of definition involved? We should have to say: "The world exists because that is what the term includes as part of its meaning." However, if we accept this reply, we should again have cut the ground from under any claim that there is a mystery that the world exists; far from having an unanswerable question on our hands, we would seem to have a question that fails of significance. It rests upon the failure to acknowledge that the meanings of the terms "the world" and "exists" require that we say "The world exists." It would appear to make no sense to ask the kind of question about a definition or a tautology that we are interested in asking about the world, namely, why it is so.

There are two points we might make by way of reply to this objection. In the first place, we might say there is something misleading in the juxtaposition of the statements "The world exists" and "Triangles have three sides." While both are tautologies, they are nevertheless different in an important respect. The term "the world" refers to something that, for certain purposes, allows us to speak of it *as if* it were an individual, whereas the statement about triangles is about a class, or type, of conceptual object. The type of tautology "The world exists" illustrates, is one which makes use of a proper name. "The world" is used as a proper name. An identifying characteristic of that to which we apply this name is that it exists. It would be a misuse of the term "the world" to apply it to something that does not have the character of existing. However, the type of tautology illustrated by "Triangles have three sides" is that of applying a common noun to a class of objects. "Triangle" is a common noun used to refer to the class of three-sided plane figures. We may speak, properly, of giving a definition to a common noun, for example, "triangle"; but it would be inappropriate to say that we are giving a definition in assigning a proper name, for example, "the world," to that which we identify in our experience as existing. Both assignments of meaning involve conventional choices of particular symbols, viz., "the world" and "triangle." However, we are not defining "the world," as if there might be many different instances of "the world," or by subsuming it under a wider genus, in the same way in which, in defining "triangle," we can refer to instances of it, or subsume it under some wider genus. The use of the term "the world" involves the use of a proper name, in a way in which "triangle," being a common noun, does not at all function as a proper name. The importance of bringing out this difference between "the world" and "triangle" is this: since "the world" identifies something that, in certain respects, may be taken to resemble an "individual," we can raise the type of question contained in the mystery of existence. For just as might properly ask about some characteristic of an individual "Why does it have this characteristic?", so the possibility is left open that there should be a meaning for the question "Why does the world exist?", i.e., "Why does the 'object' the name "the world" refers to, have the feature that it exists?"

By way of making a second point in reply to our earlier question, let us reconsider the use of "exists" as brought out by the analysis of existential statements. We could ask: In raising the question "Why does the world exist?", are we not, after all, employing "exist" in the way this term typically functions in statements asserting that there are instances of some universal, law, form, or description? Would it not, in other words, be more fruitful to say the statement "The world exists" means: *"There is* something that has the characteristics of being the kind of entity the world is"; and would it not be better, therefore, to construe the question "Why does the world exist?" as asking "Why *is there* something that has the characteristics of the world?" And the latter question, we should then recognize, need not be fruitless, since it does not raise a spurious question about a tautology or a definition, any more than we should be asking a futile question if, after having satisfied ourselves that there are crater-like formations on the moon, we should ask, "Why are there such crater-like formations on the moon?"

Let us call the use of "exists" in the type of sentence just considered, an *instantiation claim.*[17] Is the use of "exists" in the statement "The world exists," or in the question "Why does the world exist?", one that involves making an instantiation claim? This suggestion has much to recommend it, and in pursuing it we shall find

[17] Cf. Baier, *op. cit.*

that instead of its replacing our earlier analysis of "exists," as a predicate uniquely descriptive of the world, we can in fact *add* it to our previous analysis. To do this, however, it is necessary to differentiate clearly the two different senses of "exists." Let us identify the use of "exists" in which it describes (as earlier discussed) the unique "activity" of the world, as "exists$_1$" and that use of "exists" in which it can be used as equivalent to "there is an instance of so-and-so," as "exists$_2$". Then the statement "The world exists" can be expanded, in accordance with the foregoing, to mean: "There is (exists$_2$) an instance of that which exists$_1$." Similarly, the question "Why does the world exist?" can be rewritten to read: "Why is there (exists$_2$) an instance of that which exists$_1$?" With these translations, we avoid the charge that the mystery of the existence of the world evaporates, if all that we mean by "exists" is that it marks a unique property of the world, and appears as such, in a specification of the use of the term "the world." For the mystery of existence is now to be located in the fact that *there is* (exists$_2$) an instance of this property of existence$_1$.

However, we need immediately to qualify these remarks, by acknowledging certain important differences between the way in which "exists$_2$" occurs as part of the meaning of the statement "The world exists," and ordinary instantiation claims. And to do so, let us note, at once, that in using the philosophic distinction between "instance" and "universal," we normally allow that what is described conceptually, may or may not have actual instances. Thus we can characterize what a unicorn is, in general terms, without requiring that actual zoological instances be found in the world. However, if we wish to assimilate the charactersitic of existing$_1$ (the unique mode of "activity" of the world) to other universals or concepts, there is this important difference: we cannot allow the world's existence$_1$ not to be actually instantiated. Indeed, if "exists$_1$" is thought of as a predicate, on the model of other universals, it comes to be known through our having an experience of an actual "instance" of it. Unless there were this actual instance of the world's existing$_1$, there would be no "abstraction" of the predicate expressed in the statement "The world exists$_1$." The universal "exists$_1$" is exemplified in one and only one instance. In the case of the world, the characteristic "existing$_1$" is grounded in, and confirmed by, our common experience of the fact there is (exists$_2$) an actual instance of existence$_1$. And the mystery of existence can be expressed by asking the question: "Why is there an instance of that which exists$_1$?" or, more colloquially, "Why does the world exist?"

Part Three

"WHY DOES THE WORLD
EXIST?"

CHAPTER VI

The Theistic Answer

THE CONCEPT of the mystery of existence can be phrased by asking the question "Why does the world exist?" In determining the possible philosophic content and value of this question, I have thus far sought to clarify in what sense we can use the expression "the world," and what it means to assert "The world exists." Insofar as our analysis has any merit, it would serve to answer the complaint of a would-be-critic that the question is only unanswerable because it is not properly framed, in that it displays some flawed use of language. By showing how the terms "the world" and "exists" are being used, we can reject the claim that the above question suffers from the fact that it violates some linguistic rule of use. Again, in showing in what way we can affirm the statement "The world exists," as a major presupposition of the question "Why does the world exist?", I have tried to meet the possible objection that the question is unanswerable because it rests on a false presupposition, and so commits the fallacy of complex-question.

To carry forward the analysis, we have now to ask the following: The question "Why does the world exist?", by its use of the term "why," would seem to presuppose that there is some reason or explanation for the fact that the world exists. If such a presupposition is involved, is there any warrant for adopting it? Would it be possible to give a sound and acceptable formulation to the mystery of existence without subscribing to some form of *Principle of Sufficient Reason?*

There are two possible ways in which one might construe the claim that the question "Why does the world exist?" is unanswerable, and so a mystery. One of these tacitly, or explicitly, appeals to the Principle of Sufficient Reason, the other makes no appeal to this principle. The first consists in the assertion that while we may be assured *that* there is a reason for the existence of the world, we could never know *what* it is; the unanswerability constituting the mystery of existence is simply one of human inability to specify the particular character of the reason for the world's existence. The second consists in the assertion that the mystery of existence is due to our inability to say *whether* there is any reason at all for the world's existence, and not simply in our inability to specify *what* that reason is.

Now, which of these alternative interpretations should we adopt for the mystery of existence? I shall argue that only by adopting the second of these interpretations can we give an acceptable account. For, to adopt the first alternative is to maintain, for example with theism, that there is no ultimate mystery of existence: the existence of the world can be explained by a belief in God's creative power. For the theist there is no persistence of the sense of the mystery of existence of the world. One who genuinely believes in God's existence does not continue to be bothered by the question "Why does the world exist?" It is one of the marks of the presence of a genuine sense of the mystery of existence that there is no explanation, and hence no stilling of the question.

In what follows, I shall be concerned with the attempt made by those who follow in the tradition of natural theology to provide, by a process of inferential reasoning, grounds for belief in the existence of God. I shall argue that the attempt of natural theology to establish, by reasoning, the existence of a Necessary Being (whose existence can answer the question "Why does the world exist?"), is unsuccessful. However, unlike those numerous critics who, in their assault on demonstrative theism, maintain that the question from which the search for an explanation set out, must be rejected as itself spurious (because any attempt to answer it is demonstrably absurd), I shall, myself, argue that no such radical result need be adopted. There is a genuine mystery of existence —though the attempt to provide an answer, as in the case of theism, by means of a doctrine of Necessary Being, is thoroughly unsound.

To guard against misunderstanding, let me note that the following discussion will not deal with the Principle of Sufficient Reason as expressed in terms of the (so-called) Law of Causality, or as a methodological principle employed by science. I have no wish to challenge the Principle of Sufficient Reason where it takes the form of a methodological postulate serving to define the aims and interests of science. For, as Kant showed, science could not abandon the presupposition that reasons can be given for the properties or patterns things are found to have, without surrendering its very character as a continuing and endless quest for such reasons, and for continually better ways of expressing these reasons. What I do wish to challenge is the Principle of Sufficient Reason when taken as a metaphysical principle, and as applied to the fact with which science is in no way concerned, namely, the fact that the world exists.

The Leibnizian Appeal to the Principle of Sufficient Reason

A classic locus of the use of the metaphysical Principle of Sufficient Reason and, in connection with it, the cosmological argument for the existence of God, is to be found in Leibniz. Of the various places where Leibniz makes use of the Principle of Sufficient Reason, his essay "On the Ultimate Origination of Things" (1697), offers a clear and succinct statement. He there speaks of the world as an "aggregate of finite things," and of God as a "dominant unity" that "not only rules the world but constructs or fashions it." God is not only extramundane but "the ultimate reason of things." According to Leibniz, God could supply the reason for the existence of the world and the character it possesses. Leibniz, as a human being, and as a spokesman for all human rational minds, appeals to the Principle of Sufficient Reason as a *means* for arriving at the belief in the existence of God. In this capacity, the Principle of Sufficient Reason suffices to account for the truth of all those propositions whose truth could not be sanctioned merely by an appeal to the Principle of Contradiction. Other possible worlds, each of which has its own compossible (internally consistent) sets of characteristics and things, would not violate the Principle of Contradiction, any more than the present world does. What, then, accounts for the existence of this world? Leibniz does not allow that the existence of this world is either intelligible in its own right (as Spinoza maintains), nor simply, as far as its existence is concerned, unintelligible. He maintains that "the sufficient reason of existence cannot be found either in any particular thing or in the whole aggregate and series of things."

Leibniz uses an analogy between the existence of the world and the existence of a book:

> Let us suppose that a book of the elements of geometry existed from all eternity and that in succession one copy of it was made from another, it is evident that although we can account for the present book by the book from which it was copied, nevertheless, going back through as many books as we like, we could never reach a complete reason for it, because we can always ask why such books have at all times existed, that is to say, why books at all, and why written in this way. What is true of books is also true of the different states of the world; for, in spite of certain laws of change, the succeeding state is, in some sort, a copy of that which precedes it. Therefore, to whatever earlier state you go back, you never find in it the complete reason of things, that is to say, the reason why there exists any world and why this world rather than some other.[1]

The advantages of beginning with this view of Leibniz's is that it presents, in compact form, the entire range of those arguments for the existence of God that, as distinguished from the ontological proof, rest upon some appeal to fact as their starting point. Thus, Leibniz, in the above argument, attempts to prove by means of the Principle of Sufficient Reason both that God is the cause of the *existence* of the world, and that God is also the cause of the selection of this particular world from the realm of possibilities (or, that the world we find in our experience has the particular *structure* it has rather than some other.) Adopting familiar terminology, Leibniz here conjoins under the Principle of Sufficient Reason both the cosmological proof and the teleological proof for the existence of God. Of these two types of argument, however, the cosmological argument is the more fundamental, since the teleological argument presupposes the cosmological: one must first be

---

[1] G. W. Leibniz, "On the Ultimate Origination of Things" in *The Monadology and Other Philosophical Writings,* translated by R. Latta (Oxford, 1898), p. 338.

assured that there is some reason why the world exists at all, before one can attempt to account for the particular character the world has.

The Cosmological Argument; The Thomistic Version

It was the merit of St. Thomas's famous account of the five proofs for the existence of God, that, in separating and disentangling the several types of proof, he brought out the logical priority of the cosmological proof to the teleological. Since our principal interest, in the present discussion, is with the adequacy of the attempt to prove the existence of God as a way of answering the question "Why does the world exist?", and since the mystery of existence is not to be located in the fact that the world has the particular character it does (insofar as we can determine it), it will be sufficient, for our purposes, to confine ourselves to that aspect of the Principle of Sufficient Reason that takes the form of the cosmological argument. Because, too, Thomas Aquinas's arguments have been the most carefully analyzed, and historically the most influential formulations of these arguments in the entire tradition of theism, I shall, in what follows, take my point of departure for a criticism of the Principle of Sufficient Reason from these formulations.

Of the five proofs for the existence of God, the first three proofs are sometimes treated as part of one argument, called, in this broad sense, "the cosmological proof," although in a strict and narrow sense, only the third of these proofs is so named. The first argument starts from the fact of motion in the world, and argues to the existence of a Prime Mover as the source of motion in the world. The second starts from the fact of causal relatedness of events in the world, and argues to the need for recognizing a First Cause for the series of efficient causes. The third way argues for the need to acknowledge a Necessary Being, as the only means for accounting for the contingent character of the constituent parts of the world and of the world itself.

At the heart of these arguments, and of the modern restatements of them that seek to preserve their fundamental worth (when, for example, freed from their embedment in the terminology of an Aristotelian physics and cosmology), are two claims that need to be singled out for special analysis. The first has to do with the claim that there is something essentially *incomplete* about ordinary commonsensical or scientific explanatory accounts; the second has to do with the claim that not only the various constituents of the world but the world itself is *contingent*. Taken together, the facts of incompleteness and contingency point to what is regarded as the *finite* character of the world and all that it contains; they also point to the need for recognizing an Infinite Being as the ground and source of the world's existence.

The arguments for the existence of God, and the cosmological argument in particular, have been subjected to a great variety of well-known criticisms, and it is not my intention to add to their number by pretending to offer some altogether fresh or novel considerations. Nevertheless, because among the great mass of criticisms one frequently finds arguments that have as little merit as the ones they undertake to criticize, it will be of some value to single out, for brief summary, those criticisms that would seem to have sufficiently damaging worth, to make the view they attack, indefensible. I shall argue for the following results: (1) The alleged deficiency of ordinary causal explanations in science is not a genuine deficiency in the sense intended; and insofar as there is an actual deficiency in these explanations, it would not be removed, or remedied, by recourse to the type of explanation the theist proposes. (2) The claim that the world is contingent (and not simply individual occurrences within it), commits the fallacy of composition. Moreover, to say the world is contingent, is not to describe a given characteristic of the world from which the existence of a Necessary Being can be inferred. To say the world is contingent, in the sense intended, is already to presuppose that it is created out of nothing, and thus begs the question.

The Incompleteness of Ordinary Causal Explanations

It is claimed in St. Thomas's first and second arguments, that there cannot be an infinite regress in the sequence of either movers or efficient causes, and, therefore, that there must be a prime mover or first efficient cause ("which all men call God"). Father Copleston, in interpreting these arguments, tells us "when Aquinas talks about an 'order' of efficient causes he is not thinking of a series stretching back into the past, but of a hierarchy of causes, in which a subordinate member is here and now dependent on the causal activity of a higher member."[2] It is not an infinite series as such, that Aquinas rejects; there is no impossibility in the idea of a "horizontal series" (to use Fr. Copleston's phrase), in which events are arranged by an order of precedence in an infinite series of causes and effects stretching back into the past. What Aquinas means to reject, rather, is a causal series or hierarchy of a "vertical" sort

> in which a lower member depends here and now on the present causal activity of the member above it . . . (for) unless there is a 'first' member, a mover which is not itself moved or a cause which does not itself depend on the causal activity of a higher cause, it is not possible to *explain* the 'motion' or the causal activity of the lowest member . . . Suppress the first efficient cause and there is no causal activity here and now. If therefore we find that some things in the world are changed, there must be a first unmoved mover. And if there are efficient causes in the world, there must be a first efficient, and completely non-dependent cause. The word 'first' does not mean first in the temporal order, but supreme or first in the ontological order.[3]

Both St. Thomas's original statement and Fr. Copleston's restatement are couched in terminology derived from Aristotle. It is best, however, to restate the import of the cosmological argument in terms that do not make it appear it depends essentially on the use of that terminology or associated ideas. And, as a matter of fact, when we look closely at the argument, even in its original Thomistic form, it is evident that the argument has to do primarily with the general character of causal explanations given to natural phenomena. The need to avoid an infinite regress in motions or in efficient causes is, at bottom, the claim that there is something insufficient and inadequate about the kinds of explanation to be found in common sense or in science. It is not denied that these explanations are partially adequate; it is, rather, that they do not suffice for complete intelligibility. It is only by recognizing a "first cause," that does not suffer from the incompleteness of ordinary

[2] F. C. Copleston, *Aquinas* (Pelican Books, 1955), p. 118.
[3] *op. cit.*, pp. 118 f., my italics.

explanations, the argument insists, that we finally overcome this deficiency.

What merit is there in the charge that scientific explanations are unsatisfactory because incomplete? There is a perfectly obvious sense in which science is incomplete, namely, in the sense that there are many questions of an empirical sort to which there are no satisfactory answers. (To say that there are as yet unanswered questions, does not imply, however, that there need be any implicit reference to some ideally completed stage science could reach, in which all possible questions will have been answered.) At the same time, there are even now, many questions that science *can* answer satisfactorily, and where such answers take the form of *explanations*. The question at issue is whether it is true to say of these that they suffer from an essential incompleteness.

Let us consider, by way of reply, the main kinds of situations in which scientific explanations are sought. For our present purposes, these may be divided into two groups. In the first, an explanation is sought for some particular occurrence. For example, we may ask: "Why, on July 20, 1963, could one see a total eclipse of the sun at Northeast Harbor, Maine, whereas those in New York City, on the same day, could witness only a partial eclipse?" To be able to give a satisfactory answer to this question, requires that we have knowledge of two types of fact: (1) the statement of relevant regularities or laws (e.g., of mechanics and optics); (2) the data specifying the appropriate initial conditions (of time, place, etc.) of the occurrence in question. The combination of these two types of statements, the one universal, the other particular, permits the derivation of the conclusion that describes the particular situation for which explanation was originally sought. Let us call this type of explanation, "explanation of individual events by relevant laws." A second major type of explanatory problem arises whenever we ask for the reasons why an empirically confirmed *law* has the form it does. Where successful, the answer to this type of question consists in the appeal to the resources of *theory*. Theories constitute fundamental, conceptually constructed ways of regarding phenomena, at the base of which lie the use of some guiding analogy or model. The test of the adequacy of a theory does not consist in any simple correspondence with observed fact. Instead, regard must be had for such general considerations as fruitfulness for further inquiry, logical economy of conceptual means, and degree of comprehensiveness, or range, in numbers of facts systematically encompassed. A successful use is made of theory to yield an explanation of an empirical law, when, having made the appropriate translations of the empirical concepts of the law into the corresponding conceptual constructs of the theory, the empirical regularity to be explained is then shown, by a process of mathematical or logical derivation, to follow from the principles or fundamental equations of the theory in question. A familiar example is the explanation of the empirically established Galilean law of falling bodies, or Kepler's laws of planetary motion, by means of Newtonian theory (or, alternatively, by means of Einstein's general theory of relativity.) Let us call this type of explanation, "explanation of empirical regularities by use of theory."

We must now ask: Is it the case that all explanations of individual events by means of laws, or all explanations of laws by means of theories, are infected with an essential inadequacy due to their incompleteness? The answer is that this is not so. Given the question, "Why did this projectile land at this spot?", the *complete* answer can be given that removes *that* question. The answer is supplied by appealing to the relevant laws of projectiles, together with the initial conditions of its firing. If one should ask—and this is what those who use the cosmological argument, typically, do— "But why were the initial conditions what *they* were?", or, "Why is the law of projectiles what *it* is?", new and different questions are now being asked. There may, or may not, be satisfactory answers to these new questions. But whether one does, or does not, have such answers, in no way reduces the completeness of the answer to the *initial* question. Suppose one wishes to explain, for example, the occurrence of the initial conditions referred to in the answer to the original question. It may be possible, in providing such an explanation, to apply the same law, or different laws, from those used originally, together with relevant fresh initial conditions. And so on. In every case, the explanation, when given, is complete; it is not made less so by the fact that new and different questions can be asked.

Or again, suppose one asks why a particular law is as it is, and suppose an answer is available, by showing that the law in question can be conceptually incorporated within the framework of a particular theory and deduced from, or in accordance with, its fundamental principles. Now, however, if one should ask the further, new question "Why is the theory to be accepted?"—this question has no meaning, *if* what is sought is the logical derivation of the theory in question from the principles of some still further theory. Theories, unlike laws, are not deduced from other theories. Since what is essential to them, is their way of regarding phenomena, at best some features of their guiding analogies, or some principles they incorporate, may be transformed, extended, or included in the basic outlook of a new theory. In any case, when a theory does its job well—when it explains the law, or laws, in question, in a way superior to any other available, rival theory—this constitutes a *complete* answer to the question asked.

The search for various types of improvements in an explanatory schema that scientists engage in, is not spurred by the sense of "incompleteness" of which the theist (using the cosmological argument), complains. Rather, the concern of science with improvements takes the form of strengthening the evidential support for statements of fact, refining the accuracy of measurements, clarifying concepts, and finding explanatory theories of even greater logical simplicity, range of systematic power, heuristic fertility, and empirical confirmability than those already in use.

Confronted with the foregoing comments, the theist is likely to say that they are quite irrelevant to the point he wishes to make. Indeed, he might very well be prepared to grant all I have said about the different types of explanation in science. Nevertheless, he would say, this analysis really does not overcome the basic difficulty we face; even after science has done the very best it can, in explaining natural phenomena, the basic fact to which the cosmological argument calls attention, remains. Now, what is the genuine source of this dissatisfaction, and why will nothing short of a belief in God satisfy the theist?

It is easy to go wrong here. For example, C. D. Broad locates one alleged source of dissatisfaction of the theist with scientific explanations in the fact that, in appealing to empirical laws or to the occurrence of particular events, as factors in our explanations, we are appealing to items that have the nature of being only "brute fact."[4] And Broad presumes that one sort of intelligibility the theist is hankering after, is a type of intelligibility in which such appeals to brute fact would be altogether eliminated and replaced by the kind of intelligibility which, supposedly, is already present in mathematics. Such intelligibility would consist in the logical demonstration of truths on the basis of self-evident premisses. In other words, Broad attributes to theism the view that science, to be acceptable, ought to be, somehow, very much as Descartes construed universal mathematics. If only the regularities of empirical science were as perspicuously self-warranting as the laws of mathematics (supposedly) are! But, of course, Broad recognizes that they are not, and imputes to the theist the use of a criterion of intelligibility that is of this rationalistic sort. He claims the theist shares the belief that only if this were satsified, would he, the theist, stop asking the kinds of questions he does, of every answer given by the scientist; only then would he stop being dissatisfied with the present incompleteness of science.

It seems to me that this interpretation is a mistake. The theist, in his dissatisfaction with science, is not appealing to some hidden rationalist assumptions. For even if (*per impossible*) empirical laws, or the statement of particular occurrences were reducible to identities, this would still not solve the theist's problem. For he would rightly point out that this would not account for the *existence* of a succession of individual events and objects in the world, since these could not, in any way, be deduced from laws or universals, however the latter are construed. The theist (in the cosmological argument) is concerned with the existence of the world and the particularities it contains, not, primarily, with the pattern of internal deducibilities it contains.[5]

---

[4] C. D. Broad, "The Existence of God" in *Religion, Philosophy, and Psychical Research* (London, 1953), p. 184.

[5] Cf. R. Garrigou-Lagrange, *God: His Existence and His Nature*, Vol. I, p. 295: "The necessary being cannot be *the law* which unites contingent and transitory elements. For this law, in order to be the necessary being, would have to have its sufficient reason within itself and also contain the sufficient reason for all the phenomena that it has controlled, now controls, and will control in future. Now a law is nothing but a constant relation between vari-

We come much closer to understanding the source of dissatisfaction of the theist with ordinary explanations, if we revert, for a moment, to the sort of thing Fr. Copleston talks about, when he points to the need for interpreting the infinite regress of St. Thomas's arguments, not in terms of a *series* stretching back into the past, but in terms of a *hierarchy* of causal dependencies. (To the scientist, too, of course, talk of explanations in terms of a "series" of causes is highly misleading and confused. The facts of the world are not stretched out like beads on a string. Explanations are not via causal chains, in which the greater the number of links stretching into the past, the more adequate the explanation.) The theist himself, according to Fr. Copleston, is willing to abandon the imagery of a series of events, whether finite or infinite. He asks us instead to think of the structure of causal explanation in the world, after the manner of a hierarchy of causes, with orders of subordination, instead of as an order of temporal precedence.

We should not assume, however, that the theist, by this talk of a "hierarchy of causes," is seeking to express the ideal of a somehow completed science: one in which we should have *the* most comprehensive and rigorously formulated theory, sufficient to explain all items of fact. For, God as a "first cause" is not a *perfect theory*, the supreme means of expressing the intelligibility of all items of fact in the world. And why not? Here we get a clue, I think, in the very use of the word "hierarchy." The model here being employed is one that stresses an order of dependence upon authority, and the delegation of powers to subordinates. Causes are thought of on the analogy of agents; laws of nature are thought of as the outcome of the imposition of order, as enactments. The existence of the world, and all it contains, is to be understood as the product of a supreme authoritative command, or creative act. The reason the theist is fundamentally dissatisfied with scientific explanations is that, in a profound sense, he is not really interested (when speaking in terms of the cosmological argument), in the scientific explanation of individual events *at all*. What he is

---

ous phenomena or beings, and as every relation presupposes the extremes upon which it is based, the existence of a law presupposes the existence of the phenomena which it unites, instead of being presupposed by them. It exists only if they exist."

basically interested in, is *the existence of, and the explanation for the existence of, the world.* Since science never deals with *this* problem, *all* its explanations will necessarily always be inadequate. However, if science does not deal with this problem, how could it even fail to give a complete answer? The problem of the existence of the world is of an altogether different character from the kinds of problems with which science deals: one cannot measure them by the same yardstick. It follows that, if science is not an incomplete theology, neither is theology a complete science. The two are totally discontinuous.

If this be granted, then the cosmological argument fails as an argument. For the argument undertakes to show how we can make a valid inference to a first cause, from the realization of the inadequacy of other causal explanations. But the "first cause" cannot be a cause in the same sense in which other causes are causes; *they* explain the characteristics of occurrences *in* the world; *it* would explain the existence *of* the world. The term "cause" means something altogether different in both cases, and nothing we can say about causes in the scientific or ordinary sense, can ever lead to any intelligible comments about cause, when taken to mean "first cause" or Creator of the world. The cosmological argument claims to make a logical transition from one to the other. This, however, is spurious. Instead of showing that we are led by the premisses (facts about ordinary causation) to the conclusion (facts about God's causation), the argument is merely a disguised form of affirming the existence of God as the answer to the question "Why does the world exist?" The argument does not *prove* that God exists, as it sets out to do. Instead, it presupposes the truth of the statement affirming the existence of God. In short, the argument *begs the question.*

The Contingency of Finite Beings and the Necessary Existence of God

In addition to the alleged incompleteness of ordinary causal explanations of natural phenomena, another feature that marks finite entities, according to traditional theism, is their contingency. It is because we find objects and events in the world, and indeed the world itself, to be contingent, that we are led to a belief in the existence of a Necessary Being as their ultimate source and ground. The substance of this argument is contained in the third of St. Thomas's proofs for the existence of God. Its importance is so great, that it alone is spoken of as *the* cosmological proof. In the present section, I shall be principally concerned with the analysis and evaluation of the claim that the world is contingent. I propose to show that this claim cannot be sustained. Since the argument undertakes to deduce the existence of a Necessary Being from the contingent character of the world, it follows that if there is no warrant for establishing the latter, then this cannot provide a basis for a belief in a Necessary Being. It so happens that the idea of a Necessary Being is itself a confused one. But my principal concern, in what follows, is with the premises of the argument from contingency, rather than with the conclusion; if we can give good reasons for rejecting the premises, we need not bother to question the conclusion also. I shall, therefore, reserve a discussion of "necessary being" for Chapter IX, where, instead of considering it as a way of describing God's nature, I shall discuss the use of this concept as it relates to the thesis that the existence of the world is necessary.

St. Thomas's argument starts from the fact, attested to by our ordinary experience of objects and events in nature, that these, at some time, began to exist, and that whatever began to exist, at one time did not exist. Things that have this character, St. Thomas describes by saying "it is possible for them to exist or not to exist." (Thomas does not use the term "contingent" in this argument; nevertheless, since it is normally understood in this way, in what follows I shall use "contingent" to mean what St. Thomas calls "things possible to be or not to be.") The next step in the argument is the claim that it is impossible that there should be just these contingent things among the things that have being or exist. For if there were only contingent things in existence, and these have the possibility of not existing, then, we could envisage a situation in which there would be nothing at all in existence. For the coming-into-existence of each thing, or the ceasing of its existence, is caused by some other thing already in existence, and if it were the case that all the beings in existence might not have existed, then there will have been a time in which, in fact, nothing existed. (To see this last point, let us arrange contingent existences in an order of causal and temporal succession. We may conceive the most recent event not to have come into existence, since it is contingent, and there was a time when it did not exist. Moreover, the event or thing which, in fact, served as its cause, and brought it into existence, also being of the same contingent character, need not have come into existence, and indeed did not exist, until *its* causal antecedents began to exist; and, since it is possible that it, in turn, should not have existed, that it did not in fact exist, we are thus led—by eliminating each contingent existent in turn—to nothing. If all things in the world were of this contingent character, then each one, at one point, did not exist. In this case, there would have been absolutely nothing; there would be no world at all in existence.) But then it would have been impossible for anything to come into existence. For in order to do so, there must already be something in existence (since nothing can come into existence of itself.) The fact is, however, there are things in existence. We must, consequently, surrender our original assumption that the only things that exist are contingent beings. There must be a Necessary Being, one that neither comes into existence nor can *not* exist. This Necessary Being (God) confers existence on all other things, while being itself uncaused.

The main burden of the cosmological argument is not only to prove that the world is contingent, but that, as contingent, the world depends for its existence upon the existence of a Necessary Being. The failure of the argument is not simply, however, that it does not establish that there is a Necessary Being, but that it does not establish that the world is contingent. That various entities—objects or events—*in* the world are contingent, this is what the argument starts from; and adopting the language it employs, there need be no special difficulty in accepting its account of the fact that such events and objects, as one ordinarily encounters them in experience, are contingent. But the crucial step is that in which the argument proceeds to make a judgment of the same type about the world, as it makes about any individual object or event within it, namely, that the world, too, is contingent. It is this step that is open to serious doubt.

In the summary of St. Thomas's argument given earlier, the

warrant for going from statements about the contingency of particular objects and events, to the contingency of the world, was not made sufficiently clear, since St. Thomas himself is not explicit about the reasons. He says, simply: "Therefore, if everything is possible not to be, then at one time there could have been nothing in existence, because that which does not exist only begins to exist by something already existing." Focussing our attention on the first part of this sentence, we must ask: Why does it follow that if everything is possible not to be (i.e., if everything is contingent), then at one time there could have been nothing in existence? According to Fr. Copleston, we are to understand the reason as flowing from an assumption St. Thomas adopts of an *infinite time*.

> Aquinas is clearly supposing for the sake of argument the hypothesis of infinite time, and his proof is designed to cover this hypothesis. He does not say that infinite time is impossible: what he says is that if time is infinite and if all things are capable of not existing, this potentiality would inevitably be fulfilled in infinite time. There would then be nothing.[6]

However, this hypothesis of an infinite time will not do. It does not in the least sanction the conclusion intended. For, let us assume (since we are not forbidden to do so on the assumption of an infinite time) that the number of existent objects or events is also infinite. That St. Thomas indeed *has* to assume that the number of contingent existents is infinite, follows from his assumption that whatever exists, or comes into existence, has *another* being as its cause.[7] However, given an infinite time and an infinite series of objects or events to fill this time, it does not follow, if the causal rela-

---

[6] *Aquinas*, p. 120.

[7] This point has been put as follows: "Suppose that there are only four objects in the universe: 1, 2, 3, and 4; and let us suppose that the lower numerically is the cause of the higher. On the assumption that everything which existed began to exist, and hence, was caused, we can suppose successively that things numbered 4, 3, 2, and 1, respectively cease to exist in that order. But if we do, then we must *imply* that there is an "o" thing which was cause of No. 1. Hence, the assumptions 'Everything which began to exist has a cause' and 'Everything began to exist' are equivalent to saying that 'There is an infinite collection of things, at least successively.' " J. F. Ross, "God and Logical Necessity," *Philosophical Quarterly*, Vol. 11, (1961), p. 24.

tions among these objects and events is thought of in terms of a relation of temporal precedence (the cause antedating the effect), that "if all things are capable of not existing this potentiality would be fulfilled in infinite time. There would then be nothing." For to say that "all things are capable of not existing" is to say that *each and every* thing (object or event) depends for its occurrence, or existence, on antecedent causal conditions. If, as the argument presupposes, causes and effects are thought of as occupying time, with the cause preceding the effect, then not all the individual objects and events in the world will be simultaneous. They will form a set, temporally considered, that is spread out through infinite time; and, since the members of this set are infinite in number, they will fill, collectively, infinite time. They will form an infinite series of temporally overlapping events. The coming-into-existence and the going-out-of-existence of each individual event will occupy some finite temporal interval, however large or small. Let us assume, for the sake of simplicity, that the beginning of one event depends causally on the ending of another. It follows from this, if we have an infinite time in the past throughout which to trace the causal sequences of relative beginnings and endings in finite events (or durations of finite objects), that *there is no point in the past where absolutely nothing exists:* for there will always be another antecedent event for the "last" one examined.

It is simply a *non-sequitur*, then, to say that if each and every object or event in the world is contingent (begins to exist and is causally dependent on some other being), that the world, taken as composed of such entities, itself has to be contingent. The theist, as do many other metaphysicians, regards the world as an all-inclusive class or totality. I have suggested, in an earlier section of this book, why we need not be committed to speaking in this way: what we mean by "the world" need not be thought of as a class or whole. But even if we allow ourselves to say with the theist that the world is a class or whole, or to think of it *as if* it were, then we should have to conclude that the part of the cosmological argument we have been examining commits the fallacy of composition. We cannot say that, since every event or object in ordinary experience is contingent, therefore, the entire world is also contingent.

One might argue that what St. Thomas is alluding to—as a basis for the claim that if there were only contingent beings then there would be nothing in existence,—is not (as Fr. Copleston assumes) the hypothesis of an infinite time, but the need to recognize a nontemporal, omnipresent order of dependency of all contingent beings on a Necessary Being, in a causal hierarchy. In that case the argument from contingency reduces to one for the incompleteness of ordinary explanations (of common sense or science). And the reply to this objection has already been given in our earlier discussion of the first and second arguments. The point may, nevertheless, be restated, as follows, as bearing on the present context of discussion. The central question is whether the world can be spoken of as contingent: whether it makes sense to say that it might not have existed, and whether it also makes sense to say that it owes its existence to some other being. In saying that it does make such sense, the theist is taking advantage of the fact that he has already answered the question "Why does the world exist?", whereas what we need are reasons for believing that the world might not have existed. For, once grant this manner of describing the world, that it, too, is contingent, then one has not so much prepared the ground for the concluding statement that there is a Necessary Being: one has already used this conclusion in so characterizing the world. In short, we cannot say that we need, simply, to start from the realization that the world is contingent, and that we should *then* come to recognize that its existence is dependent upon God; to have characterized the world as contingent, as something that might not have existed, and whose existence is dependent on some being independent of itself, is already to use the concept of God. In saying that it is contingent, one begs the question, or presupposes what one is trying to prove, namely, that the world is created.

Some Recent Versions of the Cosmological Argument

There have been some recent attempts, both within the Thomist tradition as well as by some writers not readily identifiable with this school, to soften the impact of the many criticisms leveled against the classic proofs for the existence of God. It is claimed by these writers that what is in question, after all, is not a matter of strict *logical* inference, but, at bottom, an *ontological* relation of dependency of all finite beings on God.

In his book on Aquinas, from which I quoted earlier, Fr. Copleston writes:

> He [Aquinas] did not, of course, regard the proposition 'there are things which come into being and pass away' as logically entailing the proposition 'there is an absolutely necessary or independent being' in the sense that affirmation of the one proposition and denial of the other involves one in a verbal or formal linguistic contradiction. But he thought that metaphysical analysis of what it objectively means to be a thing which comes into being and passes away shows that such a thing must depend existentially on an absolutely necessary being. . . . It follows that for Aquinas one is involved in a contradiction if one affirms the proposition 'there are things which come into being and pass away' . . . and at the same time denies the proposition 'there is an absolutely necessary being.' . . . But the contradiction can be made apparent only by means of metaphysical analysis. And the entailment in question is fundamentally an ontological or causal entailment.[8]

In a similar vein, Dr. E. L. Mascall writes:

> . . . In practice the argument is either accepted or rejected as a whole according as we have or have not come to know the things of this world as being what they really are. And this contention is strengthened by the fact that . . . in the hands of St. Thomas the argument does not simply assert that the proposition "Necessary Being exists" is a logical consequence of the proposition "Contingent being exists," but maintains that contingent being derives its own existence from Necessary Being; in other words, that we are not concerned just with logical relations between propositions, but with metaphysical or ontological relations between existent beings.
>
> What is necessary, in short, if we are to pass from a belief in the existence of finite beings to a belief in the existence of God is not so much that we should thoroughly instruct ourselves in the laws and procedures of formal logic as that we should thoroughly acquaint ourselves with finite beings and learn to know them as they really are.[9]

[8] *Aquinas*, pp. 114-115.
[9] E. L. Mascall, *He Who Is* (London, 1958), p. 73.

Now, unless I misread entirely the intent of the above remarks, it would seem to me that they are an example of the fallacy of begging the question. Surely, we need not deny that the topic under discussion is precisely the alleged ontological relation between a necessary being and contingent beings. And the subject of concern is, admittedly, not merely the analysis of the formal pattern of an argument. The question in dispute is *whether* there is a necessary being and *whether* the world is contingent. Since the purpose of the arguments for God's existence is to avoid having to place one's acceptance of such a belief exclusively on grounds of faith or revelation, and since such arguments, if cogent, would serve to provide rational grounds for one's belief, in this sense we *do* have to have regard for relations among propositions: for this is precisely in what arguments consist. The question is: are the propositions serving as premises true, and do the propositions stating the conclusion logically follow from these premises? In any logical analysis of an argument, one is concerned with the meaning and support for statements in the argument, and not simply with syntactical transformations. And this is precisely what various criticisms of the logic of the cosmological argument have focussed on, and what my own discussion has attempted to deal with. Fr. Copleston recognizes the need for what he calls "metaphysical analysis." But is not such metaphysical analysis exactly what the arguments for the existence of God undertake to give us? And is not the calling into question of the cogency of these arguments a contribution to metaphysical analysis? We are told, moreover, that it is a metaphysical analysis that establishes there would be a contradiction in admitting the proposition "there are things which come into being and pass away" and in denying, at the same time, the proposition "there is a Necessary Being." But is not a contradiction a logical relation between propositions? And does this not, then, come down to an evaluation of the logical strength of the argument?

It must, nevertheless, be admitted that the difficulty is not simply a matter of how one chooses to define logic. And I suspect that the matter goes deeper than a question of terminology. For what is at issue, is not whether the *conclusion follows from* the premises. The issue centers, rather, on the statements that serve as premises.

When Dr. Mascall tells us that what is really called for, is that we should "thoroughly acquaint ourselves with finite beings and learn to know them as they really are," he is, I submit, in asking us to do this, begging the question. For what does it mean to "acquaint ourselves with finite beings"? This is not a matter of observation, of describing what is given. To characterize things as "finite," or to speak of the world as "contingent," is to make use of philosophers' terms, metaphysically-loaded terminology. And to characterize things as "finite" or the world as "contingent," in the way the theist does, is to use these terms in contrast with, and as correlated with, a being that is "necessary" and "infinite." The two sets of terms go together; to see the world as contingent is already, tacitly, to accept a belief in the existence of a Necessary Being.[10] If this is so, where is the argument? And where is the appeal to reason? Are we not being confronted with a *fait accompli?* And is not the belief, therefore, in the existence of a Necessary Being established independently of the argument, and then used in the statement of the premises? And is not the drawing of the conclusion, therefore, spurious and logically beside the point?

Another prominent example, in recent theology, of the same tendency to dispense with rigorous "knock-down" proofs, while continuing to claim for itself, nevertheless, the title "rational theology," is furnished by Austin Farrer's *Finite and Infinite.* According to Farrer, the traditional arguments for the existence of God are, at best, instruments or aids for the mind in bringing into clearer focus its awareness of the "cosmological relation," viz., the relation that holds between the infinite Being of God and the dependent, creaturely status of all finite existents. Dr. Farrer would contrast the methods of what he calls "analysis" and "dialectic." The latter is the method in traditional approaches that attempt to prove the existence of God; by themselves, he agrees, however, these proofs are inadequate to establish the conclusion they aim at. They are logically unsound as proofs, since they beg the question.[11] His own preferred method is that of "analysis." This consists in the attempt to make clear the apprehension of God that

[10] Cf. T. McPherson, "Finite and Infinite," *Mind*, LXVI (1957), 379-384; A. Farrer, *Finite and Infinite* (Westminster, 1943), pp. 14-15.

[11] *Finite and Infinite*, p. 7.

already is in the mind. The goal of rational theology is not to prove that there is a God: to have the belief in God emerge as the result of a process of inference. It is, rather, to start with a theistic way of regarding the world, and, by bringing out its full meaning and internal logical coherence, to show that it is the only satisfactory way of interpreting the world.

> To think theistically is both to recognise the being of God and to construe things in this order. And therefore the theist's first argument is a statement; he exhibits his account of God active in the world and the world existing in God, that others may recognise it to be the account of what they themselves apprehend—or, if you like, that others may find it to be an instrument through which they apprehend, for perhaps apprehension here is not separable from interpretation. But such apprehension is not necessarily forthcoming at once, for it is evident that deity is, like other things, e.g. the unity and freedom of the self, obscure to our vision, and may need some straining of the eyes before it is brought into focus.[12]

The major portion of Dr. Farrer's detailed analysis is concerned to help us in becoming clear about the basic, intuited apprehension of God's relation to the world of finite contingent beings. The merit of this point of view is not, then, that it would pretend to be able to show that the world is finite or contingent, and from this, infer a Necessary Being as its ground. Instead, one recognizes the essential dependence of the world as finite upon the infinite, Necessary Being as its ground and source. The two go together from the very beginning. All that "argument" and analysis can do, is to elicit, with ever-increasing comprehension, and to the limits of human capacity, the subtleties of this relation between finite and infinite.

The chief difficulty with this type of approach, however, is in its claim that we *do* have a *rational* apprehension of the concept of a Necessary Being. For the appeal to a Necessary Being is to a Being that is *self-explanatory*. (One must not ask about God, the kind of question asked about the world, viz., "what creative ground does it have?") However, to acknowledge such a being is simply to shift the location of the mystery of existence from the world to God. One can, of course, affirm that there *is* a being whose exist-

[12] *op. cit.*, pp. 9-10.

ence, if known completely, would not arouse any question as to why *it* exists. But such an idea, if not downright absurd, is, at any rate, opaque to human reason. Is not the so-called "rational apprehension" that such a being does exist, a matter therefore, of faith, not, reason? And can any adequate response be made to a sceptic who simply sees no reason for having such a faith? But if the existence of a Necessary Being cannot be upheld on genuinely rational grounds, it follows that we have as little reason to characterize the world as contingent, and as dependent on the creative agency of such a Being.

It will be said, perhaps, that if we do not accept the belief that there is a Necessary Being as the cause of the existence of the world, then we cannot hope to make its existence intelligible. However, why need we presuppose that the existence of the world *must* be intelligible? What grounds have we for asserting *that* there is a reason for its existence? It is one thing to ask, "Does the existence of the world have a reason?", and I myself am arguing, throughout this book, that this is precisely where the mystery of existence is to be located. This is a far different matter, however, from asserting, dogmatically, that that there must be a reason. Admittedly, as rational beings, we should like to have reasons for everything; but there is no metaphysical reasoning that has yet been given, of a sufficiently compelling character, to show that the world must fulfill or satisfy such demands of *our* reason. To appeal to the metaphysical Principle of Sufficient Reason for this support, is already to commit oneself to the belief that the world's existence *can be explained*. The appeal to the metaphysical Principle of Sufficient Reason, as a backing for the belief in a Necessary Being, is thus only a disguised way of affirming the belief itself.

CHAPTER VII

Can Science Establish That the Universe Had an Origin in Time?

THERE IS ANOTHER MATTER to be discussed in connection with the question whether we can describe the existence of the world as "contingent." Our attention, thus far, has been focussed on the attempts made in theology to supply reasons for so construing the world. At the heart of the theological conception of the contingency of the world, and as part of the meaning of "contingency" for it, is the claim that the world owes its existence to a being other than itself; in short, contingency implies Creation. However, there is an altogether different line of thought that might be taken to lend support to the view that the world is contingent; this consists in stressing that aspect of the meaning of "contingency" which takes it as signifying something whose existence had a temporal beginning. According to this way of regarding the matter, it is sufficient to be able to establish at least the fact that the world had a beginning, and so is the kind of entity that not only "might not have been" but actually did not exist "prior" to its beginning; nor is it necessary, in taking this approach, to presume to be able to give some causal account of how the world did begin, or to what it owes its origin. This sense of contingency, then, can be separated from that in which contingency implies Creation: it has no direct connection with traditional theology. It is this sense of contingency, and this conception of the status of the world, for which support is sought, by some writers, in the much-written-about recent theories of the origin of the universe in scientific cosmology. Here, then, is one line of investigation that needs to be examined to determine whether, indeed, it does make sense to say that the world had an origin, and so came into existence, a finite time ago.

Two points need to be made at once, before examining the worth of these claims. In the first place, the evidence from this direction will bear, at best, on the finite age of the physical universe rather than upon the world. But since, as our earlier analysis has shown, the world is at least the physical universe, and since the physical or astronomical universe may reasonably be taken as providing the natural conditions and environment for all other modes of known natural existences (e.g., of life and mind), what can be established about the physical universe will have a basic priority. If, therefore, it can be shown that the universe had a temporal origin, *a fortiori* other modes of natural existence will be bound by this fact, and the world, too, may be thought of as having had a beginning. The reasoning here is, at best, conjectural rather than demonstrative, since, as our previous discussion has shown, we cannot dogmatize about the contents of the world. It may be there are entities and processes wholly unknown (unknowable?) to us, that are not encompassed within what we call "the astronomical universe," and that these might even have some "priority" over what is now given such status. At any rate, the question is, whether the cosmologist's investigations into the temporal structure of the universe lends credence to the idea that the world, too, had a beginning.

The second point is this. The evidence from scientific cosmology bears only on the question whether it makes sense, or it is likely to be true, that the universe had an origin. If the universe did have an origin, this would only establish that the universe came into existence. It would be shown to be contingent in this sense only, namely, as having had an origin. As science, however, cosmology is powerless to make any inference to a process of creation of the world by a transcendent Creator, or to argue for the existence of a Necessary Being. If science can in some way establish that the universe did have a beginning, this leaves the way open, at any rate, for such further claims, by whatever means they might in turn be supported. It should be noted, however, that most sophisticated theologians would discount this scientific evidence of an origin of the universe, as, in any case, irrelevant to their conceptions of God and the nature of creation. For creation, they would say, should not be thought of as something that took place at some definite moment in the past.

Quite apart, however, from any theological uses (or misuses) to which the conclusion that the world did have a beginning, may be put, I wish now to argue that it is a complete mistake to suppose that scientific cosmology, *qua* science, *could*, in principle, establish that the universe *did* have a beginning.

"Origin of the Universe" and "Age of the Universe"

The introduction and use of the terms "the age of the universe" and "the origin of the universe," in discussions of current cosmological models, comes about in the following way. Well-established empirical data show a connection between the red-shift of the spectra of galaxies and their apparent magnitude or distance. This is commonly interpreted as a Doppler effect, that is, as a phenomenon due to the recession of the galaxies. The recession of the galaxies, as measured by their red-shifts, is interpreted, in geometrically-represented cosmological models, according to a scheme in which the distances separating the galaxies from one another are subject to a change in the scale-factor assigned to such distances. To get a convenient, though highly oversimplified picture of what this means, imagine all the galaxies of the universe to be uniformly distributed over the surface of a hypersphere (one whose *surface* is in *three* dimensions) and occupying *fixed* positions *on* this surface. If the "radius" of this hypersphere were unchanging in its value throughout time, the galaxies on the surface would maintain constant distances from one another. The spectra obtained by an observer attached to any one of these galaxies, of other member-galaxies of this population, would display neither a red-shift nor a violet-shift, nor indeed any change from the standard line-positions of spectra of objects at mutual rest with respect to one another. If, now, we imagine the length of this "radius" of the hypersphere to undergo changes in time, of a determinate sort, then, even though the galaxies on the surface do not have any proper motions (i.e., do not move *on* the surface with respect to one another), they will all undergo a general (or systematic) pattern of motion, due to the change in "volume" of the hypersphere. Thus, if the radius were increasing in length, as a function of time, the galaxies on the surface would recede from one another. Similarly, if the radius (also called "the scale-factor") were to decrease, the hypersphere would contract, and the galaxies on the surface would appear to approach one another.

If we now take the red-shift of galaxies as indicating a general, systematic pattern of mutual recession, this will be interpreted by means of the geometric device of a radius of space (or scale-factor) that is positively increasing in value, with increasing values of time. Indeed, the red-shift can be expressed in terms of the ratios of the scale-factor at different times in the "volume" expansion of space, namely, at the time of emission and at the time of arrival of a pulse of radiation. Thus the spectral line-displacement will be a red-shift in those cases where the value of the scale-factor (R), at the time of emission of light from a distant galaxy, is less than the value of R at the time of arrival of the particular wave-front at the observer.

In specifying the general metric (or line-element) of model-universes possessing a uniform distribution of matter, current cosmology makes use of what is known as the Robertson-Walker expression for such a line-element.[1] The use of this line-element, in the specification of a cosmological model, requires that two quantities occurring in this expression be given specific values. One of these quantities, the value k, can receive the values 1, 0, or −1; this specifies the sign of constant curvature of space, according to whether the geometry employed is, respectively, flat (Euclidean), spherical, or hyperbolic. The second quantity essential to the determination of a cosmologic model, is the value assigned to the scale-factor as a function of time. This quantity is represented by the expression $R(t)$. The scale-factor (R), theoretically, can be any assigned function of the time (t). Models

[1]

$$ds^2 = dt^2 - \frac{R^2(t)}{c^2} \left\{ \frac{dr^2 + r^2 d\theta^2 + r^2 \sin^2\theta \, d\phi^2}{(1 + kr^2/4)^2} \right\}$$

where r, θ, ϕ, are spatial coordinates, t is the time, R is the scale-factor, k is the curvature constant, c is the value for the velocity of light.

differ from one another (aside from other respects), in the particular choices they make for the space-curvature value, and for the scale-factor as a function of time. If, in addition, one uses (as most current cosmologic models do) the theory of general relativity as the physical guide in determining the mechanical behavior of the model, other quantities will also need to be determined in identifying the model. These other quantities have to do with the values assigned to the density (ρ) and pressure (p) of matter and energy in the model, and the cosmological constant (λ).

My present interest in these models has to do entirely with the way in which a temporal structure is assigned, in them, to the universe they represent. In particular, I am interested in examining the way in which we are to understand, and judge, the use of the expressions "age of the universe" and "origin of the universe," as these arise in the interpretation of the ideas present in some of these models. For this purpose, we need to focus our attention, primarily, on the different modes of specifying the quantity $R(t)$ in certain groups of models, and the conceptual interpretation of what is accomplished by these specifications.

Since, on the basis of the red-shift data, it is found that, as observed at the present time, the system of galaxies is undergoing a general expansion, if one knew the value for the "rate of expansion" throughout the history of the universe (or, more accurately, the form of the function $R(t)$ for all values of t), one should be able to retrodict to past stages in the history of the expanding system, and, in particular, to the instant of time at which the expansion began. Let us call this retrodictively inferred initial moment at which the expansion began, t_a, and let the present moment in the state of the expanding system be identified as t_o. According to some models (for example, that of Einstein-deSitter), the initial moment of expansion (t_a) is one in which all the matter in the universe was compressed into an infinitesimally small volume. Since the physical situation at t_a, with $R=0$, constitutes a physical singularity, it is customary to speak of this initial moment—of infinite density as it exists in an infinitesimal volume—as marking "the initial moment of time" ($t=0$), or as "the origin of the universe," or as "the moment of creation."

Similarly, "the age of the universe" will then be understood as the time-interval that has elapsed from t_a (or $t=0$) up to the present (t_o).

By contrast with those models that posit a unique "origin" and an ever-increasing expansion, there are other cosmological models of an oscillating type. According to these, the universe undergoes an endless series of cycles of expansion and contraction, in which the expansion phase (or the increase of R) proceeds to a maximum, and then decreases again (for some models, to $R=0$, in others, to a lower finite value of R). Finally, of course, steady-state models require that there be no unique moment of "creation" in the finite past at which the density of matter had a maximum value, since for this type of theory the time-scale of the universe is infinite. According to steady-state theories, there is a process of continuous creation of matter-in-an-elemental-form, to compensate for the otherwise decreasing density-distribution of matter, due to the expansion of the universe. It is this continuous creation of matter that maintains the universe in a steady-state of constant density.

In what follows, I am principally concerned with the interpretations given by cosmologists, and others, to those models in which a unique singularity in the past is identified, conceptually, as marking the origin of the universe. I shall concentrate, therefore, on the type of assertions than can be made with reference to the moment referred to as $t=0$, rather than on models of the universe of an oscillating type (presumably occupying an infinite time), or on steady-state models (that similarly posit an infinite time-scale).

Problems Connected with Determining the Age of the Universe

There are two sorts of problems, one technical, the other philosophical, that can be raised about the effort to determine an "age of the universe" or to fix the moment of "the origin of the universe."

There are many technical difficulties of an observational and theoretical nature that have to be satisfactorily disposed of in order to reach a determination of the age of the universe. It is questions of this sort that commonly occupy the professional cosmologist, who is concerned with making a responsible choice from among the available models, on the basis of the best available evidence. The problems here are formidable, and their analysis would involve us in highly technical considerations beyond the scope, or interest, of the present discussion. Suffice it to say, by way of hint of these difficulties, that the problem of finding a responsible determination of the quantitative value to be assigned to the age of the universe, would require either sufficient empirical data, or acceptable theoretical grounds, for fixing the form of the function $R(t)$ for *all* values of t. The available empirical data of relevance here, consist of certain values for what is known as the "Hubble parameter" and the "acceleration parameter," for the *present* value of t, i.e., t_0. These values of the Hubble parameter and the acceleration parameter, however, do not determine the function for *all other* values of t; thus they do not help to determine whether the present values of these quantities also held throughout the past, or whether these quantities assumed some other values. As a result, even with the availability of present values of the Hubble parameter and the acceleration parameter, one cannot obtain any fixed quantitative estimate of the age of the universe. Indeed, it has been shown that specific numerical values for these quantities are compatible with ages of the universe that are arbitrarily long or relatively short.[2]

Equally serious obstacles lie in the way of relying on physical theory, rather than on the immediate data of astronomical observation, to help fix such an age, since arbitrary extrapolatory hypotheses are needed to envisage, for example, the condition of matter and energy (as far as their density and pressure are concerned), for such extremely remote periods of time. It is questionable, for example, whether the laws and physical theories, now in use, to describe or explain the behavior of material systems, are of sufficient accuracy and relevance, to interpret the behavior of matter and energy under the extreme conditions of density and pressure involved in the early stages of the universe's expansion. Whether, for example, the simplifying condition of uniformity

[2] Cf. G. C. Mc Vittie, "Distance and Time in Cosmology: The Observational Data," *Handbuch der Physik* (ed. S. Flugge), vol. liii, 485-488.

of distribution would prevail, or whether one can even hope to calculate a value for the function $R(t)$, under these highly special circumstances, becomes extremely dubious.

While the foregoing obstacles in the way of assigning an age to the universe should not be minimized, and should give pause to anyone who would believe that science can reasonably hope to arrive at a satisfactory answer, it is not with these questions that I am, at present, concerned. For, there is a second and far more serious question—of a philosophic character—that needs to be explored before one can be confident of the ability, in principle, of scientific cosmology, to determine the age of the universe, or that it had an origin. This second type of problem is, for my present purpose, of greater moment, inasmuch as it has to do with the ultimate worth of such concepts as "the age of the universe" or "the origin of the universe." Let us suppose a preferred model, in which these concepts figure, came to be adopted (on whatever observational or theoretical grounds seemed compelling to the community of investigators). Suppose, in short, that, allowing for all the usual reservations of inacurracy and uncertainty, one were in a position, finally, to assign a value for the "age of the universe." Since this idea is normally interpreted, in turn, as requiring that the universe be said to have had an origin, is this now something we should also be obliged to accept, on pain of flying in the face of such confirming scientific evidence? It is this question concerning the use of the idea of an *origin* of the universe, that needs philosophic scrutiny.

From a philosophic point of view, there are, broadly speaking, two lines of approach one might adopt in undertaking a critical analysis of the concept of "the origin of the universe." The first is to ask whether the concept of the origin of the universe is *meaningful*. Opinions vary, some arguing the idea is meaningful, others disputing this on the basis of some preferred criterion of meaningfulness. A second line of analysis appeals to the regulative criteria of the *method of science*, to help decide whether any allegedly scientific theory using the concept of "the origin of the universe," satisfies those criteria. I shall, myself, adopt the second of these approaches, and argue that any cosmologic model (or interpretation thereof), seriously maintaining there was an absolute origin of the universe, fails to satisfy the criteria of scientific method, and so must be rejected as even a scientific hypothesis.

Is the Concept of "the Origin of the Universe" Meaningful?

Before turning to the latter argument, however, let me review, briefly, the types of considerations that have led some writers to uphold the meaningfulness of the concept of an origin of the universe.

(1) One way of interpreting what is meant by the "origin of the universe" is as marking a first instant of time. On this approach, it is not necessary to identify this first instant of time with the coming-into-existence of the universe, *ex nihilo*, nor as the outcome of an act of creation by some transcendent being. This view is taken by G. J. Whitrow, who writes:

> Now, it must be admitted that many people are baffled by the idea of a first instant of physical time which seems to be implied by the concept of a limited past for the universe. Nevertheless, however puzzling this idea may seem, it is *not* meaningless. For example, we can imagine a first instant of time occurring in a perfectly homogeneous and static universe formed of identical particles in equilibrium when one of them spontaneously decays. Such a first instant would not necessarily be an instant of world creation. It would be the beginning of time in the sense that it was the first thing that happened in the universe.[3]

Now while the above argument claims that the idea of a first instant of time is meaningful, it is, in fact, difficult to see in what this consists. It would seem highly doubtful whether one can adequately describe a state of the universe in which literally nothing transpires. The very concept of a "particle" (whether identified with an atom, or any other well-defined unit) already requires, for its meaning, some changes or processes within it, in order to be recognized as such. What, therefore, seems, at first glance, to refer to a possible state of affairs, a universe in which

[3] G. J. Whitrow, *The Structure and Evolution of the Universe* (London, 1959), p. 196.

nothing is happening (yet in some sense existing "antecedently" to the first instant of time), is really inconsistently posited. However, since whatever exists physically, exhibits *some* processes of change, either in itself or in its environment, the fact of such change implies the possibility of a temporal scheme to order and measure these processes of change. Hence, the idea of a "first instant of time" arising in a "pre"-existing state of affairs, and where time, supposedly, is not predicable of the latter, is self-contradictory.

(2) A second type of attempt to defend the meaningfulness of the concept of the beginning of the universe, is one that looks for support in the way the term "beginning" is used in ordinary language. It is claimed there is sufficient warrant in the ordinary use of the term "beginning," to sanction, at least, the possibility that the universe, too, had a beginning, without presupposing some previous state of affairs. Thus Brian Ellis asks us to recognize a distinction between uses of the term "beginning" in which we are obliged to presuppose some previous existence from those uses in which no such presupposition holds. He writes:

> It is quite true that in many ordinary uses of the term some previous existence or state of affairs is presupposed. Thus to speak of the beginning of a war or a revolution or a return journey is to presuppose a state of peace to be broken, a government to be overthrown or a journey already made. However, this is not true in general, for there are some temporal uses of the term "beginning" in which a previous existence or state of affairs is not presupposed. Some processes have characteristic ways of beginning and their beginnings can thus be distinguished from and contrasted with their later stages, independent of what if anything went before. For example, one might, in certain contexts, speak of the beginning of the process of tooth decay or cell division or developing (in photography) in this way, and say how this stage of the process differs from the next. Here the beginning is quite literally a stage of the process.[4]

It is argued, on the basis of the distinction here being proposed, that the concept of the beginning of the universe can be given a

[4] B. Ellis, "Has the Universe a Beginning in Time?" *The Australasian Journal of Philosophy, 33* (1955), p. 32.

proper meaning, by choosing the meaning of "beginning" which does not involve any presupposition of previous existence.

However, the distinction between these meanings of "beginning" is not a sound one, and its application to the cosmological problem is, therefore, incapable of supporting the result claimed. The distinction is not properly put by saying that, in one case, we do not presuppose previous existence, and that, in the other case, we do. There is no justification whatever for saying that, in the first case, we are not presupposing some antecedent state of affairs. On the contrary, the ability to identify the beginning of a process presupposes events prior to that process. Thus, to identify the beginning of a process of tooth-decay, presupposes the ability to identify the healthy tooth prior to its undergoing a process of decay: and, analogously, for all the other examples cited. The very notions of "cell-division" or "development" in photography, and so on, have whatever meaning they have, because they presuppose earlier states of affairs against which they can be discriminated. I see no difference whatever, therefore, in principle, between these examples and the other examples given. The difference is not in whether we have presupposed some previous state of affairs, but only in whether we choose to identify what we call "the beginning" as contrasted with *later* stages of the process, or whether we choose to identify the beginning of a process, while being conscious of its *antecedent* conditions.

The Untenability of the Concept "The Origin of the Universe"

Despite the various efforts made to show that the concept of the origin of the universe can be allowed to have a legitimate, meaningful use in connection with scientific attempts to determine an age of the universe, I shall undertake, now, to show that this idea is, in fact, incompatible with the use of scientific method.

Let us begin by recalling, first, a classic discussion of a similar theme in the *Critique of Pure Reason*. Kant's purpose was to show that, since it is possible to give apparently cogent reasons to support opposite views with respect to the question whether the universe had a beginning in time, any attempt, therefore, to reach a rational solution to this question is doomed to failure. My immediate purpose is not to consider the merit of the Kantian position from an overall point of view, but simply to recall one phase of his discussion; this occurs in his statement of those arguments that may be used to meet what he call the "thesis" of the first antinomy. According to the thesis of the first antinomy, the world had a beginning in time, and is also limited as regards to space. (I shall confine myself, in what follows, to Kant's refutation of the first part of this thesis, that which has to do with the temporal extent of the universe.)

Kant undertakes to show that it is possible to give just as convincing an argument (stated in the "antithesis") that the world had no beginning. The proof of the antithesis (and, therefore, the disproof of the thesis) is the following:

> For let us assume that it has a beginning. Since the beginning is an existence which is preceded by a time in which the thing is not, there must have been a preceding time in which the world was not, *i.e.* an empty time. Now no coming to be of a thing is possible in an empty time, because no part of such a time possesses, as compared with any other, a distinguishing condition of existence rather than of non-existence; and this applies whether the thing is supposed to arise of itself or through some other cause. In the world many series of things can, indeed, begin; but the world itself cannot have a beginning, and is therefore infinite in respect of past time.[5]

There are a number of important features connected with this proof. In the first place, it is clear that Kant, in formulating the question, makes use of an absolute conception of time. Time is conceived as a one-dimensional continuum of instants, occupied by events. This is the classic Newtonian conception. To speak, as Kant does, of an "empty time" is to think of time on the analogy of a spatial container, in which bodies may be located and in which they undergo their various changes or motions. Further, Kant's proof tacitly appeals to the Principle of Sufficient Reason, in rejecting the conceptual possibility of an empty time that preceded the coming-into-existence of the universe. He says we cannot give any satisfactory reason why one instant, of the otherwise empty continuum of time, should have been chosen,

[5] *Critique of Pure Reason*, B 454.

as *the* instant at which the coming-into-existence of the world took place. For, according to the Newtonian or absolute conception of time, the instants that make up the infinite, one-dimensional series of instants of time, possess no intrinsic differences among themselves, other than those of position in the series. In this respect, all instants are exactly alike. If, then, one were to say that the universe came into existence at one of these instants, and has endured ever since, one would not be able to give any sufficient reason for the selection of that particular instant to be the one, as it were, honored by the fact that it will now have been the first instant occupied by an event marking the very origin of the universe.

Kant thus makes use of the Principle of Sufficient Reason in connection with the fact that there is no distinguishing, satisfactory reason that can be given for the choice of *one instant of time,* rather than another. As he puts it, no part of such a time possesses, as compared with any other, a distinguishing condition of existence, rather than of non-existence. I stress this, because the Principle of Sufficient Reason, as used by Kant, does not apply to the lack of such reason as it might be applied to the existents themselves, that is to say, to the events or objects occupying these instants. Indeed, he goes on to say that this lack of a sufficient reason, because it applies to the time series itself, is quite independent of any question concerning the conditions for the genesis of the world. As Kant expresses it, this applies whether the thing is supposed to "arise of itself or through some other cause." In other words, Kant does not consider it relevant, here, to raise the question whether the origin of the universe is, in some sense, a spontaneous matter, or, on the other hand, can be credited to the creative powers of a transcendent being. As far as he is concerned, even if we were to consider, as a meaningful possibility, that the world should have arisen of itself, rather than through the agency of some divine mind, there would still be no rational explanation for the fact that the world should have originated at one particular moment, rather than at another. In short, the lack of a sufficient reason for choice of some particular instant would apply to any selection process, whether that selection process were spontaneous or planned.

We have much to learn from the Kantian analysis. The particular way in which Kant appeals to the Principle of Sufficient Reason is one that we need not accept in all its details. For Kant, as we have seen, links the failure to satisfy the Principle of Sufficient Reason, to the homogeneity of the moments of time. However, the Principle of Sufficient Reason need not, as in Kant's use of it here, be so intimately tied to a Newtonian conception of time, that, if one should find it necessary to surrender the latter conception, one will thereby have surrendered whatever merit the Principle itself has as a *methodological postulate of science;* (this methodological role of the Principle, in science, must be carefully distinguished from the use of the Principle to sanction metaphysical conclusions, of the type we have examined previously, for example, in connection with theism). The ultimate strength of Kant's position lies in extracting the fact that the belief in a beginning of the universe, however one tries to establish this, runs counter to the very conception of science. Science is grounded in the use of the Principle of Sufficient Reason and, therefore, always leaves open the possibility of finding the explanation of *any* event. To say there is some unique event, marking the beginning of the universe for which no explanation *can* be given, is to say something contrary to the method of science. It is for this reason, I should argue, that any conception of the beginning of the universe, when defended under the aegis of some supposedly scientific cosmology, is an indefensible notion.

The last point needs special stress since, if one were not to recognize it, one might be otherwise tempted to take a point of view such as the one recently defended by C. D. Broad. Broad argues against Kant's insistence on employing the absolute conception of time; if one supplants it by what he calls a relational conception of time, some of the strictures, levelled by Kant, against the position represented by the thesis of the antinomy, can themselves be undermined. Broad writes:

> I cannot see that Kant is justified in saying that the supposition that the world began involves the notion of a previous empty time, if that means an existent entity of a peculiar kind. Suppose, *e.g.,* that the relational theory of time were correct, and that time and instants are logical constructions out of direct temporal relations

between events. Then to say that the world had a beginning is simply to say that there was a certain event which was followed by others but was not preceded by any other event. To say that this event would "have been preceded by empty time" would come to this. It would amount to saying that it is logically possible that there should have been events which preceded the event which was *in fact* the first event.

On this relational view of time the question: "Why did the world begin when it did, and not at some earlier or later moment?" would reduce to the question: "Why did the particular event, which in fact had no predecessors, not have predecessors?" Certainly this question could always be asked, however far back from the present we suppose the first event to have been. And it certainly would not arise if there were no event without predecessors. But I cannot help doubting whether it is a significant question, except in a rather special theistic context; and in that context the only answer is: "God knows!". So I am not prepared to accept Kant's argument as a conclusive objection to the possibility that the world had a beginning.[6]

I should wish to take issue with Broad's conclusion that the question "Why did the world begin when it did?", is a significant one only from within what he calls "a rather special theistic context." He assumes that an appeal to the Principle of Sufficient Reason, that prompts the asking of this question, is the unique prerogative of some type of theistic philosophy. On the contrary, to ask this question is essential to any application of the very method of science itself. For, to assert that there was some unique event that had no actual antecedents, is to block the way of possible inquiry. To assert there cannot be any such antecedents, is to deny the possibility of its explanation.

Surely, nothing said thus far need be considered a reason for challenging the idea of an origin of the universe, if all that is meant by this phrase, is "the beginning of the process of expansion of the system of galaxies." For, to have retrodicted to the stage in the past where the expansion began, need not be taken as a reason for asserting that that event constituted the absolute origin of the universe—one in which the universe came into existence. Even if available laws or theories of physics do not suffice

[6] C. D. Broad, "Kant's Mathematical Antinomies," *Proceedings of the Aristotelian Society*, LV (1954-55), p. 7.

to describe events earlier than this initial moment of expansion, the possibility cannot be excluded that there were such antecedent events. The way must be left open for determining the existence and character of such antecedent events, even though, at a given stage of scientific inquiry, there are no adequate conceptual tools for conducting this analysis. The most that a cosmological model in which the idea of "the beginning of the universe" occurs, could claim for itself, therefore, is that it leads us *up to* this event, by a process of inference, but is unable to go *beyond* it. Even if there is reason to prefer a model whose account of the past history of the universe includes reference to an event called in *that* theory "the origin of the universe," it does not exclude the possibility of finding some more refined theory, in which inferences would be made to events even earlier than the one identified as "the beginning" in the theory of coarser grain. The search for a more refined theory that would explain the event considered "the beginning of the universe" (in the cruder theory) would be part of the normal interest of science.[7]

Given the choice between saying that a certain event ("the beginning of the universe") is of such a character that no conceivable cosmological theory could provide an explanation of the occurrence of that event, and saying that *all* events investigated by science are ones for which it is relevant to inquire into their causal conditions—it is the second of these alternatives that would need to be chosen, as required by the regulative ideals of science. This means that, on scientific grounds, one could never hope to establish that the universe had an absolute origin, or came into existence. Therefore, if to say the universe is *contingent* means it did have an absolute origin in the past, scientific cosmology could never establish such contingency.

[7] For further discussion of this topic, see my *Space, Time and Creation*, Chap. VIII ("The Age of the Universe").

CHAPTER VIII

The Contingency of the World

THE PRECEDING TWO CHAPTERS have dealt with the attempts made both within the framework of traditional theology and current scientific cosmology, to establish the contingency of the world. There remains one further important line of thought to be considered in connection with the view that the world is contingent. It may be said that the contingency of the world is something that can be treated quite independently of any discussion of theology or of scientific cosmology, since it is brought home to us whenever we experience what Tillich calls the "shock of non-being."[1] This may be briefly described as consisting in the realization that there might not have been a world at all, that there might have been nothing. Even theism, it may be said, starts from and feeds upon this primordial sense of the contingency of the world's existence. However, it may be further argued, even if we reject the point of view of the theist, we cannot get rid of this sense of the contingency of the world. "There might have been nothing, yet there is a world"; and the fact expressed by this statement astounds us.

That it is both meaningful and true to say that there might have been nothing, has been affirmed by many writers. One recent statement is the following:

> . . . the question 'Why does anything exist at all?' is not aroused by any particular puzzlement over the explanation of some phe-

[1] Cf. P. Tillich, *Biblical Religion and the Search for Ultimate Reality* (Chicago, 1955), pp. 6, 45; *Systematic Theology* (Chicago, 1951), Vol. I, pp. 186 ff.

am

Date 3/14/66

Aarne from

12 ⊥ 1

B. Myer M. D.

M. D.

nomenon or other, but by the shock of contemplating the possibility that nothing might exist: what Tillich calls 'the shock of non-being' . . . It *is* possible that there might have been nothing for such a state of affairs, though unimaginable, is not inconceivable—there are many true statements (in physics for example) which describe situations which cannot be visualized. To show that the proposition 'Nothing might have existed' is inconceivable it would be necessary to show that it is self-contradictory or otherwise logically malformed, and there seems no good reason to assert this.[2]

What might count in favor of the view that it does make sense to allow of the logical possibility that there might have been nothing? One possible type of reply is that which appeals to the well-known thesis that whatever is found to exist, as attested by our experience, can be conceived not to have existed. As Hume put the matter: "Nothing, that is distinctly conceivable, implies a contradiction. Whatever we conceive as existent we can also conceive as non-existent. There is no being, therefore, whose non-existence implies a contradiction."[3] It thus might be argued that the world, as with any more limited type of entity whose existence is established by ordinary experience, is something whose non-existence is conceivable as a counter-factual possibility. Just as, given the fact of a fire in my fireplace at this moment, we may conceive that there might not have been a fire there now, so, too, we can conceive of the non-existence of the world. It is the non-existence of the world that we are to understand by "nothing." It is this line of thought, we may suppose, that, among others, lies behind the claim that the proposition "There might have been nothing" is perfectly conceivable, that it is neither self-contradictory or otherwise logically malformed.

What merit is there to the claim that it makes sense to say there might have been nothing? Is it the case we need to admit the contingency of the world, insofar as we can contrast the actual existence of the world with the logically conceivable possibility that there might have been nothing? I shall argue, in what follows, that the statement "There might have been nothing," if taken to mean *no more* than "Why does the world exist?", may be

[2] N. Smart, *Reasons and Faiths* (London, 1958), p. 51.
[3] D. Hume, *Dialogues Concerning Natural Religion*, Part IX.

allowed to stand, though redundantly, as part of our way of expressing the mystery of existence. However, if the term "nothing" is intended to designate some independently conceivable possibility with which the existence of the world can be contrasted, then this manner of speaking must be rejected as being inherently unintelligible. It follows that, if the concept of the contingency of the world is made to depend on our having some intelligible and metaphysically defensible idea of "nothing," there is no warrant in speaking of "the contingency of the world."

"There Might Have Been Nothing"

As a useful preliminary step, let me summarize, in a series of simple statements, the bare schema of the argument employed by those who would defend the idea of the contingency of the world, in terms of the contrast of the existence of the world with the conceivable possibility that there might have been nothing. It can be reduced to the following four statements: (1) The statement "The world does not exist" is false. (2) Though the statement "The world does not exist" is false, it might have been true. (3) If the statement "The world does not exist" were true, this could only be the case if there were absolutely nothing, that is, if there would have been no world in existence. (4) Given the fact that the world does exist, that there is not nothing, one can nevertheless ask the question "Why does the world exist, rather than nothing?" (The intent of asking this last question, is not one of requesting the *evidence* that establishes that the world exists; rather, it expresses the need or desire for finding an *explanation* for that fact.)

My concern, in what follows, is with critically examining the worth of statements (2) and (3). We need to ask whether it makes sense to say "There might not have been a world in existence at all," or "There might have been nothing," or "The possibility that there might have been no world, is a meaningful and real possibility, though it is not, in fact, realized."

The problem we are concerned with, is one that may be considered in two ways, each supplementing the other: one is logical, the other is ontological. We may ask: "Is the statement 'There might not have been a world at all' an intelligible statement, and free from inner inconsistency?" To put the matter this way is to stress the need for bringing to bear the apparatus of logic to appraise the use of language in this statement. On the other hand, the subject matter being referred to, is some "state of affairs," some "situation" of an ontologic sort: the alleged contrast between a state of non-being and the actual existence of the world. The question is: Does the language used in a statement such as "There might not have been a world" describe an ontologically real possibility?

In undertaking a critical analysis of the statements "There might have been nothing," and "It is conceivable that the world might not have been," I shall review, first, those critical arguments that center their attention on the concept "nothing"; later, I shall consider a line of criticism that takes its departure from an analysis of the expression "might not have been."

Critique of the Concept "Nothing"

One favorite line of attack on the kinds of statements we have been mentioning, that many philosophers have adopted, is to try to show that the idea of *absolute nothing* is thoroughly muddled or inconsistent. Such has been the tradition of criticism that began with Parmenides, and continues down to Bergson, and, even more recently, to the methods of linguistic analysis and formal logic. I shall review, briefly, three such lines of criticism, as drawn from contemporary writers.

(1) Bergson argued that the idea of absolute nothing is vacuous, because it contains an inner inconsistency, just as in the case of the idea of a square circle. His argument is couched largely in psychologistic terms. He maintains we can neither imagine Nothing, nor conceive it. The attempt to form an image of Nothing is self-defeating, according to Bergson, since whenever I extinguish, or suppress, an image of some item of my experience of the external material world, by eliminating, in turn, each sensory avenue of access I have to the world, I find there still remains the whole domain of my inner life. Should I now try to suppress or extinguish each of the items of this domain of experience—for example, my memories of the past, or my awareness of my present consciousness, I can never completely succeed in this. For, even if I should now imagine all sources of outer or inner

consciousness removed, there will have remained, to take its place, another act of consciousness to witness the extinction of the earlier set. Therefore, I can never form the image of Nothing, in the sense that literally everything has been removed from the range of my awareness. For, in the very act of trying to imagine the extinction of everything, I have already allowed something to remain as present and actual, namely, this very act of consciousness itself.

In the face of this criticism, however, it might be contended, we can at least form the *idea* of absolute nothing, even if we do not succeed in forming an image of it. We can always suppose each item or object of our experience to be annihilated, and the nought (absolute nothing) can be defined as the limit approached, and finally reached, when this operation of annihilation is carried out completely. To this, Bergson replies by charging that the claim to be able to form a consistent idea of Nothing is just as incapable of being realized as the attempt to form an image of Nothing. For the idea, too, contains a latent inconsistency. Once more, he appeals to what we mean by an "annihilation in thought" of something, and shows that the meaning this phrase has, prevents it from being extended to the totality of whatever exists. Bergson says we mean by "annihilation" an act of the mind by which the mind *replaces* one object by another. The possibility of regarding things as absent, is realized in creatures like ourselves who possess the power of memory and expectation. A being not endowed with the capacities to recall and to anticipate, would not use terms like "void" or "nought." The sense of absence (or what Bergson calls "the partial nought") rests upon the comparison of something in the past, or in the future, with something in the present. We never experience a total nought. At best, we make a substitution of one thing for another, or express a preference for one thing over another. Always, there is something present and actual that takes the place of what is absent, void, or out of existence. For Bergson, therefore,

the absolute nought, in the sense of the annihilation of everything, is a self-destructive idea, a pseudo-idea, a mere word. If suppressing a thing consists in replacing it by another, if thinking the absence of one thing is only possible by the more or less explicit representation of the presence of some other thing, if, in short, annihila-

tion signifies before anything else substitution, the idea of an "annihilation of everything" is as absurd as that of a square circle. The
absurdity is not obvious, because there exists no particular object
that cannot be supposed annihilated; then, from the fact that there is
nothing to prevent each thing in turn being suppressed in thought,
we conclude that it is possible to suppose them suppressed altogether. We do not see that suppressing each thing in turn consists
precisely in replacing it in proportion and degree by another, and
therefore that the suppression of absolutely everything implies a
downright contradiction in terms, since the operation consists in
destroying the very condition that makes the operation possible.[4]

(2)   A more recent, popular type of criticism of the use of the
concept "Nothing" undertakes to show that, as used by metaphysicians, statements such as "Nothing exists," or "Nothing might
have existed," represent a gross linguistic confusion. It is pointed
out that the metaphysician falls into the error of assuming that
since the term "Nothing" is a noun-substantive, it must be understood, along with other noun-substantives, as designating some type
of thing or entity. Just as we use the terms "book" or "moun-
tain" to designate types of things, so, the assumption is made, the
term "Nothing" also designates some type of entity. It is this type
of confusion that is at the bottom of the strange-sounding locutions one finds, for example, in Heidegger. Heidegger would have
us accept the view that "negation" (in the sense of the denial of
some positive fact) is by no means the fundamental concept, as
contrasted with "Nothing." Rather, negation itself derives its
"being" from the Nothing. "The Not does not come into being
through negation, but negation is based on the Not, which
derives from the nihilation of Nothing."[5]

Carnap, in his well-known criticisms of Heidegger's use of the
term "Nothing," called attention to the mistake involved in using
this term as if it were a name for some special type of entity.[6]
To use language in the way Heidegger does—for example, to speak

[4] H. Bergson, *Creative Evolution*, translated A. Mitchell (New York,
1911), p. 283.
[5] M. Heidegger, "What is Metaphysics?" in *Existence and Being*, edited
W. Brock (London, 1956), p. 372.
[6] R. Carnap, "The Elimination of Metaphysics Through Logical Analysis
of Language," reprinted in A. J. Ayer (ed.), *Logical Positivism* (Chicago,
1959), p. 71.

of "Nothing nihilating," would make it quite obvious that Heidegger has fallen into the trap of assuming that "Nothing" can be treated as if it had the same type of role as the term "swimmer" has in "the swimmer swims." He would appear to think that one can treat "Nothing" as if it were an entity that can "do" something, or as if it were a "real object" of some sort (though admittedly a very queer one), that has relations to other types of entities. This use of language shows an utter muddle and complete violation of the rules of use that determine the proper use of the term "nothing."

This proper use is brought out when "nothing" is used to mean "not anything of the sort . . ." Thus we might ask: "What happened at the meeting last night?" and the reply might be: "Nothing happened," where this means "not anything of importance or relevance happened." To interpret this statement ("Nothing happened"), as meaning that some very special sort of "something" happened, namely, "Nothing," would be an utter misuse of the term "nothing." In the hands of Heidegger and others who use the term "Nothing" as a noun-substantive, the error that results, moreover, does not even have the virtue of comic nonsense that a similar confusion has, in the well-known passage of *Alice Through the Looking Glass,* where the play is on the term "Nobody."

"I see nobody on the road" said Alice.
"I only wish *I* had such eyes," the King remarked in a fretful tone. "To be able to see Nobody. And at that distance too! Why it's as much as *I* can do to see real people, by this light!"

(3)   There is still another type of objection to the concept "Nothing," this time, from the side of formal logic.[7] The criticism consists in showing that any attempt to state, in a coherent language, that there is no world, is self-defeating. If we require (as seems plausible), that what is conceivable should at least be capable of being expressed in some language, then the terms "nothing" or "the non-existence of the world," can be shown to be logically defective: they do not describe any possible situation; they cannot be given any meaning in any logically definable language.

[7] The following analysis is based on N. L. Wilson, "Existence Assumptions and Contingent Meaningfulness," *Mind,* XV (1956), 336-345.

Whatever else the world may be said to contain, it does contain individuals. These can be referred to by proper names. In order to refer to individuals, one must have a language containing individual constants to serve as such names. Let us use the letters "x," "y," and "z," etc., for individual *variables,* and the constants "a," "b," "c," etc., for the values that can be used to replace these variables. To say there is a world, in the minimal sense of this term, is to say that at least one individual exists. In the language of *Principia Mathematica,* one may express this by the formula: $(\exists x)(x=x)$; this can be read "There is (exists) an x such that x is identical with itself." If one were to try to express, by the use of this symbolism, what it would mean to say there is no world, or that the world does not exist, this would have the form $\sim(\exists x)(x=x)$, read as: "It is not the case that there exists an x, such that x is identical with itself." But this expression would be strictly meaningless. The positive assertion $(\exists x)(x=x)$ is necessarily true, since the possibility that it might be false, that is, that there should not be a world, is a possibility that cannot even be stated meaningfully.

For, suppose it were the case that the statement "There is an x such that x is identical with itself" (that is, the statement "There is a world") were not necessarily true. This would mean that it might be false. And this, in turn, means that the statement "There is a world" might be *falsified.* But, how *could* it be falsified? In order to falsify a statement, we must find that there is some state of affairs different from what the statement, whose truth we are investigating, says it is. But we cannot find, or examine, a state of affairs in which there is nothing—in this case, no individuals at all. Another way of putting this, is to say that if there were no individuals, then a language containing individual variables would not have applicability: the range of values would be empty. In order to use the language containing individual variables, the range of values for such variables must be non-empty; there must be a world containing at least one individual.

The same point may be made by considering what is meant by a *language,* from the point of view of logic. For this purpose, we may contrast a language with a *pure calculus.* A pure calculus consists of a system of uninterpreted signs, whose combinations are governed by various explicitly introduced rules of formation and transformation. To construct a language, by using the pure calculus as a basis, it is necessary to give the non-logical signs of the uninterpreted calculus an interpretation, that is, to supply them with rules of designation for items in some domain. As Wilson remarks, however,

> if there were no concrete world there would be no possibility of providing an interpretation. Again, therefore, if no world, then no languages.

It follows from this,

> that the sentence 'No individuals exist' (or its symbolic translation, '$\sim(\exists x)(x=x)$' does not describe a possible state of affairs. If by 'conceivable' we mean 'verbalizable' (i.e., 'expressible in a synthetic sentence of an empiricistic language') then we cannot conceive of the non-existence of the world, we cannot significantly wonder why the world exists at all.[8]

The three types of criticism of the concept "Nothing" we have just briefly reviewed—that of Bergson, Carnap, and Wilson—for all the differences in approach, are united in their agreement that the concept "Nothing" has no legitimate place in philosophical discourse. While employing different reasons for pronouncing their common judgment, they would expose the inconsistency and confusion on which the use of this concept rests. Although one may admire the acuity with which these criticisms have been carried out, one cannot help suppressing the belief, nevertheless, that somehow they do not go to the root of the matter. It is not in the least likely that those who are given to using the concept "Nothing" will, in any way, be deflected by these attacks, or moved to alter their ways of expressing their philosophic insights or claims. Nor is this to be set down to sheer perversity of mind, or to the incorrigibility of some metaphysicians and their unwillingness or inability to learn from the exposure of their errors. This hypothesis is itself too simple and naive.

Nor would it do to try to give, as some writers have, a psycho-

---

[8] N. L. Wilson, *op. cit.*, pp. 342, 343.

logical explanation of the persistency of use of the concept "Nothing." It has been suggested, for example, that

> For some reason, which may go quite deep psychologically, the metaphysician is seriously dissatisfied with the fact that the word "nothing" has the grammatical function of a substantive but does not, so to speak, get enough linguistic credit for its grammatical work. He is discontented with its being *merely* a grammatical noun and sees the possibility of assimilating it into the class of semantic nouns, without making it the name of anything. What he does to correct the unsatisfactory linguistic state of affairs is to make more pronounced the similarity between the functioning of "nothing" and that of words like "moon" and "ghost." He gratifies his wish to have "nothing" as a thing-denoting substantive, instead of as a noun which does not name, by *creating* a bit of language in which "nothing" is used *as if* it were a name.[9]

Such a "psychological explanation" leaves one wholly dissatisfied. In the first place, it is difficult to see even the plausibility of the proffered explanation. Secondly—and more seriously—this explanation gives us no clue whatever to the *philosophic* motivations that prompt some writers to give the importance they do to the concept "Nothing." What we should need to know is the reason for the persistent use of this concept, despite all the efforts of the logician, or the ministrations of the psychologizing philosopher.

We come closer, I believe, to answering this question, when we realize that the use of the concept "Nothing" cannot be easily dislodged by the above means because, in the minds of those who employ it, it is indissolubly linked with the need to voice the mystery of existence. They cannot, and would not, suppress their sense of wonder at the existence of the world, and as one device, among others, they use the expression "Nothing" to reinforce and convey their sense of astonishment at the fact of the existence of the world. It is only if one were able to show how to give a proper formulation to the mystery of existence without using the concept "Nothing," that one might constructively serve the interests of philosophy. Under those conditions, the term "Nothing" might still continue to be used—no longer, misleadingly, as a name for

[9] M. Lazerowitz, "Negative Terms," *Analysis*, XII (1952), pp. 60-61.

some special type of entity—but merely as a way of underscoring the mystery of existence. And under those conditions, there no longer need be any objection to the use of this concept.

". . . Might Not Have Been"

I should like to develop the foregoing remarks, in connection with another commonly-used phrase: "There *might not have been* a world altogether." I turn to the analysis of this locution, since it provides the opportunity to make some points not readily made in connection with the use of the concept "Nothing." The problem is to answer the challenge laid down by those who maintain that the statement "There might not have been a world at all," is neither logically self-contradictory nor logically malformed. In undertaking to meet this challenge, I shall consider, first, the analysis to be given to the expression "might not have been," and I shall then attempt to show that the statement "There might not have been a world" is indeed malformed. It is malformed because it implicitly contains certain unwarranted presuppositions; to grant these is to commit the fallacy of begging the question. Without these presuppositions the phrase "might not have been," as employed in the statement "There might not have been a world," is lacking in certain crucial features normally present in other contexts of use, and so renders the statement in which it here occurs, vacuous or indeterminate.

To sustain these criticisms, let me begin by noting the factors present in the ordinary, straightforward use of the expression "might not have been." There are at least two ordinary contexts in which the phrase "might not have been" finds its frequent and appropriate use. The first has to do with matters in which human agents are involved; the second has to do with the occurrence of natural events, not involving human agents. As examples of the first type of case, we say: "If I had not chosen to visit Florence, I might not have been able to see Michelangelo's *David*," or, "If Michelangelo had not been given a piece of marble that had already been partly gouged and carved, he might never have been induced to produce a statue with the particular body stance of his *David*." As examples of the second type of case, we say: "If there had not been a strong wind last night, this tree might not have been uprooted," or, "There might not have been a tree here at all, if a wind, years ago, had not blown the seed from which it grew, and deposited that seed in this spot."

In these ordinary uses of the phrase "might not have been," there are two important features present, those of *conditionality* and *temporality*.

(1) To say "Such and such might not have been done (or made)," or "Such and such might not have happened," does not, ordinarily, form a complete sentence by itself. Rather, it occurs as the consequent of a counterfactual statement, whose antecedent clause (whether explicitly stated or tacitly understood) states some part, at least, of the conditions for what did, in fact, take place. The conditions mentioned in the antecedents of these complete statements may be of various types. Where human action, or making, is involved, these may include reference to the factors influencing choice from among possible alternatives, the circumstances affecting such choice, or the motives or purposes of the human agent in accomplishing what he did. Where some non-volitional natural event is involved, the antecedent of the counterfactual states some condition, from among the range of possible initial conditions or circumstances, that helps to explain the event that finally did occur. This condition, whether simple or complex, is compatible with the range of possibilities allowed by the known law (or laws) applicable to this kind of event.

To say that something might not have been the case, means that what did, in fact, happen is one of a set of possible cases. Thus, in the case of natural events in which no deliberate human intervention is involved, besides the event that did take place, other initial conditions or circumstances are permitted by the law used in the understanding of the event. To say that other events might have taken place is simply to say that the law used in the explanation of the event, allows, as values for its variables, an entire range of individual circumstances different from the one that belonged to the event under consideration. In an analogous fashion, where some action was performed, or an object was made, as the outcome of deliberate human choice or intervention, to say that the event that did, in fact, take place, "might not have taken place," is to say there was a range of possible alternatives available to the agent or designer from which he made his selection. Just as the law used in the explanation of a natural event allows for a range of possible values, not restricted to the case under investigation, so, too, the range of free action, or designing intelligence and skill of some human agent, includes other individual alternatives besides the one in fact chosen. In summary, then, the element of *conditionality* present in the use of the phrase "might not have been," implies (1) what did happen is the consequence of some particular set of antecedent conditions; (2) the actual antecedent conditions belong to a range of alternative conditions compatible with either an explanatory law, or the freedom of choice of some agent.

(2) A second important feature of the use of the phrase "might not have been," has to do with the temporal aspects of what is being discussed. To say "*x* might not have been," implies that there was a time at which *x* came into existence, and that prior to the moment at which *x* began, other initial conditions or choices (as discussed previously, under (1)) existed as possible alternatives.

Temporal predicates are basically of two types. Either, (1), they specify the *durational interval* throughout which some process, action, or continued existence of some object lasts, or, (2), they specify the *date* at which something happened. The first type of predicate (e.g., "three hours," "a million years" etc.,), tells us *how long* something endures; the second (e.g., "at noon, February 19, 1867,"), tells us *when* something occurred. One type of time-predicate is appropriate to some types of events or changes, and inappropriate to others, while other events and processes can be described by the use of both types of predicates. Thus, we can ask *how long* a race lasted. Similarly, we can ask *when*, i.e., at what point (date) it began, or ended. Where an object, activity, or process had a beginning, endures for some stretch of time, and then ceases, or goes out of existence, we ask for the duration; however, for an activity that does not have a temporal beginning, duration, and end, one cannot ask how long it lasted. As Ryle pointed out, while we can ask how long it takes to run a race, we cannot ask how long it takes to win it.

The point of recalling these well-known distinctions, is that whether we are dealing with one type of event (a process of change, or an event that occupies a durational stretch of time), or the other (an "achievement" event, that can only be dated, but not clocked as to its duration), we can meaningfully relate the time *at which* (the date) the process began, or when the "achievement-activity" took place, to events that preceded and followed it, in some temporally ordered series of events. Similarly, where explanations are provided (particularly, causal explanations in which temporal terms are used in the very formulation of the explanation), time-coordinates and predicates of the relevant kind can be specified for the conditions present either before, or at, the moment that the process under investigation, began.

Given these ordinary uses of temporal predicates, as reflected in the use of tensed verbs in ordinary language, the way the expression "might not have been" is to be used, can now be analyzed as follows. In the first place, there was a moment, in the past, at which some process began, or some event took place. Secondly, one could give an account of the conditions either prior to or simultaneous with the occurrence of the beginning of the event or process under discussion. To say that the event or process that has already taken place, might not have happened, is to make reference to the situation that prevailed prior to, or simultaneous with, that process or event.

"*The World Might Not Have Been*"

How much, if anything at all, of the ordinary meaning of "might not have been" is retained and presupposed in the statement "There might not have been a world"? The first, most obvious point to note, is that, unlike its ordinary uses, the statement "There might not have been a world" is presumably complete. As we have seen, the ordinary use of "might not have been" normally occurs in connection with the consequent of a conditional counterfactual statement. We do not say, "There might not have been an explosion," and intend this to be a complete statement. If we do use this expression, without adding anything further, there is usually some tacit understanding as to the unexpressed antecedent condition necessary to complete this statement. We say, "There might not have been an explosion, *if* there had been a thorough search of the premises for all explosive

materials (or for gas leaks, or for faults in the boiler, etc.)." In the
case of "There might not have been a world," however, "might
not have been" displays a truncated use. What would normally be
the consequent of a compound statement, becomes itself a complete
statement. Instead of "If such-and-such had not been the case,
there might not have been a world," we are given, simply,
"There might not have been a world." But how are we to understand this use of "might not have been," if it is no longer governed
by its ordinary meaning?

One possible way of replying to this last question, is to say that
we are being confronted, in this case, with a degenerate form of
the ordinary use of the expression "might not have been."
Whereas, in ordinary uses, the phrase "might not have been" is
employed as part of the consequent of a compound counterfactual
statement, in the present case, it might be argued, though we are
not given any statement of the conditions for the existence of the
world, it is, nevertheless, perfectly meaningful. This reply, however, is not altogether satisfactory. We should ask: "Why is there
need at all for this truncated and degenerate mode of using the
expression 'might not have been?'" Now, this last question *can*
be answered, but in giving the answer, we shall see how the statement "There might not have been a world" *became* a degenerate
statement; the statement cannot be understood independently of
its original meaning. And if one were to retain reference to its
original meaning, the statement "There might not have been a
world," contains presuppositions that beg the question.

At this point, it is worth calling attention to an important
historical fact, previously noted in this book, and frequently com-
mented on by others.[10] Greek philosophers, from the pre-
Socratics to Plato, do not look for an answer to the question
"Why does the world exist at all?"; they ask, rather, the question
"How did the world get to be the way it is now?" It is a question they answer by appealing to some pattern of development, or
transformation, out of antecedently existing stages or materials.
(Even when Plato makes use of the imagery of "making" rather
than "development," within which to cast his cosmogony, his

[10] Cf. E. Gilson, *The Spirit of Medieval Philosophy* (New York, 1936),
pp. 68-69.

language makes clear that the Divine Craftsman, as any other craftsman, transforms pre-existing material, by imposing a "rational" form on it.) Between the time of the Greeks and Leibniz (who phrased the question "Why is there something, rather than nothing?"), however, there had intervened the momentous development of creationalistic theism. At the core of this philosophy was the dogma that God created the world out of nothing. (The expression "creation out of nothing" can be interpreted in various ways. An interpretation given by many theologians, that avoids the difficulty of treating "nothing" as if it were some type of special "material," is to say that "God created the world out of nothing" is equivalent to "God did not create the world out of anything.")[11]

For the creationalistic Hebraic-Christian theist, then, the question "Why does the world exist, rather than nothing?" is not only a meaningful question, it is one he answers directly by saying: "God created the world, and had it not been for God's creative agency, there would not have been a world." Once the theistic answer becomes available, there is a tendency to forget that the question "Why does the world exist, rather than nothing?" is a question dependent on theism for its meaning. People ask this question as if it had an independent meaning. They begin with what they take to be the basic question, "Why does the world exist, rather than nothing?" and assume that this already has a meaning quite apart from the available theistic answer. For example, Leibniz not only had theism behind him, historically, but himself accepts a theistic metaphysics as an answer to his own (basically similar) question. It would be a mistake, however, to assume that this question is meaningful apart from the context of theistic metaphysics.

The *statement* "There might not have been a world" is derived from the *question* "Why does the world exist, rather than nothing?", and this question, it is assumed, *must* have an answer. It would be incorrect, therefore, to assume that the statement "There might not have been a world" is intelligible apart from this par-

[11] Cf. Thomas Aquinas, *Questiones Disputatae de Potentia Dei*, Q. 3, *De Creatione*, Article i; A. N. Prior, "Identifiable Individuals," *Review of Metaphysics*, Vol. 13 (1960), p. 691.

ticular context. In saying the statement "There might not have been a world" is a degenerate expression, I mean to call attention to this total historical context of discussion. The apparently complete statement "There might not have been a world," if it is to be given its full meaning, requires use of the conceptual framework of theistic metaphysics. To do so, however, is a gross example of begging the question. Among other things, it implies that the only way of giving meaning to "There might not have been a world" is by presupposing the Principle of Sufficient Reason, and that we need to assume, therefore, a causal agency for the existence of the world. For this, however, there are no good philosophic reasons.

Some support is given to the above account, in considering the temporal implications of the ordinary meaning of "might not have been." To say "something might not have been," is to make reference to the fact that what now exists (or has existed), did not always do so; if the conditions present at its inception were not operative at the time, the object or event would not have come into existence. The bearing of this on our present topic is the following. While not all forms of theism rest on the belief that the world had an origin in the past, some forms of theism, particularly the most primitive and unsophisticated, do rest on this dogma. It is from these unsophisticated forms of theism that the use of the expression "There might not have been a world" is derived. It is an expression taken over, first, by more sophisticated forms of theism, that, themselves, no longer insist the world had a finite origin *in the past*. What is retained, however, in these more advanced forms of theism, is the meaning "might not have been" has, when stress is placed on the fact of *conditionality*. A final step in the attenuation and evacuation of the full meaning of the phrase "might not have been" (that includes, in its normal use, reference both to conditionality *and* temporality), is to be found in those writers who eschew theism altogether. They would deny any explicit, or tacit, reference to the fact of conditionality; for them the statement "the world might not have been" is, allegedly, complete and intelligible. For these writers, the phrase "might not have been" is intended to express, simply, the fact of the pure contingency of the world; it is not presupposed that the world either came into existence at a finite moment in the past, or that it has a causal ground.

I have been arguing that this depleted or degenerate use of the phrase "might not have been" cannot be understood apart from its use in connection with those events that did have both a beginning and an assignable causal ground. It is this use that appears in theism, in its attempt to explain the existence of the world. For those forms of theism that retain the use of language normally applied to events, as extended to the world, the statement "The world might not have been," is to be understood in its full, ordinary meaning. Once we have removed, however, *all* the normal components of the meaning of the phrase "might not have been," it is not at all clear what it means to say "The world might not have been." It is for this reason that one would have to conclude this statement is malformed. It is the most primitive form of theistic philosophy that gives whatever meaning there is to this statement. In the absence of this background, the statement lacks meaning; with the use of this background, it begs the question.

If it should be insisted that the statement "There might not have been a world" is entirely significant without presupposing the background of theistic philosophy, then, I submit, this can only be the case, if we regard the use of the statement "There might not have been a world" as a rhetorical means for giving extra emphasis to the question "Why does the world exist?" It does not, however, in any way, enlarge or add to this question. The expression "There might not have been a world," just as the use of the term "nothing" (when used as a substantive), is harmless enough, if one appreciates its vacuousness, when taken literally, and admits that it is being employed simply as a device for phrasing the mystery of existence.

CHAPTER IX

Is the Existence of the World Necessary?

THE LAST THREE CHAPTERS have dealt with those arguments that seek to show the existence of the world (or the universe) to be contingent. We have seen that the traditional routes followed by rational theology to establish such contingency, as a preliminary step to proving the existence of God as a Necessary Being, are beset with insuperable difficulties. Similarly, the appeal some writers make to particular cosmological models, to uphold the claim that the universe is contingent (in the minimal sense that it had an absolute origin in time), is also without merit. Finally, I have explored the claim that the world is contingent, as this is experienced in our sense of "the shock of non-being," and again, I have argued, there is no warrant on this score to say the world is contingent.

I shall now examine an altogether different type of proposal as to the manner in which we are to regard the existence of the world. It may be said that there is no genuine mystery of existence since the existence of the world is *necessary*; there is no reason to regard the existence of the world as contingent, whether upon the creative energy of a transcendent deity, or in any other sense of contingency, since the world's existence is necessary in the sense that its existence is entirely self-sufficient and self-explanatory. I propose to examine this claim, and to show that we are not helped, in the slightest degree, by this line of thought, to dispense with the need for recognizing a mystery in the existence of the world, and that, moreover, there are no good reasons for saying that the existence of the world *is* necessary, in the sense indicated.

Spinoza's View of Nature (or God)

Of the various thinkers in the modern period who have explicitly defended the view that the existence of the world is necessary, Spinoza is, by far, the most important and influential. In one way or another, those contemporary writers who reject a supernaturalistic world-view, and who would assert, therefore, that Nature is self-sufficient, find a principal source of support for their views in the writings of Spinoza. I shall, therefore, in what follows, focus my attention on the way in which Spinoza undertakes to defend this position, hoping thereby, in my criticisms of these efforts, to show the weakness of all those views that bear any kinship to his.

Before turning directly to this task, however, there is need for a brief preliminary comment. For the purposes of the present discussion, I shall assume there are sufficient points of similarity between Spinoza's account of Nature and my own account of the world, to justify the assimilation of the conclusions I shall reach about the necessary existence of Nature, as holding, also, for any attempt to impute necessary existence to the world. I am fully aware that much of what Spinoza builds into his conception of *Natura sive Deus* would not coincide with my own account of the world. In particular, Spinoza attributes a far greater degree of order and intelligibility to Nature, than I have allowed, on purely methodological grounds, in my own characterization of the world. Nevertheless, both Spinoza's conception of Nature, and the present account of the world are in agreement, at least to the extent that, negatively speaking, they both rest on a common rejection of the metaphysical view of theism, and the denial that we have a clear rational warrant for positing a transcendent being as the ground of the existence of Nature (or the world). One major, important point of difference between Spinoza's view of Nature and my own account of the world, is that Spinoza does not recognize any mystery in existence. For him, the existence of Nature is necessary, and so does not contain any element of unintelligibility, whereas I should wish to insist on the fact of the mystery of the world's existence. In the sense in which Spinoza uses the term "necessary," I shall argue, the existence of the world is *not* necessary.

In Proposition XI of his *Ethics*, Spinoza asserts that "God, or substance consisting of infinite attributes, each of which expresses eternal and infinite essence, necessarily exists."[1] To support this proposition, Spinoza offers four proofs for the existence of God (where "God," in his system, is taken synonymously with "Nature" and "Substance"). These four proofs are modeled on the traditional proofs for the existence of God (as conceived in the theistic traditions of Judaism, Islam, and Christianity). Of these four proofs, only the second will occupy us, since it is in this proof that Spinoza seeks to establish the necessary existence of God.

In order to understand the reason for our so restricting the present discussion, we need to call attention to the fact that, although all four proofs seek to establish that God necessarily exists (in the Latin, *necessario existit*), actually, the statement "God necessarily exists" is amphibolous, and has two basic meanings.[2] In one of these meanings, to say that God necessarily exists, means that the statement "God exists" can be established by following rigorous, demonstrative reasoning from unexceptionable premises, or that it itself is an apodictic statement. According to the second meaning, to say that God necessarily exists, is to attribute to God the property of *necessary existence*, as distinguished from possible existence. Thus, while in the first meaning, to say "God exists" necessarily, is to make a claim about the logical status of a certain proposition, namely, the proposition "God exists," the second meaning intends that the phrase "necessary existence" be used to designate a property of God, in contradistinction to those entities that have the property of *possible existence*. Since the attempt to assign to God the property of *necessary existence* also, if it succeeds, will establish that God

---

[1] B. Spinoza, *Ethics*, translated by W. H. White.

[2] Cf. H. A. Wolfson, *The Philosophy of Spinoza* (Cambridge, Mass., 1934), Vol. 1, p. 160; R. E. Allen, "The Ontological Argument," *Philosophical Review*, LXX (1961), 56.

exists, it follows that *all* the proofs Spinoza gives are, in this sense, concerned to establish the *existence* of God. Insofar as they are valid demonstrations, again, all four proofs would succeed in establishing that the statement "God exists" is logically necessary, or apodictic. However, only the second of the proofs given by Spinoza, in Proposition XI, is concerned to establish the necessary existence (as distinguished from the existence) of God, and it is, therefore, this proof that is of special interest for our present discussion.

The reason for not considering the other proofs is that, for the purposes of the present analysis, I take it as already sufficiently well-established, by our own previous discussion, that we are entitled to say, without any manner of doubt, the world exists. Moreover, I have also given reasons for saying it would be wholly otiose to try to *prove*, by argument, as Spinoza does, that the world exists. *That* the world exists, we can take to be perfectly well-established by ordinary experience, and need not be supported by an elaborate argument, or inferential process of deduction.

Spinoza's proofs for the existence of God (Nature) include forms of the ontological and cosmological arguments. Some commentators have pointed out that, in particular, the ontological argument is not essentially, or strictly, an argument, but at best only a way of making explicit (in the "conclusion") the full meaning of what is already contained in the premiss, and that, in turn, the statement "God exists" is taken to be known intuitively, by an act of immediate knowledge. It might be thought that this treatment of the ontological argument applies, as well, to the way in which, in my own account, the statement "The world exists" is supported. I should be willing to accept this interpretation, on one proviso: the awareness of the existence of the world is not to be taken as based on an intellectual intuition, of the sort intended by classic rationalism in its appeal to the paradigm cases of mathematical axioms, and as containing such allegedly intuitively warranted truths. The knowledge that the world exists, is a matter of direct experience; it requires neither an intellectual intuition nor an argument to establish it. At best, an "ontological argument" for *the world's* existence only serves as a discussion that helps clarify what one means by saying that the world exists, and what kind of warrant this assertion does have.

The claim, however, that the existence of the world is a *necessary existence* is another matter altogether. One could certainly *not* appeal to any ordinary experience to establish this assertion, and if it is to be accepted at all, would need considerable discussion and analysis. This is, however, what Spinoza himself wants to assert of God or Nature, and we must, therefore, stop to examine whether his proof that Nature has the property of necessary existence is a sound one, and whether it might also be transferred, as having a similar validity, to the conception of the world developed in this book. It is to this task that I now turn.

"Necessary Existence"

Spinoza's proof of the necessary existence of God, as does much of his philosophy, makes use of locutions and distinctions that he had taken over, not only from Descartes, but, more generally, from the traditions of medieval philosophy (which, in turn, of course, had their roots in ancient Greek philosophy). These are made to serve the purpose of expressing his own distinctive philosophy. I shall first call attention to some of these relevant locutions and distinctions, and then later show how, despite his attack on medieval supernaturalism, Spinoza retained in the very terminology he employed, the lineaments of a system of thought that a more thoroughgoing critic would also have found objectionable, and would have discarded.

Spinoza begins by expressing his own complete acceptance of the Principle of Sufficient Reason. He says: "For the existence or non-existence of everything there must be a reason or cause." As a next step, he introduces a classification of various types of being. This classification employs distinctions that had already been worked out by such medieval writers as Avicenna, Maimonides, and Crescas.[3] One such traditional distinction is that between *internal* and *external* causes: "the reason or cause must either be contained in the nature of the thing or lie outside it." Spinoza, furthermore, draws a distinction (also traditionally recog-

[3] Cf. Wolfson, *op. cit.*, I, 184-199.

nized) between those causes which, being positive, explain why something exists, as distinguished from those causes which, as impedimental, prevent something from happening or existing. Thus if something exists, for example a particular triangular-shaped object, "there must be a reason or cause why it exists; and if it does not exist, there must be a reason or cause which hinders its existence or which negates it."

Another set of distinctions, finally, Spinoza uses, is that according to which all beings are divided into those that are *necessary*, *possible*, and *impossible*. By making use of the earlier distinction between internal and external reasons or causes, Spinoza describes what he means by an *impossible being* as one that, because of reasons deriving from its internal nature, cannot exist at all. On the other hand, a being is *necessary* when its existence follows from its own nature—when the reasons for its existence are, again, wholly internal to itself. As an example of an impossible being, he instances the square circle: "the nature of the thing itself shows the reason why a square circle does not exist, the reason being that a square circle involves a contradiction." On the other hand, to understand clearly the kind of being that possesses necessary existence, we need but think of the definition of Substance (Nature or God). For "the reason why Substance exists follows from its nature alone, which involves existence."

With respect to the class of *possible* existences (as distinguished from those that are either impossible or necessary by virtue of their own nature), we need to introduce *external* causes or reasons, "from the order of corporeal nature generally," to account for the fact that something happens, or exists, or that it does not. For example, "the reason why a circle or triangle exists or does not exist is not drawn from their nature." Thus, that a particular triangle or circular-shaped object should exist, is possible: it might exist or it might not exist; if it does exist, then, as a possible existence, it follows (Spinoza would say) necessarily, i.e., by a sequence of determinate *external* causes. Similarly, if it does not exist, it follows, equally necessarily, by external reasons, that it is impossible that this particular possible thing should exist. The class of "possible existences" thus includes those that are "necessary possible existences" and "impossible possible existences" (where the "necessity" or the "impossibility" resides in the external causes that determine their existence or non-existence.) In any case, of course, such possible existences have to be distinguished from the class of "internally impossible existences," illustrated by a square circle, and from an "internally necessary existence," exemplified by Substance.

At this point, it might be useful to remind ourselves of Spinoza's views on necessary causation (although he does not, himself, elaborate on this matter in the particular proposition we are examining.) These views on necessary causation, the fruit of Spinoza's reflections on what science and metaphysics can achieve, will be of importance to us in the analysis of the concept of necessary existence.

For Spinoza, causal relations are necessary, in the sense that when properly identified, the effect follows from the cause with the same type of necessity as that with which a validly deduced theorem follows from unexceptionable premisses. Causal necessity is a species of logical necessity. Given the appropriate antecedent conditions for some event, and in the absence of any impedimental conditions, the consequent event *has* to occur. Since, for Spinoza, the world is thoroughly rational in structure, the order and connection of things is the same as the order and connection of ideas. If one knows, in advance of the occurrence of some event, its antecedent conditions together with the relevant causal laws, then it will be possible to deduce and thereby predict, the inevitable outcome; at the same time, the course of nature itself, ontologically considered, is also determined by the same conditions and laws. For Spinoza, therefore, there is no separate category of logical necessity as applying to propositions or other symbolic expressions, and another species of necessity that holds for events or objects. These are, rather, two different ways of looking at the same fact. The discursive necessity articulates the ontological causal necessity; and the same requiredness or necessity that warrants our inferences, also determines the sequence of events. Not only is rational thought able to predict, when it has relevant knowledge; it can also retrospectively explain any given event by the same procedure of logical deduction. For Spinoza, *all* occurrences in Nature—past, present, or future—are causally necessitated.

The understanding of the causal necessities that account for ordinary objects and events always makes reference to factors that are external to the nature of the object or event in question. By "the nature" of an object or event, Spinoza means the essential characteristics that make the object or event the *kind* of thing it is. However, in gaining a *causal* understanding of the occurrence or existence of some particular object or event, one needs, not a definition, but a specification of the conditions or circumstances whose presence and concatenation lead (necessarily) to the existence of the object or to the occurrence of the event in question. In this sense, causal conditions and circumstances are normally external to the definition of the *kind* of thing being examined, and require reference to the environmental factors that bring about the object or the event. In dealing with God (or Nature), however, there is, by definition, nothing external. Whatever understanding, then, is to be had of this "object," must be wholly of an internal character; it is achieved by turning to a clear and adequate *definition* of its essential *nature*. It is for this reason that Spinoza, in describing the "causal" understanding of God, says that it is *causa sui*. While entities other than God need still other entities or circumstances to give a causal understanding of their existence or occurrence, a causal understanding of God can only be obtained from God's own nature.

Another way of bringing out the important difference between God and all other (finite) entities is this. Whereas, when we attempt to understand the occurrence, or existence, of ordinary objects and events, we make reference to the external circumstances of their genesis or continued existence, these other circumstances are themselves, in turn, precisely of the same finite character. Though the occurrence of a given event is causally necessary, this necessity is of a conditional character. Given the conditions, the event in question necessarily follows. But what about the conditions themselves? According to Spinoza's philosophy, these conditions, in turn, must be causally understood in terms of their necessary dependence on still other circumstances. The existence and occurrence of all such finite conditions can ultimately be traced back to the unconditioned nature of God (or Nature), from which they derive their intelligibility and causal relatedness. God (or Nature), however, cannot be causally understood in terms of anything more ultimate. Therefore, if it is to be intelligible, it would have to be *causa sui;* it would not only explain everything that it derivatively contains or encompasses, but itself as well.

The Necessary Existence of God (or Nature)

To return to the proof of God's necessary existence, in Proposition XI: Spinoza's purpose is to show—by a *reductio ad absurdum* argument—that God necessarily exists. (On the basis of the distinctions previously discussed, one could say the proof undertakes to show, by necessary reasoning, the truth of the statement: "God, as a being possessing necessary existence, exists.") The proof is as follows. Spinoza begins by pointing out that "if there is no cause or reason which hinders a thing from existing, it exists necessarily." He applies this principle to the case of God's existence. "If, therefore, there be no reason nor cause which hinders God from existing, or which negates His existence, we must conclude absolutely that He necessarily exists." A reason for God's non-existence, however, could not lie outside God, in another substance, for the supposition of another substance is either of one of like nature to God, or of a different nature. If it is of like nature, then by this fact, we should already have admitted the existence of God. On the other hand, if the "other substance" were of an altogether different nature," it could have nothing in common with God and therefore could not give Him existence nor negate it." "Similarly, if one supposes that God's own nature internally contains the reason for His own non-existence, this would only betray a self-contradiction. "Therefore neither in God nor outside God is there any cause or reason which can negate His existence, and therefore God necessarily exists."

To properly evaluate this proof, I shall offer, first, a restatement of it, as given by Professor Wolfson, who points out that the argument, in its barest essentials, reduces to one type of ontological argument. The argument may be restated as follows:

> If we have a clear and distinct idea of God as a being whose existence is necessary by His own nature, then God is immediately perceived by us to exist. But we have a clear and distinct idea of

God as a being whose existence is necessary by His own nature. Therefore, God is immediately perceived by us to exist.[4]

Critique of the Concept of "Necessary Existence"

The standard criticisms of the ontological argument point out that one cannot legitimately infer *existence* from the *idea* of a perfect being. However, in what follows, I shall not raise any question about the legitimacy of inferring the existence of God from the *idea* of God's necessary existence. While this may be a useful line of criticism to follow, it presupposes that we already have understood clearly enough what is meant by saying that God has necessary existence. This, however, is precisely what cannot be granted. It is the antecedent of the conditional of the very first premiss of the above restatement of Spinoza's argument, that I wish to examine. For, I should maintain, we do *not* have a "clear and distinct idea" of a being whose existence is necessary by its own nature, or that is *"causa sui."*

For Spinoza, "necessary existence," as describing a property of God, has a double meaning—or, if one prefers, a negative and a positive aspect. On the one hand, to say God necessarily exists means that God's existence is unlimited, i.e., not contingent on something else. On the other hand, to say that God necessarily exists means that God's existence is intelligible, i.e., to be explained by reference to His own nature: God is *causa sui*. Of these two aspects, it is the second that calls for our special critical attention. My own discussion, in earlier chapters of this book, has explored the different kinds of argument that could be employed to uphold the claim that the world's existence is contingent; although my analysis has not coincided with Spinoza's reasons, nevertheless, the result has been substantially the same. If by saying that the world's existence is contingent, one means only that the existence of the world is not causally dependent on some transcendent reality, there need be no objection (in this special, *negative* sense of "necessary existence") to saying that the world has necessary existence.

The fact is, however, Spinoza does not intend simply to use the phrase "necessary existence" in this limited, negative, special

[4] *Ibid.*, p. 199.

sense. He wishes also to affirm that the world has necessary existence in the positive sense: its existence is intelligible in terms of
its own nature. This, however, as I shall now undertake to show,
is as little capable of being supported by sound argument, as the
statement that the world's existence is contingent.

(1) The first point to be noticed is similar to one that has already
been made in connection with the theist's position. It needs to
be repeated here, even though Spinoza's philosophy is radically
opposed to that of theism. For there is a common presupposition,
in both philosophies, of the Principle of Sufficient Reason. Spinoza,
in common with the theist, presupposes that for the existence of
the world, as indeed for any specific characteristic or fact of a
more limited status, some explanation is to be found. As I have
previously argued, there is no reason for questioning the reliance
on the Principle of Sufficient Reason, when this is interpreted as
a regulative (or methodological) postulate that defines the continuing interest of science in finding intelligible connections among
events. However, when taken as an axiom of a metaphysical character, that is, when taken to describe constitutively the supposedly
pervasive intelligibility of the world, there is nothing but faith
to warrant the adoption of this axiom.

Neither Spinoza nor any theist can provide convincing reasons
for adopting the Principle of Sufficient Reason as a metaphysical
principle, to guarantee an explanation for the existence of the
world. The world's existence *may* have a reason, but there is no
way in which we can know this, or be assured that it must be so.
To assert that the existence of the world, along with everything
else, *must* have a reason, is something for which we have no
philosophic warrant. In one direction, Spinoza's adoption of the
Principle of Sufficient Reason marked his own allegiance to the
Cartesian ideal of disclosing the mathematical orderliness of
the world of natural events. In another direction, Spinoza's adoption of the same principle marked his affinity with this aspect of
theism, generally, that is, as a way of solving the mystery of the
existence of the world. If Spinoza had been more thoroughgoing
in his rejection of supernaturalism, he need not, in any way, have
disturbed or weakened his enthusiasm for the prospects of rendering Nature intelligible by scientific means, by also rejecting

the metaphysical Principle of Sufficient Reason as a way of accounting for the existence of the world. By retaining this use of the metaphysical Principle of Sufficient Reason, even though it is, for him, no longer made to support a belief in a transcendent Deity, Spinoza compromised his position and rendered it, to that extent, philosophically unsound.

(2) A second point of criticism to be made of Spinoza's conception of necessary existence is that there is no contribution whatever to our understanding of the existence of the world, in saying that the world necessarily exists or (as Spinoza also puts it), that Nature is *causa sui*. The expressions "necessarily exists," "necessary existence," and *"causa sui"* (as well as similar expressions in use by more recent naturalistic philosophers, for example that the world is "self-sufficient"), far from serving to make the existence of the world intelligible, are, in fact, verbal disguises for the failure to contribute to such understanding.

For Spinoza, there are two ways in which we can state our understanding of something: by the use of definitions, and by causal analysis. A definition, for Spinoza, is the statement of the essence of some concept. Spinoza adopts the traditional Platonic-Aristotelian view of definition; it is not a verbal stipulation or conventionally agreed-to equivalence of terms. Rather, the *definiens* or predicate of the definitional statement gives the *correct* analysis of the meaning of the *definiendum* (or subject). Causal analysis, on the other hand, states the relations between events in terms of antecedent conditions and consequent effect. The necessity of causal relations is both logical (the denial of a correct causal analysis would be self-contradictory), and ontological (the events in Nature cannot deviate from the logically analyzed order). In saying that Nature is *causa sui*, and that a *causal* understanding of the existence of Nature is to be found in realizing that necessary existence is part of the essence or *nature* of Nature, Spinoza would seem to be saying that our understanding of the existence of Nature is both a matter of definition (in his sense of definition), *and* of causal understanding. The causal understanding of the existence of Nature is encompassed by means of, or within, the definition of Nature. In this respect, as previously remarked, the causal understanding of God is wholly different from the causal understanding of some ordinary object or event, since, for the understanding of the latter, it is always necessary to allude to some external conditions or circumstances. An explanation of why *this* event occurred, would not be obtained simply by means of a definition of the type of event this instance exemplifies. However, in the case of God (or Nature) such a causal understanding, not having anything external to refer to, is wholly internal; and this is contained in the statement of the *definition* of the essence of God.

Now, I submit, this attempt to import the idea of *causal* intelligibility within the framework of a definition, as Spinoza understands definition, is unsatisfactory. It does not yield an explanation of that for which an explanation is wanted—the existence of the world. Take a paradigm case of causal understanding: a statement describing the effect is shown to follow logically from other statements describing relevant causal conditions. (One may also use the language of more recent philosophies of science, and describe causal explanation as the inference based on a conjunction of relevant laws and initial conditions). In any case, the effect is distinct from the cause. Given the particular body, dropped from a particular height with such-and-such an initial velocity, and the statement of the law of falling bodies, one can deduce, and thereby explain, causally, why the body took the number of seconds it did, to reach the ground. The statement that the body reached the ground in so many seconds (the effect), is different from both the statement of initial conditions, and the law of falling bodies, or their conjunction (the causal conditions). We explain the first statement by means of a simple mathematical calculation, in which the first statement follows from the second set of statements (or formulae).

Consider, however, the situation in finding an explanation for the existence of the world. We are told that it is part of the essence of the world that it necessarily exists. If there is any remnant of the pattern of causal understanding to be found in the use of a definition (i.e., if there is any meaning to "*causa sui*"), what, now, corresponds to the *cause* from which the effect (the existence of the world) is to be inferred? I fail to see any. The use of causal terminology, under the cloak of the expression *causa sui*, is wholly devoid of meaning. There is neither a distinct cause, nor a process of inference by which to logically deduce the effect from the cause. In asserting that the essence of the world includes the trait of necessary existence, the term "necessary" is an idle one; it does not, in any way, reflect the meaning of the term "necessary" when used to describe the logical deducibility of an effect from its cause.

How, then, is the statement that the world *necessarily exists*, any different from the statement that the world *exists*? The latter statement we already know to be true. Though true, however, we still ask the question—which the truth of this statement in no way makes irrelevant: "*Why* does the world exist?" We are not helped in answering this question, by being told the world exists because it has necessary existence. All that is being done, in the absence of a genuine explanation, is to repeat the very fact to be explained, and to offer this fact as its own explanation. We should surely be completely dissatisfied, in asking "Why did this body reach the ground in 10 seconds?" to be told, by way of explanation, "It reached the ground in 10 seconds." We have, in the use of the expression *causa sui*, precisely the same failure of explanation. We don't know any more, in the sense of having an *explanation* of the existence of the world, in being told it is part of the essence of the world. To say it is part of the essence of the world, is merely to restate the fact which calls for an explanation; it is not to give the explanation.

Part Four

MYSTERY AND AGNOSTICISM

CHAPTER X

"Reasons" and "Rational Method"

A PRINCIPAL THEME of the past several chapters has been the way in which the question "Why does the world exist?" would be interpreted on the presupposition that there must be an answer to this question in accordance with the Principle of Sufficient Reason. We have seen that this principle is tacitly or explicitly invoked whether one thinks, with traditional theism, of the world's existence as contingent upon the creative power of a transcendent deity, or with Spinoza, as necessary and self-sufficient. Our discussion has sought to bring out the difficulties not only in adopting the Principle of Sufficient Reason as a metaphysical principle, but also with the view that the existence of the world is contingent, as well as with the view that it is necessary. What remains to be considered now is this: is there any way in which we can formulate what the mystery of existence is, without adopting either the Principle of Sufficient Reason, or one or another of the views that the existence of the world is contingent or that it is necessary? If this can be done by means of a question, how shall this be expressed? And what considerations are there to support the claim that the question, thus chosen, is unanswerable? These are the topics that will occupy us in the present and following chapters.

The view I shall argue for, may be summed up as follows. There is no harm in continuing to use the expression "Why does the world exist?", provided it is recognized that the use of the term "Why" is not to be taken as committing us to the presupposition that there must be a reason for the existence of the world, or, if there is such a reason, that this can in any way be known to us. Since, however, it must be admitted that the use of the term "Why," in the formulation of ordinary questions, is normally accompanied by the presupposition that there are reasons to be found to answer such questions, it is better to drop the use of the term "Why," altogether, from the question "Why does the world exist?" However, we shall need some other way of phrasing the question, so that the unwanted normal associations of the term "Why" will not be present to mislead us. One way of doing this, is to put our central question in the form: "Is there a reason for the world's existence?" I shall, therefore, use this question, rather than the question "Why does the world exist?" to convey our sense of the mystery of existence. I shall argue that this question, too, is unanswerable, and so expresses the proper mystery of existence. In saying that it is unanswerable, I mean that there is no rational method already known to man by which this question can be answered.

In upholding these claims, it will be necessary to explore the uses of the terms "reason" and "rational method." It will also be suggested that a more precise formulation of our question would be: "Is there a reason-for-the-existence-of-the-world?" (rather than "Is there a reason for the existence of the world?"). It will be seen, as a result of our analysis, the reason for saying the question "Is there a reason-for-the-existence-of-the-world?" is unanswerable, is that we have no way of assuring ourselves either as to an affirmative or a negative answer to this question. It follows that the only sound philosophic view to adopt in connection with this entire matter, is one of agnosticism.

The Meanings of "Reason"

As a first step in elaborating the above suggestions and developing the arguments in their support, let us consider the use of the term "reason." Our goal is to try to understand what meaning, if any, can be assigned to the expression "reason for the world's existence." Confronted with the welter of uses of the term "reason," both in ordinary language and in the technical vocabularies of psychology and philosophy, it would clearly be futile to seek for some single meaning that might be extracted and encapsulated within some definition. It will be more profitable to select, for our present interest, that group of related meanings in which we use the term "reason" in connection with the giving, finding, or obtaining of reasons for something or other. This meaning of "reason" is normally indicated whenever we raise a question in which the term "why" occurs. (I do not wish to deny that questions in which other interrogatory terms figure—such as "which," "how," "who," etc.—might also lead us to expect, by way of answers, the giving of reasons. I simply want to begin with the obvious fact that the normal use of "why"-questions does call for reasons, by way of suitable answers.)

Yet, having delimited the domain of our inquiry in this rough way, we find no single and easily detectable uniformity within what remains. Even when we confine ourselves to the analysis of the term "reason" as it functions in the matter of giving or finding reasons, there is a great variety among its different senses, and different sorts of things with respect to which it makes sense to use the term. Once more, instead of attempting to formulate some definition that would give the "essential" meaning of reason in all these cases, it would be more profitable to enumerate the major types of cases in which we use this term, and note the similarities and differences, as we go from one meaning to another.

Consider the following typical questions whose answers would consist in giving reasons:

(1) "Why are you taking a course in computer-programming?"
"I wish to prepare myself for a position in this field."
(2) "Why are you spraying these trees?"
"To prevent caterpillar nests from forming."
(3) "Why do automobile tires have ridges on their surface?"
"To give better traction."
(4) "Why did the radiator crack?"
"You forgot to put anti-freeze in, and when the water froze it expanded and cracked the radiator."
(5) "Why do unsupported bodies fall to the ground?"
"There's a force of gravity that's exerted on them by the earth."

(6) "Why do you think General Motors is a good stock to invest in?"
"All the market analysts I've read, seem to agree it is."

(7) "Why was the development of Lobachevsky's geometry so important?"
"Well, for one thing, it showed there was something mistaken in believing that mathematics is founded on self-evident axioms."

(8) "Why was my answer marked incorrect on this exercise?"
"You said the syllogism was valid, but actually it commits the fallacy of undistributed middle."

In examining typical cases such as the foregoing, it will be convenient to sort out three principal groups of meanings of "reason," viz., "purpose," "explanation," and "evidence."

(a) *Purpose.*—One group of cases has to do with those situations in which men are engaged in acting in a certain way in order to make possible some sought-for result (or to prevent something from happening.) Cases (1), (2), and (3), in the above list, would fall under this category. In the case of the person who takes a course in computer-programming in order to prepare himself for employment in this field, we say the individual has a selected end-in-view, for which his taking the course is a chosen means. Having deliberated as to what he wants to achieve, and how he wishes to go about realizing it, the individual reached a decision and can now *give* his reasons, when asked, for his actions. The giving of reasons by the individual engaged in the action, serves as a justification (or, in one sense of this term, as an explanation) for his action.

In case (2), again, there is a deliberate end-in-view for the individual; his spraying the trees is another example of purposive behavior. In this case, as distinguished from example (1), the agent seeks to bring about certain changes in his environment rather than, primarily, in himself. He sprays the trees in order to prevent certain things from happening. Once more, the reasons for this action can be supplied by the agent.

In (3), reasons are sought for a manufactured article (the automobile tires) having a certain feature (a ridged surface). Such reasons can be obtained from the maker (or user) of the object, who points to the results to be achieved—better traction—by employing the means selected, and as embodied in the construction of the object. In all similar cases of craftsmanship or manufacture, the transformation of raw materials into finished products can be justified by calling attention to the sought-for results, in the use and enjoyment of those products. The reasons for the object being what it is, are supplied by the maker, and can be exhibited in the way in which the object "works."

The foregoing cases of the use of "reason" are all straightforward, elementary instances of how we go about satisfying our interest in obtaining answers to questions of a certain kind. The questions asked look for reasons in the sense of *purposes* or results sought-for by some agent, or maker, who deliberately does things, or makes things, in a certain way. In these cases, the agent can, under questioning, justify or explain his behavior or his constructions, by himself supplying the reasons. There are, of course, many cases where one or another of the features present in straightforward examples may be lacking, doubtful, unclear, or controversial. And for such cases, we may not have any definite basis for speaking of reasons at all, in the present sense, or for expecting that we shall obtain satisfactory answers to our questions. "Why were the stones at Stonehenge placed the way they were?" "Why do beavers build their dams?" "Why was President Kennedy assassinated?" "Why didn't Bach indicate for what instruments he intended his *Art of the Fugue?*" Answers to these questions are not readily available or free of controversy. For present purposes, however, it is unnecessary to dwell on these difficult, unsettled, or obscure cases, since my main interest is to distinguish the major senses of the term "reason," and not to deal with borderline or controversial instances of their application.

(*b*) *Explanation.*—A second group of cases in which the term "reason" has relevance, is exemplified by (4) and (5), in the above list. In these cases, the questions look for reasons, in the sense of *explanations* for observed events. Explanations may take various forms. Causal explanations of a common-sense sort belong to this group. Such explanations may be wholly satisfactory without the need to introduce technically formulated laws or theories of a scientific sort. Thus, to the question "Why did the tree fall down?", it would be thought sufficient, normally, to reply: "There was a hurricane last night, and the wind was very strong." In this case, no explicit reference is made to the laws of physics, as part of the explanation, although they would be relevant in a more refined scientific explanation.

The more refined explanations of natural events given by science are of two principal types: one consists in the subsumption of individual events under empirical laws, the second consists in the explanation of empirical regularities by means of theory. (1) According to the first type of explanation, the occurrence of some individual event is shown to be an instance of some law or regularity. Thus to the question "Why did the pipe burst?", one may reply by showing that the statement reporting this event can be deduced from premises that include, on the one hand, the laws having to do with the tensile strength of different materials, and the behavior of water at different temperatures, and, on the other, the particular circumstances that obtained in the present case—the amount of water in the pipe, the temperature it reached, the specific tensile strength of the pipe, and so on. In some cases of explanation, the laws state strict invariances, in others they may be of a statistical character. (2) The second major type of scientific explanation consists in the kind of reasons offered to make the empirically observed regularities themselves intelligible. We ask, for example, why unsupported bodies fall. In providing an explanation, the physicist shows how the empirical regularity can be deduced in accordance with the principles of a constructed theory whose distinctive conceptual constructs (e.g., "gravitational force") are introduced on the basis of some guiding analogy. The principles of these theories are not to be confused with empirical laws; they do not have any direct observational warrant.

Insofar as science succeeds in supplying reasons of the above principal kinds, it serves the human need of rendering our environment intelligible. As distinguished from the first group of meanings of "reason," scientific explanations do not involve reference to the purposes of some conscious agent. What distinguishes the scientific mode of thinking is the refusal to share with animism or theism the belief that only by considering ultimately the in-

tentions of some agent, can we understand why natural phenomena have the patterns or qualities they manifest. The scientific
quest for intelligibility does not rest on the attempt to find out
the reasons some superhuman agent or maker might give, that
justifies or explains what he has done or is planning. It is we,
human beings using common sense or the refined methods of
the sciences, who give ourselves reasons for what happens in Nature. We cannot consult some non-human agent or maker to
ascertain his reasons, as we normally do, when we turn (as in
the first group of cases) to some human agent or craftsman to
find out *his* reasons for his performances or constructions.

The foregoing account of the character of "reasons" in the
sense of explanations of natural events, has again concentrated on
simple and straightforward cases. Not only would a more thoroughgoing discussion add many refinements and qualifications—
it would also deal with the problems that arise from consideration
of special, borderline cases. As an example of the latter, we may
mention the problem, frequently encountered in the study of
human behavior, as to where to draw the line between those cases
of behavior that call for an analysis in terms of causal laws, and
those that call for analysis in terms of the purposes of the agent.
We can explain why a particular individual, in a stuffy room,
fainted, by assigning as a *cause*, the lack of oxygen; similarly,
we explain why we open the window in that room by stating our
purpose: "to let in some fresh air." But is the reason that would
answer the question why this man is having his ninth martini, a
cause or a purpose? The notorious difficulties of casuistic questions in ethics, or the daily problems of the law court and the psy-
chiatrist's office, remind us of the absence of clear-cut distinctions,
and yet of the need to reach decisions with respect to these cases.

   (*c*) *"Cause"*.—Before turning, finally, to an analysis of "evidence," as the third major sense of the term "reason," let me
pause to comment on the use of the term "cause" with respect
to our present theme. Does "cause" belong exclusively to one or
the other of the senses of "reason" so far discussed, or to neither?
The answer is that the term "cause" does not stand for a single
idea, but for a complex of different ones. When its principal
meanings have been distinguished, these can be accommodated by

assignment to either the category of "purposes" or "explanations."
Consider the following typical uses of the term "cause": (1) "The
toppling of the tree was caused by the strong wind"; (2) "Exces-
sive smoking is one of the chief causes of lung cancer"; (3) "The
engineer applied the brakes suddenly, and this caused the train
to come to an abrupt halt"; (4) "Detectives established that the
cause of the fire was a case of arson on the part of a disgruntled
employee."

We sometimes use the term "cause," as in case (1), to describe
a relation between two particular events not involving deliberate
human intervention; sometimes, as in (2), to describe a relation
between two classes of events; sometimes, as in (3) and (4), to
describe a sequence of events that has some features in common
with (1), though it also involves the deliberate action of a human
being.

While (1) has to do with the causal connection between two
particular events, some tacit appeal to a regularity of connection
between classes of events is required, especially on the level of
scientific explanation. In (2), the term "cause" occurs in the statement of a regularity holding between classes of events, without
(as in example (1)) its being applied to some particular instance.
Since, in both cases, the meaning of "cause" makes tacit or explicit appeal, at some point, to some regularity or law, we may,
therefore, consider the fundamental meaning of "cause," illustrated in both (1) and (2), as being "regular connection."

In examples (3) and (4), however, the word "cause" is best
understood in its role as an active, transitive verb. We say "So-and-
so *caused* such-and-such to happen." This meaning is based on the
common experience that a person can *make something happen* by
manipulating his environment in some way.[1] The simplest and
most familiar case is that in which a person deliberately moves
some part of his body in order to bring about some change in the
arrangement of bodies in his environment: the engineer pulls the
brake; the arsonist sets fire to the building. These acts are normally
done for a reason by the agent—to achieve some result. In acting,

[1] Cf. D. Gasking, "Causation and Recipes," *Mind,* LXIV (1955), 479 ff; M.
Black, "Making Something Happen," in *Models and Metaphors* (Ithaca, New
York, 1962), 153 ff.

he sets in train a sequence of events; these events may also be explained, in part, by applying relevant causal laws: to explain the stopping of the train requires reference to the interaction of frictional and other forces; to explain the burning of the building's flammable materials involves use of the chemical laws of oxidation, etc. However, the principal meaning of "cause" in these last examples, is that which calls attention to an agent's intentional action rather than to explanatory causal laws. The term "cause" when used to designate an act by which a human being makes something happen, has, accordingly, a different meaning from that which is brought to the fore by emphasis upon causal laws. In their study of the causes of human actions, historians and lawyers are normally concerned with the use of the term "cause" as purposive action, not with the meaning that concerns the natural scientist.[2]

In order to avoid any confusion between these two different meanings of "cause," we may assign one set of meanings to one of the meanings of "reason," viz., "purposive action by a conscious agent," and the other, to another meaning of reason, viz., "explanation of events by means of empirical laws." For purposes of the present discussion, I have differentiated the meanings of "cause" into two main groups. A more thorough discussion—particularly of the historical development of these several uses—would show how the meaning of "cause" embodied in the scientist's appeal to causal regularities, is itself a refined and attenuated transformation of the meaning of "cause," as used to designate a human act of manipulation of objects in the environment of the agent. There are various transitional phases in this transformation. For example, to say "The woodsman chopped at the tree and caused it to fall," is to employ the term "cause" in its primitive and original meaning. To say "The blowing of a strong wind caused the tree to fall," is to extend the original meaning of "cause," by analogy, to the wind: it, too, can "cause" things to happen. Hume argued that the essential meaning of "cause" is to be found in the notion of regularity; one must purge the concept of cause of all remnants of anthropomorphism as, for example, in thinking of cause as having anything to do with exerting force or power. In saying these

---

[2] Cf. H. L. A. Hart, *Causation and the Law* (Oxford, 1959); W. Dray, *Laws and Explanation in History* (Oxford, 1957).

things, Hume showed how far the idea of cause had developed under the pressure of scientific interests, and had been removed from its original meaning. The notion of causal *laws* now dominates the meaning of "cause." Even the original meaning of the term was taken up and absorbed within this new meaning—so that the notion of a freely acting human agent causing something to happen, is widely thought to be a relic of primitive ways of thinking; many would say it is no longer possible to take seriously the conception of a free action, in the face of an increasing awareness of the universal reign of causal laws in all phenomena, human as well as non-human.

A new stage in the career of the concept "cause" is reached with the realization that the category "causal law" itself does not have the central importance for science that, according to older theories of scientific method, it is thought to have. What is important for science, it will be commonly argued, are patterns of invariance in which relations of cause and effect are of little importance compared to the need to state functional relations among selected quantities. Moreover, in place of the dominance earlier accorded to strictly invariant causal laws, it is now seen to be the case, in certain areas of study, that statistical regularities have an independent status of their own, without their being thought to be merely inexact approximations to causal laws. Finally, the realization of the importance of the role of theories in science, as fulfilling a function quite different from those belonging to empirically established causal laws, functional equations, or statistical generalizations, has reduced the status of importance of causal laws even further; the latter are no longer thought to have the significance for an understanding of the goals and achievements of science they were once thought to possess, as in the days of Hume or Mill.

(*d*) *Evidence.*—A third major class of uses of the term "reason" is made up of those cases in which the reply to the question "Why?" is given by supplying reasons in the form of *evidence for particular statements or beliefs.* Examples (6), (7), and (8), in the list given earlier, belong to this group. (The range of examples to which the term "reason," in the present sense, applies, could be extended to include other types of statements or beliefs. My present purpose is not one of exhaustive analysis, however, and I content myself with mentioning a few representative uses.) Let us first be clear about what distinguishes the present group of uses of the term "reason" from the two previously distinguished families of uses. In the first group, the term "reason" is used in connection with actions and constructions, and their results or products. In the second use of the term, we speak of "reasons" as having to do with explanations for events. In the present case, reason has to do neither with actions nor events, but with *statements*. Men affirm, deny, judge, appraise, predict, interpret, and explain an endless number of things; and they express, through language, their convictions, views, beliefs, and conclusions in great varieties of ways. Whenever the question is put to someone why he accepts or affirms a particular statement, the request is for the reasons, in the sense of *the evidence*, for the statement in question.

That men very often accept all sorts of things for which they are unable to provide any evidence whatever, is too well-known a feature of human behavior to need any elaboration. Nor does the fact that a particular individual is unable to give any evidence for his beliefs exclude the possibility that reasons might be given by someone else who shares the belief. And again, of course, the fact that a person is unprepared, unwilling, or unable to give evidence for his beliefs, does not preclude the possibility of treating his *having* the belief as a fact of his biography, and so as something for which it is relevant to ask for reasons, in the sense of *causes*. However, knowledge of the causes that would explain his having the belief in question (causes that may be psychological, social, etc.), does not take the place of considering the evidence for the same belief. We are concerned, then, in our present analysis, with those cases in which men recognize the need for supporting what they accept as true, by giving evidential reasons.

An "argument" is a sequence of statements in which certain statements serve as reasons (or evidence) for other statements. The first-order activities (and results) of giving arguments, and the second-order activities (and results) of evaluating and classifying the first-order arguments, in their different ways, are occupied with the matter of giving or examining reasons in the present sense of this term. The analysis and classification of different types of statements and arguments belongs to the province of logic. This discipline includes not only the study of the formal canons of validity and consistency, but the distinctive uses of discourse in diverse areas, e.g., in empirical science, mathematics, law, ethics, history, philosophy, theology, and esthetics. Considerations relevant to this study deal with the distinctions that would clarify, for example, the appropriate types of evidence needed in a mathematical proof, philosophical argument, empirical generalization, legal decision, moral evaluation, esthetic appraisal, and so on. The study of logic is thus essentially an inquiry into the manifold applications of the use of the term "reason" as signifying "evidence."

We now have before us a three-fold set of families of uses of the term "reason." With respect to human actions of a voluntary or intentional sort, we look for and find reasons (when we can) in the sense of *purposes*. With respect to individual occurrences and empirically established patterns of natural events, we look for and find reasons (when we can) in the sense of *explanations*. With respect to statements and beliefs of all sorts, we look for and find reasons (when we can) in the sense of *evidence*.

It remains to note briefly with respect to the foregoing distinctions, some relations among them. (1) Among beliefs for which evidence is required, are beliefs about the desirability of achieving some end, or the effectiveness of using certain means to reach it. These statements and the arguments in their support ("reason" as "evidence") clarify the reasons (purposes) of action. Again, consider the species of belief consisting in the giving of reasons (explanations) for natural events. As with all other beliefs, it is relevant to examine the reasons (evidence) in their support. (2) In similar fashion, both actions and makings (for which reasons as purposes can be offered), when treated as natural events, provoke a search for reasons, in the sense of explanations. This is the type of interest taken in these phenomena, for example, in anthropology or in psychology. Or again, the *having* of beliefs, as previously noted, can be treated, along with other aspects of the behavior of the human animal, as a matter for causal analysis, i.e., as something to be explained. (3) Finally, one may approach the activity of looking for explanations, or the activity of supplying evidence for beliefs, as examples of purposive actions. In this type of teleological analysis, one considers the reasons (purposes) these activities manifest and the value they possess.

Rational Method

I turn next to the analysis of the expression "rational method." The adjective "rational" is best understood in connection with the activity of giving reasons. It is because man can give reasons for his actions, for the phenomena he observes, and for his beliefs, that he is a rational animal; because he can give reasons, a human being can be said to have the faculty of reason. The use of the adjective "rational," as in the expressions "rational actions," "rational beliefs," and "rational explanations," (or any species of these, e.g., "a rational way of running a government," "a rational scheme of insurance," etc.) suggests something further: not only can reasons be offered, but the reasons are good ones.

The term "method" may be used to describe a number of related but variously different things, viz., a way, technique, or series of steps for doing something or other, or a set of rules, criteria, or policies for guiding what is done.[3] We speak of methods of putting on horseshoes, playing the violin, conducting a meeting, pursuing a scientific inquiry, teaching, performing a surgical operation, etc. Each of these may, or may not, be rational, i.e., capable of being supported by reasons, or by good reasons.

Our present interest is in a rational method of knowing the reasons for anything. This, of course, is a very specialized kind of method. To say that a method of determining reasons can itself be rational, is to say that one can give reasons for using that method rather than some other. It is, in other words, to apply *to* a method of determining reasons, one or another of the meanings of "giving or finding reasons" which, in other respects, is the *subject matter for* the method. It is to bring to bear, reflexively, upon the method, the kind of thing the method is concerned to investigate. Here the use of the adjective "rational" in con-

[3] Cf. J. Buchler, *The Concept of Method* (New York, 1961).

nection with "method," involves the use, in particular, of one of the discriminated senses of "reason," namely, the giving of evidence. A rational method of determining reasons, is one for which evidence can be given to support the belief that that method is a sound one. The term "rational" further suggests that to the question "Why do you prefer this method for determining reasons?" one can not only supply reasons (in the form of evidence), but that the evidence is convincing or supportive in a superior degree to that which may be adduced in favor of a belief about the use of some other method for the same purpose. The term "rational," as used in connection with "method," is thus both descriptive and evaluative. This is to say that the belief that such-and-such a method is to be preferred to other methods, is a belief for which we are not only prepared to give evidence (support by relevant reasons), but for which we take the evidence to be convincing.

In what does a rational method of knowing reasons consist? There is no single formula that adequately serves as an answer to this question. We need to take into account not only the previously distinguished range of meanings of "reason," but the fact that what constitutes a "rational method" for obtaining knowledge about such reasons, exhibits shifts in meaning as we go from one set of cases to another.

The first important fact to be noted about the different senses of "reason" is this. With respect to reason in the sense of "purpose," those engaged in some action or construction can be questioned why they act in a cerain way, or why they make objects with such-and-such features. Again, where a man defends some belief or other, he can be asked for his reasons or evidence. Where "reasons," however, means "explanations of natural events," of the kind given in science or common sense, one cannot ascertain what those reasons (explanations) are, by interrogating a responding human being or conscious agent. It is the *investigator* who *assigns* reasons for his subject matter; it is he who offers explanations. He does not receive these reasons—he gives them (by invention or conceptual construction). In short, one looking for a reason in the sense of an explanation, does not arrive at it simply by asking another human being what it is. (I am, of course, dealing here with those cases in which—confronted by some phenomenon for which there is not already a satisfactory explanation—the person searching for an explanation, for example the scientist, has to provide one. I am not considering the case of learning an already accepted explanation, by turning to some expert, teacher, textbook, or encyclopedia. For even these sources of explanation will ultimately derive from some *original* act of *giving* an explanation *to* some subject matter by an investigator who employed some particular resource of creative imagination and insight in arriving at the explanation.) Reasons, in the sense of explanations, are not extracted by interrogation of the subject matter being studied, in the way in which reasons as purposes, or reasons as evidence, can be determined by interrogation of conscious, rational beings.

A second point to be made in clarifying the expression "a rational method for knowing reasons," is this. We might ask: "When one speaks of 'obtaining knowledge,' is this to be understood as a matter of obtaining information, or is it also evaluative of reasons as well?" Once more, there is no single formula that will encompass all cases. For in some cases we mean one, in other cases, both of these elements.

(1) Take the matter of what we mean by "a rational method for knowing the reasons, in the sense of purposes, of some conscious agent or maker." Our interest may simply be one of finding out what, in fact, were the reasons (purposes) had by the agent or maker in question, for doing or making what he did. We may have no special interest in judging the results—in extending our approval or disapproval to what was done or made. If our interest were simply one of obtaining information about the agent's reasons, a rational method of knowing these reasons would consist in employing whatever tested, reliable skills and devices we have for obtaining this information. In simple cases, it may be sufficient to ask the person directly, why he is doing what he is doing. In other cases (as in historical inquiry), it may be necessary to resort to all sorts of indirect techniques of comparison, inference, or guesswork.

(2) Similarly, one may ascertain the reasons (evidence) why a person holds the beliefs he does, by asking him. His reply may

be simple in character, or, if the matter is of a more recondite nature, as, for example, the complicated proof of a mathematical statement, the reasons may lie hidden, and need to be disentangled. (Sometimes, as in the case of Fermat's famous "theorem," we don't know why a man says what he does. Fermat asserted that the equation $a^n + b^n = c^n$ is not solvable in integers for any n larger than 2. He tells us, however, that the proof he had found for this was, unfortunately, too long to be written out in the margin of the book in which he was writing!)

In the sphere of action, as well as in the sphere of the technical and fine arts, a rational method for knowing reasons is, in part, a method for ascertaining the actual reasons men had in acting the way they did, or making the objects they did; it is, in addition, the use of a set of rules and criteria for evaluating those reasons. The application of the latter side of a rational method of knowing reasons, involves the use of the particular rules and criteria that belong to the various practical arts and skills (e.g., medicine, shipbuilding, etc.). In the case of reasons for beliefs (evidence), again, in addition to knowing what the reasons are by which a person attempts to support his views, there are more or less well-defined rules and criteria for appraising the worth of these reasons. This is the concern of logic, broadly conceived. In addition to the general rules of consistency for determining formal validity, and that can be applied to all discourse, there are (insofar as they have been worked out) special rules and criteria that define, for specialized disciplines, the probative force of different types of evidence for the area in question (e.g., in mathematics, law, empirical science, etc.). A rational method for knowing reasons, in the sense of knowing the evidence for beliefs, is thus a matter of having information as to what a person's reasons are, and how effective or sound they are.

(3) In the case of obtaining knowledge of reasons, in the sense of explanations, for natural events, we cannot (as previously remarked) simply obtain such knowledge by interrogation. Explanations are brought to the subject matter by the investigator. Since, however, different explanations may be offered for the same phenomenon, the problem becomes one of appraising the worth of various proposed explanations. To *give* a reason, in this case,

is not to *find* a reason by asking: it is achieved by sifting and weighing different proposed answers. What is called "scientific method" defines the rules and criteria for judging proposed explanations of natural phenomena; these rules and criteria are worked out (though never, of course, with finality) for different types and levels of explanation. Scientific method is, par excellence, a rational method of knowing reasons, in the sense of giving explanations for things.

CHAPTER XI

Reason and the World's Existence

Now that we have explored the different senses of the terms "reason" and "rational method," we need to consider what relevance they have in connection with our principal theme. In what way, if at all, do they help to clarify the meaning of the phrase "reason for the existence of the world," or the claim that the mystery of the existence of the world consists in the fact that there is no rational method by which any possible reason for the existence of the world could be known? Let us consider, first, the use of the expression "reason for the existence of the world." Do any of the senses of the term "reason," previously discriminated, contribute in any way to our understanding of this phrase? This is the topic of the present chapter. The question of rational method, as applied to our present problem, will be discussed in the following chapter.

THERE IS NO REASON FOR THE WORLD'S EXISTENCE

The World Is Not a Statement

As a first step in narrowing down the possible relevance to our topic of the meanings of "reason" already considered, it will readily be granted, I should expect, that there is no plausible connection between what we might wish to refer to, in using the expression "a possible reason for the existence of the world," and what we mean by "reason" when we speak of evidence for some belief. We do not regard the existence of the world as a belief or a statement. In saying this, I do not wish to deny that we may investigate, as I had myself done earlier, the evidence for the *statement* "The world exists," and that, in this sense, we may examine the reasons for the statement "The world exists." I am now concerned, however, not with the statement "The world exists," but with that to which the statement refers—the ontological fact these words describe. We are asking with respect to this ontological fact, whether there is any reason for *it*. And my first point is that there is no good reason for identifying the kind of fact to which we refer when we speak of the existence of the world, with the utterance of a statement or the having of a belief. We should not group these together as belonging to the same category or type. The existence of the world is not comparable to what is said or believed. Hence, it would make no sense to ask for reasons for the existence of the world in the way in which, when we are given the affirmation of some statement or belief by a person, we ask this person for his reasons, i.e., for the evidence or arguments by which he would support his statement or belief. The world is neither a statement nor a belief. (Even when, as in traditional theism, it is said "In the beginning there was the Word," or, "God said 'Let there be light' and there was light," etc., the existence of the world is not identified with God's utterance; it *results* from it—much as if some act were carried out at the command of some powerful ruler or magician.)

Although there is no warrant for speaking of the world's existence as an example of an utterance, statement, or belief, it should be noted, nevertheless, that according to some philosophic systems, there is an implicit (though as we shall see, also misleading) *analogy* of the existence of the world with a special type of statement. Such, I believe, is the case with the philosophy of Spinoza. Spinoza, it will be recalled from the previous discussion, attempts to show that there is a reason for the existence of the world in the fact that God is a being whose existence is necessary by His own nature. If we ask what it means to say this sort of thing, it would seem that it derives whatever plausibility it might have, from bringing to bear the kinds of things we would assert of statements in a mathematical, or other strictly necessary argument, and applying them to the world.

Consider the statement "The sum of the angles of a triangle is 180 degrees." The reasons for this statement—the evidence and argument in its support—are to be found in the proof by which this statement can be shown to follow, demonstratively, from other statements. In making explicit all the premises of this proof, it is necessary to include some statements for which no proof can be given in the system. These unproven or primitive statements are the axioms; they include the definitions, postulates, and rules of transformation. Together, they characterize the distinctive axiom-set of Euclidean geometry. Included in this axiom-set, will be a statement to the effect that "through a point not on a given line, there is not more than one line which does not meet the given line." Similarly, certain terms in the system will be undefined, for example, the terms "point," "line," "point on a line." Other terms, for example, "triangle," "parallel," "circle," etc., will be explicitly defined in terms of these primitive, undefined ones.

An axiom, being a statement, can be said to be necessary in the sense that, in the system in which it occurs as an unproven statement (along with other axioms), it must be accepted, if we are going to derive other statements from it. Similarly, to say a definition is necessary, means that it must be accepted because that is how it is stipulated the term in question is to be used—as a replacement for another expression containing (ultimately) only undefined primitive terms. But can the existence of the world be treated either as an axiom or as a definition? If one should want to say that the world's existence can also be regarded as necessary, there is an implicit appeal to the analogy between the existence of the world and an axiomatic or definitional statement. It is sufficient to call attention to this *misleading* analogy, in order to expose the basic fault that lies in this way of thinking; for there is no basis whatever in thinking that the existence of the world is in any respect like an axiom or a definition. To use the term "necessary" in connection with the existence of the world, in the way in which this term is used in connection with axiomatic or definitional statements, can only breed confusion.

The foregoing criticism takes advantage of the analysis of the language of mathematical or axiomatic systems commonly accepted in our own day. Spinoza himself, of course, did not have the advantage of this analysis, and his views are expressed in terms of the classic rationalistic philosophy. For that philosophy, the axioms of a rational system (such as mathematics) are self-evident truths; moreover, definitions state the essential properties of a concept, and are not simply stipulations or conventions as to the use of words. Spinoza thought, therefore, that in saying the existence of the world is necessary, just as in uttering an axiomatic or definitional truth about triangles, he was asserting something about an objective ontological state of affairs, reporting something that is the case. In this, however, his view was misguided. If we should reformulate in what the necessities of a mathematical system genuinely consist, and then say that the existence of the world is necessary in a similar sense, namely, that the reason for the existence of the world is comparable to that by which we say that an axiom or definition is necessary, we are employing a misleading analogy: for the existence of the world is in no way like the adoption of an axiom or a definition.

The World Is Neither an Occurrence Nor a Regularity

Of the previously discriminated major senses of "reason," I turn, next, to the second major group of meanings of this term— that in which it is used to stand for the explanation of some observed natural phenomenon. It will be recalled that in the present sense of "explanation," there are two principal forms: (1) that in which some observed individual occurrence is explained by reference to some empirical law or regularity, and (2) that in which some observed regularity, whether strictly invariant or statistical, is explained by reference to some theory. The question we must ask, then, in connection with our present theme, is this: is there any way in which we can suitably apply either of the above types of explanation to clarify the use of the phrase "reason for the existence of the world"? Let us consider each of the above meanings of explanation, in turn. (I shall reverse the order of treatment of the above enumeration, and consider the second meaning first, namely, that in which the reason for an observed regularity is found by appealing to the guiding analogy or model of some theory.)

There would seem to be little plausibility in thinking of a possible reason for the existence of the world as being at all similar to the type of reason provided in a theory, i.e., an intellectual device that makes use of hypothetically constructed entities in a conceptual model to explain empirically observed regularities. The difficulty is not so much that we would find it far-fetched to think of a "theory," in this sense, to serve as a reason for the existence of the world, but that there is no warrant, to begin with, in assimilating the existence of the world to the kind of thing we construct scientific theories to explain, namely, *empirical regularities*. There is, in other words, no plausibility in treating the existence of the world as itself an empirically observed regularity.

Consider, once more, a typical case of an observed regularity for which a theoretical explanation is sought. Let the well-worn example of Boyle's empirical law of gases serve the present purpose. Boyle established, through repeated laboratory observation, a regular connection between the volume-changes in a gas and changes in the pressure of the gas when the temperature was kept constant. This connection was formulated as an inverse relationship between the quantities volume and pressure. It was a pattern or relationship observed to hold in repeated instances of gases experimentally subjected to the appropriate changes. To say, in general, a regularity has been established, means, at the very least, that a pattern has been found (whether invariant or statistical) to hold in a *plurality* of separate instances of some phenomenon. Unless there were such a plurality of instances, there would be no meaning to the very concept of regularity. There are, of course, many other aspects to what is meant by "an empirically observed regularity." However, let us fasten our attention, for the moment, on this one feature.

It will be clear that even this rudimentary requirement is absent, if we should wish to extend to the existence of the world the meaning of "reason" relevant to observed regularities. For the existence of the world *is not* a regularity. The world, among other things, *contains* regularities. It contains, for example, gases that exhibit the kind of regularities Boyle noted. But there is no reason for identifying what we mean by the existence of the world as *itself* a regularity. What we mean by the existence of the world is, by definition, unique. There are not multiple instances of "the existence of world." The existence of the world is not some kind of phenomenon, or object, of which multiple instances have, in fact, been empirically observed. Since the way in which we understand the term "existence of the world" precludes any assimilation to the way in which we think of objects or events, of which there are multiple instances empirically identified, it makes no sense to think of the existence of the world as a regularity. It follows from this, that the sense of "reason" employed in looking for an explanation of an empirically observed regularity, has no relevance to the existence of the world.

Is the situation any better when we turn to the second of the meanings of "reason" as "explanation"—that in which we explain some individual occurrence (or the possession of some property by a particular object) by reference to a law of which it is taken to be an example? The prospects of employing "reason," in this sense, as the relevant one to use in analyzing the meaning to be given to "a possible reason for the existence of the world," seem just as dim and unpromising. Let us consider, again, a typical example of explanation in the present sense. Question: "Why did ice form on the top of the pond in Central Park last night, and not at the bottom?" Answer: "Whenever water is subjected to a temperature of 32 degrees Fahrenheit, or lower, it freezes, and when it does so, it expands—its volume increases. The density of frozen water, or ice, is less than that of liquid or unfrozen water, and when immersed in a fluid, a body will be buoyed up with a force equal to the weight of the liquid it displaces; the body in question will float in that liquid. Last night, the temperature in Central Park dropped to 10 degrees Fahrenheit. The water in the pond was exposed to this drop in temperature. Therefore, some of it froze, and when it did, it floated to the surface of the pond." In this explanation, the fact to be explained is shown to follow as a consequence of two sets of statements: (1) those which state regularities among observed characteristics (e.g., the Archimedean law of floating bodies, the behavior of water at different temperatures, etc.), and (2) those which specify the relevant initial conditions holding in the particular case under investigation (e.g., the drop of temperature to 10 degrees, etc.).

Is there any way in which the above *type* of explanation might also explain, i.e., provide a reason for the existence of the world? That our answer has to be negative, is supported by the following considerations. In the first place, it seems extremely strained to think of the existence of the world as some kind of "event" or "occurrence." We recognize events or occurrences as taking place *in* the world; but to say the world itself is an event or occurrence would stretch the use of these terms beyond any recognizable meaning. Also, an event or occurrence is something that takes place in time. This means that temporal predicates of positional location with respect to other events, given by the relations "earlier," "later," or "simultaneous with," can be specified; it also means that an event's duration (i.e., the time "how-long") can be measured. It is by no means clear that either of these types of temporal predicate has any relevance, or applicability, to the existence of the world.

This, in turn, leads to a second and perhaps more obviously damaging point of criticism. The law (or laws) forming part of a normal explanation of the above-considered type, state a relationship between certain changes or occurrences that can be observed. Similarly, the statement of the initial conditions, relevant to a normal explanation, specifies the particular circumstances that were present in the case in question; as initial conditions, these were different from the fact to be explained. We say, for example, that temperature-changes are correlated, according to a law, with volume-changes in water. Or, we say, as a matter of specifying initial conditions, "This body of water was exposed to a temperature of 10 degrees Fahrenheit." We distinguish temperature-changes from volume-changes; we also distinguish the temperature-change to which *this* body was exposed, and the changes in *its* volume and density.

Suppose, now, we try to think of what it would mean to speak of a reason for the existence of the world, with the above model in mind. In order for there to be a reason for the existence of the world, there would have to be, in the first place, some "law" or "laws" that would connect the existence of the world with some other fact or situation. Secondly, in applying these "laws," we should have to introduce into the statement of our "initial conditions" some relevant circumstances other than the fact of the existence of the world itself. But clearly, neither of these requirements makes any sense in the present case. What possible meaning can be given to the idea of a "law" that would connect the existence of the world with some other *observable* fact or conditions, in a regular manner? As we have seen, it makes no sense to say that the existence of the world is an event. Nor is it an event of which we know multiple instances. However, even if we should waive these difficulties, we find another obstacle to applying the present notion of law to explain the existence of the world. In order to satisfy the normal meanings of "law," any connection of the existence of the world with some "other factors" would have to include these "other factors" as part of the world itself. Just as temperature-changes and volume-changes are both observable traits of physical phenomena, and are both found in the same world, so any conceivable circumstances or changes with which the existence of the world could be correlated, would have to be found in the same world. But if we adopted this pattern of speaking, we should not have advanced our need to find a reason for the existence of the world one bit. For if any "reason" is part of the world, it, along with everything else that forms part of the world, is to be included under the heading "existence of the world." And we could not obtain an explanation for the existence of the world by including that which is to serve as the explanation, as part of that which is to be explained. It is the existence of the world for which we are seeking a reason. Hence, if there is such a reason, it would have to be different, in some way, from the existence of the world, and yet correlated with it. The model of reason provided by appealing to "law" and "initial conditions," simply does not serve, nor is it intelligible, in the present case.

The World Is Not Something Made

Of the threefold clusters of meaning of the term "reason" previously enumerated, we have now examined two: reason in the sense of "evidence for a belief," and reason in the sense of "scientific explanation of an individual occurrence or of an empirically established regularity." We have seen that in neither of these senses of the term "reason," can we find any plausible ground either of applying directly, or extending, the normal use of these terms, to serve the purpose of clarifying what might be meant by "a reason for the existence of the world." We have now to examine the remaining group of these meanings, that in which "reason" stands for some purpose or intention possessed by some freely-acting agent who makes something happen, either by doing something (acting in some way), or by fashioning or making something in order to accomplish his purposes.

Surely, if we bear in mind the past history of speculations on "reasons for the existence of the world," it would have to be acknowledged that the bulk of the direct applications or analogical extensions of the term "reason" in such speculations derive their meaning from exploiting this third sense of "reason." The clearest and most familiar examples are those belonging to various forms of theistic philosophy, in which God is thought of as an infinitely powerful and creative mind, or First Cause, in the sense of a *maker* and sustainer of the world and all it contains. The imagery of the Divine Craftsman in Plato's *Timaeus* feeds on the same broad source. But we need not restrict our examples to these. Many primitive cosmogonies and mythologies, the world over, have sought to account for the world's existence by using now this, now that, analogy of how men act or make things, as the basis upon which they would explain the existence of the world. Even, therefore, those cosmogonies that see the coming-into-existence of the world as the fruit of the mating of a primeval pair, or as the outcome of the authoritative command of some all-powerful ruler, would fall within the same group of meanings of "reason" in our present sense. Wherever, in short, there is an attempt to account for the world's existence by the use of such terms as "creation," "making," "genesis," and the like, we shall find a use of "reason" in the way we are now concerned to examine. In light of the rich fund of examples to be found employing the third of the meanings of "reason," we cannot afford to assume that this mode of interpretation will be just as easily dismissed as those resting on the other two main groups of meanings of "reason," when used in the interpretation of the phrase "reason for the existence of the world."

The root idea we have to examine is that in which some conscious and freely-acting agent makes something, or makes something happen. For this is the primitive sense around which cluster various examples to be taken from ordinary experience. We say, for example: "The hunter shot the animal with his bow and arrow; he cut up the carcass and used some of it for food, and out of the hide he made clothing for himself." Here is a simple case of a human agent deliberately making something happen in the environment by using some part of his own body to manipulate material objects. He pulled the bow with his arm; he stripped the hide from the carcass; he shaped it to serve as a covering for his body; he cut the meat and cooked it. Other cases of "making things happen," in ordinary experience, are readily assimilated to this paradigm. By having sexual intercourse, one initiates a series of changes whose outcome is the birth of a child. Clearly, one does not "make" the child—in the sense of directly controlling all the changes and transformations necessary to its birth and growth—in the same straightforward way that the hunter makes his food or makes his coat. The connection between the initiating cause (the actions of the agent) and the ultimate outcome, is more remote and indirect; the intervening sequences of change are less subject to control by the agent, than are the more primitive and less complicated cases of making an inanimate object for use. Despite these differences, there is enough in common to justify the use of the same general model. The human agent, through his body, interacts with another, and, in so doing, initiates a sequence of changes which he may be said to have made to happen. Similarly, the case of "something made to happen," in which one human being controls the actions of another human being, can be assimilated to the same pattern. The powerful ruler or master-craftsman need not himself manipulate the materials he wants transformed in certain ways. He gives orders to his subordinates, and they, in turn, do his bidding. Among the "tools" the ruler or master-craftsman uses are other human beings—apprentices or lackeys. He does not manipulate with his hands; he does so with his voice and gestures. Once more, the chain of connection between the intention of the principal acting human agent and the resultant product or outcome may be indirect, and involve highly intricate linkages. But the same model of "making something happen," that we derived from such primary examples as that of the hunter will serve adequately, and in a general way, to lend meaning to this type of case as well. Other cases in which we continue to use the language of "making" or "creation" are even further removed from the simple case in which a man literally manipulates a material body in his environment and thereby achieves a useful result. We say the composer "creates" the symphony. Yet the tones and rhythms he works with are not "there" in the same way that the carcass lies before the hunter; he does not obviously transform some antecedently given material object.

Let us take, as a major special case of "making something happen," those cases where we say someone *makes something.* Whether the case be elementary, uncomplicated, and paradigmatic, or of a more indirect, complicated, and analogically extended sort, certain features are to be found. Not all of these features need be found in all these cases; some may be altogether lacking, while others may be at best inferred, controversial, or only suggested. However, there are, normally, a sufficient number of these features present, to say, with some degree of plausibility, that here, too, is a case of someone making something. There is no fixed rule as to what constitutes sufficiency, here: this varies with the context. If we take the hunter and his prey as a clear and unmistakable case of someone making something, the following features will be found in this sort of occurrence to suggest the criteria for judging other instances; if any other case exhibited all these features in an unmistakable way, it, too, would be a clear case of making something: (1) There is a conscious agent who (2) uses some identifiable tools or means, (3) according to some method and with some degree of skill, which he applies (4) to some existent, given, raw materials (5) to transform it into a resultant product, possessed of certain qualities (6) he or others can use or enjoy in ways that (7) were intended by the agent.

Let us consider, now, some examples in which we do not hesitate to say "someone made this," even though not all of the foregoing listed features are present, or present unmistakably. Let us begin with a familiar example: suppose I find an object that has all the marks of a watch, and performs as one. Although I may not have seen the watch being made, nor examined the raw materials out of which it was made, nor confronted the craftsman who made it, I have no hesitancy in *inferring* that all these features of watchmaking were present in this case, too. I confidently believe there was a watchmaker, that he made this object, and that it was intended to function as a watch. My confidence is supported by the common experience that watches are made, and neither "grow on trees" nor are thrown up by the unplanned interactions of natural processes. Consider, now, a slightly different situation: let us suppose I gain access to a factory in which a top-secret piece of apparatus is being made for the government. I see men busily at work, manipulating and fashioning some object. I ask what they are making, and am told (supposing, too, I have not been already unceremoniously ushered out by this time): "It's none of your affair; the matter is top-secret. We can't tell you what this is for, nor how it is to be used." Again, despite the fact that I should be lacking in some vital pieces of information, I should not hesitate to describe this situation, too, as a case of something being made by identifiable agents to serve some specific, intended purpose.

Now suppose I wander into the studio of a musical composer, and I find him busily at work, as he informs me, in writing a symphony. Once more, I may find certain features to be absent that I normally find in other cases of making something. For one thing, while I see that it is he who is doing the writing, and I might even elicit from him what he is trying to do, namely, to write a symphony with such-and-such general qualities, it is by no means the case that—before he has found "by inspiration," or "by trial and error," the themes, tunes, rhythms, tonal combinations, etc., he proceeds to operate on—he can be said to have started with some already existent, raw materials in the way other craftsmen do. Nor need he (or anybody else, for that matter) be very clear about what are all the methods or techniques he uses.

Consider a final example: Suppose a museum, originally standing near a beach, and housing "modern sculpture," were bombed, and that, in the process, some of its treasured art objects were scattered far and wide. As I walk along the rock-and-pebble-strewn beach one day, my eye is caught by an interesting piece of stone.

I pick it up and ask: "Could this be something made by a sculptor, or is it just another rounded piece of stone, like so many others, which were made by no man, but were the result of the inter-action of wind, water, and sand over the centuries?" All clues to classifying it as one, rather than the other, are missing. I did not see the sculptor work on the piece; I have no record of a sculptor's intentions to make an object of this sort; nor any of the other normal, minimal features that would be present in order for me to be able to say that this is a case of someone having made some-thing. Obviously, in this case, the extension of the terminology "a thing made," to classify this particular object, would be wholly speculative, far-fetched, and arbitrary.

Where *all* features, normally present, are entirely absent in some particular case, we should find it wholly inappropriate and im-plausible to say that this, too, is, nevertheless, a case of something having been made. The greater the number of features absent or doubtful, the more attenuated the model of "making some-thing" is, in its application to a particular case, the less fruitful is the analogy with the paradigm case. Where we reach a point of extreme attenuation—where only on the most dubious, contro-versial, or hypothetical grounds, could we argue that some agent made something—the point of continuing to use this way of describing the situation makes little sense.

Despite the wide prevalence in mythology, poetic cosmogony, and theistic metaphysics, of accounts of the reason for the ex-istence of the world that fall back on the model of creation or procreation, all such accounts lack any inherent plausibility (what-ever entertainment value they possess as interesting stories) when once we approach them with the requirement that some, at least, of the features commonly associated with how things are brought into existence by deliberate acts of contrivance (or by sexual re-production), be shown to be literally, and clearly, manifested in what we know of the world. Here, the classic criticisms of Hume have pointed the way to the essential weakness in all these views, if taken at all seriously. Wherever we have a bona fide case of a craftsman making something, a biological process being initiated by some deliberate act, or a case of something being accomplished through the utterance of a command by some directing agent, *some* features (if not all) of those previously enumerated, will be found—non-controversially, and by direct inspection. If I have an object which, on the basis of previous experience with similar objects, I know to possess a structure that is the outcome of deliberate making, I am prepared to acknowledge that this, too, was made. It has a structure and use I can inspect and compare with other objects of a similar sort. If I see a craftsman at work, yet neither he nor I are clear about all the details of his techniques by which he accomplishes his results, I can at least see the craftsman at work; I see the resulting product to have such-and-such properties; and I can confirm the uses to which it can be put, by asking the craftsman to tell me about his intentions. Again, if a sexual act is performed that issues in a child, I may not understand all the intervening stages, nor need they be under any direct control by the one who initiates the action. Once more, however, the agents or progenitors, the process of parturition and birth, and the child, have characteristics that can be directly observed and that stamp them as the kinds of thing of which many other examples exist. Or, finally, I may see a craftsman at work, see him manipulate his materials in a certain way—yet I may never know, when I see the finished product, what it is for. In each case, while we are lacking in some item, or items, of information, at least enough facts of similarity with known cases are present, and are readily identifiable in experience, to justify the application of the model and terminology connected with "something made."

However, in the case of the existence of the world, it must be insisted that *none* of the features of the standard case of making something are present. *All* the features are conceived by analogy; none are present in any ordinary, literal, and non-controversial way. Let us first recall Hume's words:

> And will any man tell me with a serious countenance, that an orderly universe must arise from some thought and art, like the human; because we have experience of it? To ascertain this reasoning, it were requisite, that we had experience of the origin of worlds; and it is not sufficient surely, that we have seen ships and cities arise from human art and contrivance . . . Can you pretend to show any such similarity between the fabric of a house and the generation of a universe? Have you ever seen nature in any such

situation as resembles the first arrangement of the elements? Have worlds ever been formed under your eye? and have you had leisure to observe the whole progress of the phenomenon, from the first appearance of order to its final consummation? If you have, then cite your experience, and deliver your theory.[1]

The force of Hume's criticism can best be appreciated if we stress what, in the above passage, Hume himself would also seem to stress, namely, the requirement that we be able to point to something in our *experience* of the world, that warrants our saying its coming-into-existence can be compared, fruitfully, with the way in which we say such objects as a house come into existence—by art and contrivance. (It is not a matter of fundamental importance, I should say, though for Hume it is, that we have *repeated* experience of *worlds* coming into existence. For Hume, to assign a cause to something means to be able to fall back on repeated experience. However, as our earlier discussion of "cause" has brought out, the notion of "causal making of an object by some agent" need not be grounded in the performance of similar acts in our experience, over and over again.) What is essential, is that we have some basis in our experience for saying that such-and-such a feature of the act of making something was observed, even if it was observed only once.

With this empirical requirement as our guide, it is obvious that none of the features commonly found in the experience of objects as having been made, are found in the existence of the world. To begin with, there never has been any experience of the maker or creator of the world. Plato insists that the Father and Maker of all things is "hard to find." And traditional theism has always insisted on God's transcendence—the fact that God cannot be an object of ordinary experience. Also, of course, those mythical cosmogonies that assign the coming-into-existence of the world to the mating of a primeval pair, or to some other generative act, do not assert this to have been an event actually witnessed in human experience. It is, at best, only imagined. Moreover, not only is there no experience of God as the maker or progenitor of the world, there is no experience of his process of creation, either. In traditional theism, creation is said to be

[1] D. Hume, *Dialogues Concerning Natural Religion*, Part 2.

wholly unlike any act of human making, since it is something no
finite creature can understand, let alone witness.[2] Nor are we
in any better position when we look for unequivocal evidence
that the world displays some marks of its having been designed
—that its features were intended by its maker for use or enjoyment. Though we are given the world as existing, we are not
given the world as designed. To insist on the latter as a deliverance
of experience is to beg the question. There is no satisfactory
evidence that the world was designed. It does not follow that,
insofar as order and beauty are discovered in the world, these
were intended; the fact that there is some order in the world does
not guarantee that this is a beneficent or designed order.

At no point, therefore, in our analysis of the kinds of things
that warrant us in saying, normally, that we are confronted by
something deliberately made, do we find these features to be
unmistakably present in the existence of the world. It follows
that to say the existence of the world can be given a type of
reason which is appropriate for things designedly brought into
existence by a conscious maker, has no plausible ground in its
favor. (Although the preceding analysis has focussed on that
phase of the third group of meanings of "reason" in which we
apply it to made objects, the same type of analysis could be
carried out, and with the same results, for the other direction
of application of "reason," viz., in connection with purposeful
actions. And though there are, perhaps, fewer instances in man-
kind's mythologies of attempting to understand the existence of
the world under the model of purposeful action (rather than purposeful making), the upshot of our criticism would be substantially the same, and basically for the same reasons.)

The Irrelevancy of Reason to the Existence of the World

We have seen, in the preceding analysis, if we take "reason"
to mean the sort of thing man is accustomed to give reasons for,
then, in none of these meanings of "reason" does it make sense
to say there is, or might be, a reason for the existence of the
world. We should need to stretch the meaning of "reason" so

[2] Cf. St. Augustine, *Confessions*, Book 11, secs. 4, 5; F. R. Tennant, *Philosophical Theology* (Cambridge, 1930), Vol. II, p. 125.

far from its normal or standard uses, in order to incorporate this extension of its meaning in the phrase "reason for the existence of the world," that we should thereby have reached, or passed beyond, the limits of useful and fruitful application of the term. The world is not a belief, or a statement; it is not an event, or a regularity; it is not a deliberately made object, or a purposeful action. We speak of "giving reasons," in the sense of giving "evidence for beliefs or statements," "explanations for events or regularities," "purposes for things done or made." However, the existence of the world is not sufficiently similar to any of the standard cases to which these terms are applied, to warrant our saying we can find, or give, a reason for the existence of the world.

One way, then, of summing up this phase of our discussion is this: the expression "the mystery of existence" describes an unsuccessful search for a reason for the existence of the world. The mystery of existence means, in part, "There is no reason for the existence of the world, *because* it makes no sense to look for it."

It may be asked, however: "Why add 'in part'?" Should we not, rather, take this as exhaustively characterizing what is meant by "the mystery of existence"? And if we do so, should we then not realize that the phrase "the mystery of existence" actually cloaks a confusion of thought? Since there is no appropriate sense in which one can even speak of giving a reason for the existence of the world, there is no point in the quest for such a reason, or in the puzzlement at the lack of finding a reason for the existence of the world. We should, according to this way of thinking, actually dissolve our original problem altogether. We should be obliged to say that the use of the phrase "the mystery of existence" no longer identifies a genuine human experience of the world; it expresses a misguided and confused way of thinking about it. In saying "There is no reason for the existence of the world," we should be saying *all* that can properly be said from a critical, philosophical point of view.

Nor need this result be taken as saying: "The world is irrational." For this, too, would be just as incorrect and fruitless a way of describing the world, as to say there is some reason for it. The existence of the world is neither rational nor irrational.

These adjectives are appropriately applied to man's judgments, actions, and explanations. Neither of them has any relevance to the existence of the world. To say, therefore, "There is no reason for the existence of the world," is not to say it is irrational, in the sense that it displays little or no evidence of rational planning, decision, action, or believing—whereas, we think, it might have shown more, or more clearly, such evidence. This use of "irrational" is appropriate enough in connection with a man who can think or act rationally, and whose performance, in some particular case, we appraise as being irrational, because it failed to live up to his capacities, or what we should expect of him. In the case of the world, however, since we do not find any signs of rational powers used, or misused, in connection with its existence, it makes no sense (in this normal use of "irrational") to say the world is irrational.

If we adopted the foregoing line of thought, as altogether convincing, we should terminate our discussion at this point. It would serve as the answer to the question posed at the very outset of our inquiry. We asked, then, it will be recalled, whether the common use of the phrase "the mystery of existence" marks a confused and misguided way of thinking—a cramp in our philosophic outlook on the world—or whether, on the contrary, when clarified and reconstructed, it stands for something that is of positive conceptual value, and should be incorporated in any sound philosophy. If we were to stop at this point with the type of judgment summarized above, we should opt for the first of these alternatives. However, to do so would be unsatisfactory.

IS THERE A REASON-FOR-THE-EXISTENCE-OF-THE-WORLD?

There is more to be said about the use of the phrase "the mystery of existence." While part of its meaning is summed up in the negative conclusion we have reached ("There is no reason for the existence of the world"), this does not suffice for a complete analysis; it does not give us any clue as to what, in addition, the phrase can be taken to connote. This other part—that rescues the phrase "the mystery of existence" from disappearing as a useful conceptual shorthand for a genuine philosophic idea—is what we must now try to explicate. One way of doing this, is to say that the analysis of "the mystery of existence" involves, in addition to the negative result thus far reached, the further statement that we do not know whether there is a reason-for-the-existence-of-the-world. The hyphenated expression is intended to designate something quite different from the expression "reason for the existence of the world." Insofar as it can be differentiated from the previously discriminated senses of "reason," and yet not rejected as being altogether vacuous, it deserves a special place on the logical map of useful philosophic locutions. However, what is just as essential as the need for introducing this idea, is the complementary realization that there is no rational method, known to man, by which it could be established that there is (or is not), in fact, anything to which this idea can be applied, as a referent for it. It is for this reason that the inclusion of the element of agnosticism—with respect to this possible reason-for-the-existence-of-the-world—has to be insisted on, in any analysis of the constructive, positive side of the idea of "the mystery of existence." The complete idea of the mystery of existence—if our analysis proves to have any merit—can then be summed up by the following two statements: (1) There is no reason for the existence of the world; (2) We have no way of knowing, by any rational method, whether there is, or is not, a reason-for-the-existence-of-the-world.

What, then, is to be understood by the expression "reason-for-the-existence-of-the-world"? In the very nature of the case, since we cannot lay claim to know either that there is such a reason, or, if there were, what its specific characteristics would be, all that can be done, by way of giving this expression enough in the way of a "definition," so that we can use it intelligibly, is to give it such meaning by means of a contextual analysis.

In the first place, by contradistinction to the meanings of "reason" examined earlier, a reason-for-the-existence-of-the-world would be related uniquely to the existence of the world. If there were a reason-for-the-existence-of-the-world, it would be so distinctive, that it could not be assimilated to any other types of reason known to us. It would be a cosmological reason exclusively. It would not have to do, in any way, with actions, constructions, beliefs, statements, events, or regularities. It would have to do exclusively with the existence of the world and with nothing else. It would not be a typical reason, or a reason that would apply to a class of objects, as is the case with other senses of "reason." There would be no recurrent or mutliple instances of some type of entity to which it could apply.

A second thing we might say about a possible reason-for-the-existence-of-the-world, is that it would serve to explain the existence of the world. Here we may take advantage of a broad use of the term "explain." For while, earlier, we used the term "explanation" in connection, specifically, with the kinds of reasons that science gives, to make intelligible the occurrence of individual events or regularities, the term "explanation" can also be understood more broadly, so as to describe what is accomplished by supplying reasons in *any* of the senses we previously discussed. Thus, we may ask someone who accepts a certain statement as true, or who holds a particular belief, to explain why he does so, i.e., to give his evidence and his arguments. Again, confronted with some deliberate action or made object, we may ask to have the features of the action or the object explained to us, that is, why such and such features were chosen to be realized or embodied. And, of course, as we have seen, in the case of the scientist's interest in giving reasons in the sense of explanations for observed phenomena, the term "explanation" already has a well-defined and special set of meanings in this context. Wherever, then, we have a reason of any kind, it can be said to explain, in some distinctive way. We have already examined three broad types or species of explanation, each of which confers a mode of intelligibility upon its subject matter, and yet where each has specific differences from the others. Now, if there were a reason-for-the-existence-of-the-world, it, too, if known, would explain the existence of the world. It would not explain in the way beliefs or statements are explained, in the way actions or made objects are explained, or in the way events and regularities are explained. It would explain in the way that would be uniquely tied to the fact of the existence of the world. It would explain *that* existence, and nothing else. Since we do not know whether there is such a reason-for-the-existence-of-the-world, we cannot say, in advance, in what the specific and unique mode of explanation would consist. We cannot, therefore, reduce the explanation it would provide, to one or another of the types of explanation previously considered. All we can say is that, if there were such a reason-for-the-existence-of-the-world, and it were known, it, too, would explain in its own distinctive way, its distinctive object—the existence of the world.

With the foregoing "definition" of what is to be understood by the expression "reason-for-the-existence-of-the-world," we may now return to the formulation of the question which, it is being suggested, expresses the positive side of the mystery of existence. This question can be put in the form "*Is there* a reason-for-the-existence-of-the-world?" This question amounts to asking whether there is anything to which the above characterization of what it is to be a "reason-for-the-existence-of-the-world," applies. The thesis I wish to defend is summed up by saying that this question is unanswerable, because there is no known rational method by which this question can be answered. We have no way, that is, of establishing the truth either of the answer "There is a reason-for-the-existence-of-the-world," or of the answer "There is no reason-for-the-existence-of-the-world." In this sense, the question "Is there a reason-for-the-existence-of-the-world?" is unanswerable, and so an essential part of what we mean by the mystery of existence.

The expression "reason-for-the-existence-of-the-world" is best viewed as a gap-schema. It is a "place" in the "logical space" of explanations or reasons. If there were something that occupied that place, and, if it were known by some mind, it would serve as the answer to the question "Why does the world exist?" (understood as, "Is there a reason-for-the-world's-existence?"). But we don't know that there is anything to fill that gap, and, *a fortiori*, what it is. For, if we knew both of these items, there would be, of course, no need to ask the question "Is there a reason-for-the-existence-of-the-world?" All that we are entitled to do, therefore, is to leave room for such a reason, if it exists. The mystery, then is precisely that we have no knowledge of whether it is occupied, or what it is occupied by, if it is. Moreover, we have no known way by which we can find out whether it is occupied. This is the "agnosticism" feature of mystery.

Let us consider, however, before going on, the following possible objection to this entire way of putting the matter. It may be said that there is an inconsistency in the very concept of a reason which may exist and yet which could not be known. Is not a reason of any kind something that would have to be known, to exist at all? However, if we say that the question "Is there a reason-for-the-existence-of-the-world?" is unanswerable, this allows that there may be, as one of the possibilities, a reason-for-the-existence-of-the-world that is not known, though it exists. How can this be, on the above analysis of what it is to be a reason? Are reasons not something men give, and if *they* cannot give a reason, does this not mean there is no reason? Therefore, would not the proper way of putting the matter consist in saying "There is no reason-for-the-existence-of-the-world," rather than, "We have no way of knowing whether or not there is a reason-for-the-existence-of-the-world"?

In order to reply to the foregoing objection, we need to recall certain distinctions relevant to the use of the term "reason." We sometimes speak of finding or obtaining reasons, and sometimes of giving or assigning or constructing reasons. Suppose we are considering a clear case of a human action we know to have been motivated or undertaken for a reason, though we do not know, at some point in our inquiry, what the reasons were that the agent had in undertaking the action. Again, to vary the situation slightly, suppose we are confronted by an object we know to have been made for a certain purpose, though we do not know, at a certain stage in our inquiry, what the purpose was. In these cases, we, as inquirers, having the assurance that these actions or constructed objects were accomplished for a reason by some human agent, set about trying to find or obtain knowledge of these reasons. We say there were these reasons on the part of other conscious human agents. Though we may not find out what these reasons were, this does not affect the independent existence of these reasons as they existed, or continue to exist, in the minds of those other human agents or makers. The fact that we do not know these reasons, or cannot express in statements what they were, does not make it meaningless to say that such reasons nevertheless exist (or existed) in the minds of these other individuals. We say, with confidence, there was a reason, although it is not known. Should we succeed, at some point in our inquiry, in *finding* an answer to our question, this would consist in our discovering what, in fact, were the reasons had by the agents or makers in doing what they did. *We* should then state in language, and say we know, the reasons *they* had, or would have given, if asked, for what they did. And we say our knowledge of what these reasons are, is correct, when our statement of these reasons coincides with the reasons the agent or maker himself would have given. Here, then, is a case where it makes perfectly good sense to say that a reason for something exists, or is believed to exist, without our knowing what it is, at a certain point in our inquiry. We can say that the existence of such a reason is independent of our knowledge or formulation of it; successful rational inquiry results in our being able to say we have found out what the reasons were. We have obtained answers to the question "What was the reason so-and-so had for doing (or making) what he did?"

Now let us consider a quite different situation, though, again, one in which our interest is to determine the reasons for something. Take the case, considered earlier, of the scientist who offers a theory by which to explain certain empirical regularities (laws). The theory provides reasons, in the sense of an explanation, for the laws. But here, obviously, the scientist—for example, a Newton or an Einstein—does not find, or obtain, the reasons had by some other mind or conscious agent. He himself constructs, or gives, the reason, in the form of a theory. The success of his theory is not judged—as it is in the case of reasons we considered, a moment ago, in connection with human agents acting for a reason—by seeing whether the reasons the investigator gives, coincides with the reasons had by the agent. Rather, the reasons given by the investigator do not have to match anything antecedent to, or independent of the inquiry. They have to meet certain criteria of success imposed by the scientific community for theories, e.g., comprehensiveness or range of data incorporated, pragmatic utility or predictive power, logical simplicity of conceptual means, logical consistency, conceptual clarity, and so on.

Competing theories are judged in terms of their relative adequacy with respect to *one another*. In this type of situation, it makes sense to say the investigator *gives* a reason; he does not find it, or obtain it, by looking to see to what extent his proposals agree with what is already there. In connection with this type of reason, it would not be acceptable to say that this reason exists independently of the inquirer, and could continue to have an objective status, even though it were not known. This type of reason can only exist *as* known, or *when* known. A theory not invented, constructed, tested, and accepted in place of its rivals, is not known, and, therefore, does not exist at all. Scientists construct theories, and thereby give reasons for empirical facts.

Now consider, finally, as a third case, one which may be said to lie somewhere between the two foregoing examples. Suppose I have turned on the water in my garden hose, but find that, upon opening the nozzle, it does not flow. I want to know the reason. And in examining the length of hose stretched over the ground, I discover, at one point, that the hose was twisted and formed a sharp bend. I untwist the hose and find, now, that the water flows freely. I say the reason why the water did not flow at first, was that there was an obstruction, and now that I have removed it, it flows freely. Have I "discovered" a reason or "given" it? I haven't discovered it, surely, in the sense in which I find a reason by asking somebody who is doing something, why he is doing it. My son, as a prank, might have deliberately bent the hose, and in this case I do discover his reason for stopping the water from flowing. But suppose my prankish son were not involved at all in this case. In unfurling the hose, it became twisted through no intention of mine. In finding the trouble spot, I say I know the reason. But what I know, is something in the arrangement of the hose—there, for all to see. In this sense, the "reason" is independent and objective, a matter of the arrangement of the hose. It is, in *some* ways, just as objective as the reason that someone has for doing or making something, and that, as a reason, may exist even though I do not know it. The hose-situation, however, is not quite like the case of my discovering a reason that exists as an intention in the mind of some other human being. The hose does not have a reason (intention) for being twisted (as an acrobat might have in twisting his own body), nor did I deliberately twist the hose. Is it, then, like the case of the scientist constructing a theory as a reason for some observed regularity? Again, in some respects it is, at least to the extent that I, as an investigator, have to *give* the reason: I have to formulate it in words before it exists as a reason; it cannot be known and does not exist until it is put into language and confirmed. However, in other respects it is clearly unlike the matter of constructing a scientific theory. In the latter case, we recognize (as the crucial factor) the opportunity for a creative act of imagination in the suggested use of analogies or models of some degree of illuminative power. To realize the twist in the hose as being the cause of the failure of water flow, is not a matter of creative imagination, or the use of an analogy for conceptual purposes. It is a matter of looking and seeing; this is where the trouble was, and nothing else. I discover, or find, it to be the reason, in a way that does not apply to the "finding" of a theory. I find the kink in the hose as an objective, observable fact; however, I do not find, in the same way, for example, that what accounts for the gravitational acceleration of bodies is the variable curvature of space. In connection with this third type of "reason," the reason can be said to exist, in some respects, even though we might not have succeeded in finding it: the kink in the hose is there, and holds back the water; in other respects, however, it does not exist as a reason, until we formulate the matter in language, and give it or assign it.

Let us return, now, to our original question. When we speak of a possible reason-for-the-existence-of-the-world, does it make sense to say that it might exist, even though it were not known? Clearly, *if* such a reason were altogether like the kind of reason that makes up theory-construction in science, it would not exist unless it were given or constructed by men. And in this sense, to say that men might never know that there is a reason-for-the-existence-of-the-world, would be inconsistent and, therefore, vacuous. A reason that could not be given, if the only way it could exist is *as* given, is a contradiction in terms. Suppose, however, we allow that, in some respects, the reason-for-the-existence-of-the-world might be like a reason had by some conscious mind for acting or doing something, though it is unknown to us. In this case, it would make sense to say that such a reason-for-the-existence-of-the-world need not be known by us, in order for us to say, nevertheless, that it might exist. Or again, if such a reason-for-the-existence-of-the-world were, in some respects, like the kind of reason previously illustrated by the twisted-hose situation (which, in some respects, may be said to exist independently of us, even though we do not know it), once more, it might make sense (to this extent) to say there is a reason-for-the-existence-of-the-world, without our knowing it.

It is one of the principal theses of my argument that we do not have any knowledge of the specific character of the reason-for-existence-of-the-world, if any exists at all. Therefore, we cannot rule out, in advance, the possibility that *if* it existed, it might exist without our discovering it or knowing it. The objection, therefore, that in order to be a reason of any kind, it must be known, does not hold. It need not hamper us in our account of what we can construe as the mystery of existence, namely, as a lack of knowledge as to whether there is a reason-for-the-existence-of-the-world, and if there is, what it is.

CHAPTER XII

Philosophical Agnosticism

OUR NEXT TASK is to see what can be said by way of support for the contention that there is no rational method by which an answer can be found to the question whether there is, or is not, a reason-for-the-existence-of-the-world. If there were a rational method by which to establish whether or not there is a reason-for-the-existence-of-the-world, we should want to know, of course, in what this method consists. As a preliminary inquiry, therefore, we shall have to canvass the various theoretically available possibilities, from among known types of intellectual experience, to see whether, among them, there is any one having greater promise of success than the others. This, accordingly, is the procedure I shall follow.

In any such broad survey of the types of human experience in which intellectual activity of one sort or another is carried on, and in which one might conceivably find a suitable method for dealing with the question we have set ourselves, it would be necessary to include (a) common sense, (b) science, (c) religious experience, and (d) philosophy. However, as we shall see, none of these domains of experience is capable of providing the rational method we are looking for; even philosophy, which might be thought to possess the greatest promise in this regard, fails us in yielding a rational method for answering our basic question. We shall, therefore, be obliged to defend, ultimately, the viewpoint of agnosticism.

Common Sense

The term "common sense" does not have a single meaning, and it will be sufficient for our purposes to single out the following principal uses of this term. (1) We sometimes use the term "common sense" to designate those beliefs whose warrant is found in a more or less universally shared sense-experience of such an uncontested character, that to challenge their truth brings down the charge that one is "flying in the face of common sense." That fire burns, that there is a regular alternation of night and day, that eating food will normally allay hunger pangs, and so on—these and countless other statements are accepted on the basis of funded sense-experiences normally available to all human beings. (2) A broader use of the term "common sense" refers to beliefs shared by some group (whether the latter be as relatively restricted as some local, isolated community, or as wide as the human race itself, throughout its history and spread over the face of the globe), whose warrant is not restricted to what can be found in more or less direct sense-experience of an elementary and relatively unsophisticated kind. In this second sense of the term, what belongs to common sense will be all sorts of beliefs derived from various sources. Thus, what belongs to common sense frequently marks the assimilation of what in fact were the fruits of some highly sophisticated, specialized system of beliefs of a religious, philosophical, or scientific kind. The contributions of Aristotelian philosophy, Newtonian mechanics, or the Biblical conception of human destiny, to the persistent "common sense" ways of thinking of men during various epochs of Western culture, are familiar examples. The well-known upheavals and bitter controversies that followed upon the attempts to challenge these enshrined orthodoxies of "common sense," on alternative philosophical, religious, or scientific grounds, are too well known to need any more than the briefest reminder.

Can common sense, in either of these meanings, serve as a likely source for finding a rational method by which to ascertain whether there is a reason-for-the-existence-of-the-world? That the answer must be in the negative, would appear from the following elementary considerations. It will be clear that any hope of establishing that there is a reason-for-the-existence-of-the-world by turning to common sense, when taken as a fund of beliefs founded on universal and uncontested sense-experience, is utterly futile. Surely, if there is a reason-for-the-existence-of-the-world, it is not to be expected that we shall find it by the use of any one, or a combination, of our sense-organs. At best, what sense-experience establishes are the qualities and relations of some given object, event, or process as found *in* the world. However, the reason-for-the-existence-of-the-world, if it existed, would not be something we should find in the world by our sense organs. For, whatever we should find by this means would be part of the world. And along with everything else in the world, it would provoke the very question we are trying to answer. It could not, itself, therefore, serve as a reason-for-the-existence-of-the-world.

Let us turn, next, to the second meaning of "common sense"— the shifting set of accepted beliefs that are the funded amalgam of ancestral experience of all sorts, including the various deposits of religious, philosophic, and scientific thought. Rather than consider these beliefs in their common-sense versions, however, we do well to turn to the primary sources from which these were derived. We should need to examine the power that science, religious experience, and philosophy have in their most developed forms, to yield the answer to our question, rather than in terms of their results when assimilated, as they normally are, in a simplified, uncritical, and unsophisticated way on the level of common sense. This, accordingly, is what we shall now do.

Science

First, a brief word as the use of scientific method as a candidate for our present problem. It is clear that it promises no help whatever. Science concerns itself with the understanding of the phenomena empirically observable in the world. In no way, does it concern itself with the fact of the existence of the world itself. The criteria for judging hypotheses used in explaining natural events, are wholly fashioned in order to help evaluate the soundness of such hypotheses. The criteria for judging the relative adequacy of candidates to serve as law-statements, theory-statements, observation-statements, and the probative force of the

types of arguments into which these enter (all of which constitutes "scientific method"), have no relevance to the kind of
problem posed by the mystery of existence. What might serve
as a statement of a possible reason-for-the-existence-of-the-world
cannot be classed as an observation-statement, a law-statement,
or a theory-statement. No possible argument, therefore, in which
a statement relating to the reason-for-the-existence-of-the-world
appears, can be one to which the criteria (or method) or science
are in any way relevant.

Religious Experience

I turn next to the sphere of religious experience. This phrase
will be used to designate whatever in the entire complex phenomenon of religion, has to do with a non-inferential mode of awareness of some Supreme Being. Such experience is regarded as having
transcendently important cognitive worth by those undergoing
the experience. It is an experience, moreover, commonly recognized to be wholly different in character and subject matter from
other modes of experience—for example, the esthetic, sensory, or
scientific. Though the term "religious experience" itself covers
a fairly wide range of cases, I shall consider, as a primary example,
what Rudolf Otto calls "the sense of the numinous" (or what
others refer to as "mystical experience"). Thus, all that is comprised, traditionally, under the heading "natural (or rational)
theology" can be regarded as a form of theistic *metaphysics;*
it would *not* be included under the present designation of "religious experience." The validity of religious experience is taken
to be quite independent of any appeal to rational *argument.*

What value does mystical experience (or the sense of the
numinous) have, as a method for establishing that there is a
reason-for-the-existence-of-the-world? Although mystical experience is non-inferential and immediate, this does not, by itself,
justify our condemning it as non-rational. Not all rational methods
for establishing the truth of some belief or the existence of some
entity need be inferential. Suppose, for example, I have just
received a package, and before opening it, try to establish its
contents. I might *infer* from its size, the label on the outside, and
the fact that I remember having ordered an art book, that this

is, indeed, what the package contains. These would be relevant
evidence in an argument I might offer to support my prediction.
Once I open the package, however, and look at the book, I no
longer have any need to fall back on an argument. I *see* that it
is the very art book I ordered. To establish by one type of rational
method appropriate to these circumstances, that the book is an
art book, all that I have to do is to look. It might very well be,
therefore, to employ a similar argument, that the rational method
for establishing that there is a reason-for-the-existence-of-the-
world, if such existed, consists in "seeing" it, in some act of direct
mystical vision.

The term "sense of the numinous" has received wide currency
ever since the appearance of Rudolf Otto's important study, *The
Idea of the Holy*.[1] The term covers a complex of factors, at the
core of which is to be found an attitude of worship and a feeling
of awe toward the Wholly Other, the divine source and creator
of the world. The sense of the numinous is (in Otto's phrase) a
sense of the *mysterium tremendum et fascinans*. Otto stresses the
fact that the Divine Power (whether called "God," "Allah,"
"Brahman," "Jehovah," etc.) transcends all natural and human
phenomena; God cannot be described satisfactorily by means of
rational concepts. Only in the adoption of a worshipful *attitude*
toward the Holy Being, and in the cultivation of the *feelings* of
utter separation from it, do we have the means for being genuinely
aware of God. The numinous experience is "the emotion of a
creature, abased and overwhelmed by its own nothingness in contrast with that which is supreme above all creatures." To one who
has experienced the sense of the numinous in some more or less
adequate degree, God's holiness is, first of all, a *mysterium*—a
profound mystery that baffles and defeats all attempts at rational,
conceptual understanding. God, being Wholly Other, is at an
infinite remove from the status and comprehension of finite
creatures. God is a being "before which we recoil in a wonder
that strikes us chill and numb." The *tremendum* aspect of the
numinous object is what we feel with "an inward shudder of
the soul" as we respond to the aweful, utterly overwhelming

[1] R. Otto, *The Idea of the Holy*, translated by J. H. Harvey (2nd ed.,
Oxford, 1950).

might and majesty of divine power, Finally, the awareness, or experienced feeling, of God as *fascinans,* is the correlate and opposite of "the fear of the Lord." God as *fascinans* arouses the sense of adoration and praise for his infinite worth and value; we experience a sense of the infinite glory, goodness, and perfection of the divine.

The existence of religious experiences of the type described by Otto, is a well-attested phenomenon of human history. That men have undergone and shared in the various feelings of awe, dread, and fascination, that they have responded with an attitude of prayerful worship to a Being they regard as the creator of the world—all this need not be doubted in the slightest degree. The important, central question is what *cognitive* value these experiences have, what epistemological worth they possess. Are they nothing more than feelings and attitudes belonging to individuals undergoing the experiences in question, or are they, on the contrary, revelations of some independently existing, objective reality?

For Otto, and for all those for whom religious experience is taken to have genuine, unique cognitive worth, the second alternative, of course, is chosen. Otto spoke, for example, of what he called a "faculty of divination" as that which men possess by which they are made aware of the existence and character of the transcendent, numinous object. The difficulty with this view, however, is the familiar one: to speak of a "faculty of divination" is already to beg the question. It takes for granted that the experiences in question are in fact possessed of cognitive worth. To say that these experiences are genuinely revelatory of an independently existing, transcendent Being, and are not merely expressions of deeply felt human yearnings, or the projections of human imagination and its myth-making propensities, is precisely what needs to be established. One cannot appeal to the experiences themselves to establish this; they are not self-authenticating. For, even the sceptic is perfectly willing to acknowledge the existence of the experiences. "What reason is there, however," he would ask, "to accept the mystic's claim about the objective existence of the God he worships, and whose holiness he feels? What supporting, public tests, or independent criteria of corroboration are there, by which to separate the spurious claims of the visionary from the possibly authentic?"

The moment, however, we recognize the need for corroborative sources of judgment to support the mystic's claims, we have passed beyond the domain of feeling and private experience altogether; and one way of doing so is to appeal to philosophical *arguments*. The *interpretation* of immediate religious experience can thus be made to feed on a scheme of metaphysics or theology (as, in fact, it usually has). However, the truth of the doctrines thus appealed to, and the arguments on which these doctrines rest, would need to be independently warranted; they could not—on pain of circularity—be made to depend exclusively on the existence of "religious experience."

If there were, therefore, a reason-for-the-existence-of-the-world, its existence could not be established simply by an appeal to the kind of experience the mystic undergoes. The sense of the numinous could not, by itself, constitute a rational method adequate to establish that there is a reason-for-the-existence-of-the-world. If there were a rational method adequate to this purpose, it would have to be something more than an expression of *feeling*, however deep or sincere the latter might be.

Philosophy

We come, finally, to the domain of philosophy proper, to see whether here, if not elsewhere, we might find an adequate means for establishing whether or not there is a reason-for-the-existence-of-the-world. The first fact that needs remarking is that "philosophy" does not stand for a single enterprise, uniformly conceived. There is a wide range or cluster of intellectual activities that share the name "philosophy." Indeed, some adherents of one or another strand of this complex will be found, who strongly deny the privilege of using the name to those with an altogether different conception of philosophy from their own. It is not within the scope of my present interest to engage in any evaluative analysis of these various claims. I shall, instead, identify two major members of the family of intellectual activities that share the name "philosophy," and simply ask with respect to each of these, how competent it is to yield a rational method for determining whether or not there is a reason-for-the-existence-of-the-world. The two types of philosophic activity I shall consider may be grouped under the headings (1) "conceptual analysis" and (2) "construction of a metaphysical world-view."

(1) *Conceptual Analysis.*—The term "conceptual analysis" is a convenient handle by which to designate a whole group of examples of an approach to philosophy that takes the primary task of philosophy to be the higher-order analysis of language as used in various domains, or types, of discourse. Prominent examples, in recent philosophy, of what would fall under this broad rubric, would include: the analysis given by logical positivists of the logic of scientific statements; G. E. Moore's analysis of moral concepts, and of the statements made in everyday discourse about the perception of material objects; the analyses offered by Wittgenstein, Ryle, Austin, Wisdom, and their numerous followers, of terms such as "know," "believe," "intend," "understand," "remember," "recognize," etc., as used in everyday language. Excellent examples of conceptual analysis, in this broad sense, can also be found scattered thoughout the writings of virtually all the great philosophers of the past—for example, in Aristotle, Hume, Locke, or Kant—though frequently embedded in discussions that are not primarily, or exclusively, devoted to conceptual analysis as such, and that, consequently, betray other dominant conceptions of philosophy.

There are, of course, important differences in techniques and results for these different practitioners of what I have lumped together under the umbrella term "conceptual analysis." Thus, the method of analysis practiced by Moore needs to be differentiated from the mode of logical analysis, developed in association with the doctrines of logical atomism, of the "early" Wittgenstein and Russell, and these, in turn, need to be marked off, in certain crucial respects, from the quite different methods used by the "later" Wittgenstein, or by Austin. Again, there are important respects in which the entire movement of logical positivism was the target of much criticism by adherents of "ordinary-language philosophy" ("linguistic analysis"). Nor do I wish to give the false impression that logical positivists confined themselves exclusively to the analysis of scientific language, or that Wittgenstein, Ryle, or Austin are exclusively concerned with the analysis of psychological or epistemic concepts. There is much overlapping, in a variety of ways, among these different "schools," as well as significant divergences among them—all of which would have to be brought out in any more refined discussion of this complex movement of thought.[2]

While all who think of philosophy as "conceptual analysis" would, in some way, be concerned with getting at the meaning of concepts, they would go about this in different ways. For some, analysis is conceived as a process of paraphrase, translation, or replacement of a given sentence in which some key term, word, phrase, or concept occurs, by means of a sentence in which the original concept no longer appears. The new statement, containing the analysis of the concept, is couched in language preferred (for some particular reason) to the original, or is set out in precise and reconstructed logical form. Many who adopted this approach emphasized that analysis meant reduction of a complex or unclear concept to irreducible, perspicuous simples. Within this group, in turn, some took these simples to be "atoms" of sensation, while others took them to be atomic statements as defined in *Principia Mathematica*. An entire wing of the development of linguistic analysis (largely under the inspiration of the work of the later Wittgenstein) has, however, renounced altogether the attempt at achieving the goal of "analysis"—in this sense of "logical atomism." For these philosophers, the process of conceptual clarification means not reduction to simples, but disentangling the strands that make up the various families of discourse to which different concepts belong. What is called for, they would say, is not reduction, replacement, or paraphrase; rather, what is looked for is some way of bringing out—by countless examples—the similarities and differences between the concept under analysis and others, closely, or more distantly, related to it. The outcome would not be the replacement of the original statement in which the concept occurred, by some other. Everything would be "left the way it was." However, as a result of

<hr>

[2] Cf. J. O. Urmson, *Philosophical Analysis* (Oxford, 1956); A. J. Ayer and others, *The Revolution in Philosophy* (London, 1956).

having put the statement (or concept) in question next to all sorts
of neighbors, and seeing to what extent it had some things in common, others markedly, or subtly, different from them, one would
be the wiser—because the clearer—about the uses and meanings
(i.e., "the logic") of the concept or the statement.

I shall not attempt here to enter into any more detailed account
of the points of comparison and contrast among those who treat
or "do" philosophy as conceptual analysis, since I am primarily
concerned to single out, as of sole relevance to our present problem, one feature that runs as a common thread throughout all
these diverse strands.

In the minds of those who are committed to the view that
philosophy is conceptual analysis, it is necessary to differentiate
the interest philosophy takes in concepts and language, from the
kind of interest other studies have in *using* concepts, or even—as
in the case of philology and linguistics—in taking language as
their subject matter. One way of putting this, is to say that
philosophy is not concerned to make statements about the world
or some part of it; it is not involved at all in making factual assertions. Thus, each of the sciences carves out some domain or
subject matter which it investigates, and about which it makes
various factual statements. For example, physics, biology, psychology, or linguistics, use a variety of concepts to describe or
explain the phenomena of some particular domain of Nature.
They are concerned to make factual discoveries and provide insights with respect to the entities and processes they study. Not
only the sciences, of course, but much of ordinary language is
employed, similarly, in everyday situations, to make factual assertions about objects and events encountered in ordinary experience. Also, one important traditional conception of philosophy
took philosophy itself, in the form of ontology or metaphysics,
to be engaged in the task of making various factual claims about
the world. Those who take philosophy to be concerned exclusively with conceptual analysis would say, however, that
philosophy, as they restrict the use of this term, does not have
to do with the world, either in some comprehensive way (as in
traditional metaphysics), or in some piecemeal way, as in the various sciences, or in the factual references of ordinary language.

Philosophy is not properly concerned to make factual claims of any sort whatever.

Instead, philosophy takes, for example, the language in which the scientist couches his reports or explanations of empirical phenomena, and examines that language. Its study is a second-order one; it examines the logic of factual assertions. It does not engage, as a first-order activity would, in making factual assertions, in defending or criticizing, or searching for adequate ones by which to give an account of the world. Further, with respect to the first-order activity of metaphysics in undertaking to give us factual truths about the world—those who regard the business of philosophy as conceptual analysis take different attitudes. Logical positivists would dismiss metaphysics altogether as a bogus effort to establish meaningful and true statements about the world. Others are prepared to recognize some legitimate domain of inquiry for metaphysics, but would clearly distinguish, and keep separate, the first-order factual interest of metaphysics from the properly philosophical task of conceptual analysis. Philosophy as conceptual analysis would take the first-order assertions of the metaphysician as grist for its own mill.

It should be added that the practice of philosophy as conceptual analysis is not restricted to the analysis of concepts that occur in statements whose primary function is to make factual assertions about the world. Conceptual analysis is not only a study of the logic of fact-asserting statements; it is a study of the roles of language for various other purposes as well, and of the concepts that are introduced in connection with these other uses. Thus, it is just as much within the province of philosophy to study the logic of religious language, of moral discourse, of the use of concepts in the spheres of law, esthetic appraisal, political policy-making, or historical narrative. In each case, the task of the philosopher is to examine the way in which language is being characteristically used, in order to note its similarities and differences from other uses. To set out the "logical geography" of each type of discourse results in an enormously increased sensitivity to the nuances and elements of distinctiveness belonging to these different areas of discourse; it results, too, in the elimination of many confusions resulting from running together the logic of different types of discourse; finally, it results in the untying of a great number of intellectual knots and puzzles.

It is not the task of the philosopher, *qua* conceptual analyst, to engage in the use of language to utter moral appraisals, make legal decisions, express religious sentiments, declare political allegiances, formulate esthetic judgments, provide historical insights —any more than it is his job to make a contribution, as a scientist, to the store of factual knowledge, or as a mathematician, to perform calculations and demonstrative inferences. Each of these uses of language may be left to the specialist concerned, or, if it is not a matter of specialization at all, to whoever wishes to use language in a given way; and this would include the philosopher himself, though not in his role as philosopher. The task of the philosopher, in reflecting on these various modes of language-use, is to become clear about their distinctive roles, their manifold relations of similarity and difference within the broad range of human discourse and thought. When he has done his job well—and there is, admittedly, no uniquely correct or final way of setting out the matters in question—we are all the beneficiaries of this service. The study of logic, in this much-broadened sense, will not tell us what to say, but in making us conscious of what is involved in any mode of saying, we shall be the less apt to fall into confusion and error. The philosopher *qua* conceptual analyst is ideologically neutral; he does not favor one or another factual claim, moral appraisal, religious attitude, and so on. But when he, or others, in their non-philosophical moments or involvements, do "take sides," what the philosopher has done, by way of conceptual clarification and the sharpening of tools, will be of inestimable value in accomplishing our various moral, scientific, legal, political, religious, esthetic, or historical purposes.

Can philosophy, understood as conceptual analysis, in any way help to answer the question we are interested in, namely, "Is there a reason-for-the-existence-of-the-world?"? One reply that might be given, takes the form of saying, "Yes, conceptual analysis is relevant to the question you raise, but only in order to show that it represents a confusion in thought. A proper straightening out of the logical issues would show that there is no question left. The question represents a muddle that needs to be dissolved." I have tried to anticipate this type of objection, in my earlier discussion. I do not propose to repeat my grounds for being dissatisfied with this way of dealing with the question. I have tried to show in what sense one can say the question *cannot* be dissolved, and does not represent an obsessive entanglement in the snares of language, one to be dissipated by the therapeutic ministrations of the analyst. If there has been any merit to this rejoinder, the question remains. And if the question remains, we must now consider whether the method of conceptual analysis can itself provide an answer *to* the question.

It will be clear, however, that this prospect is incapable of being realized, either. For if the question "Is there a reason-for-the-existence-of-the-world?" is not a bogus question, conceptual analysis cannot answer it, by giving grounds for either an affirmative or a negative answer. And the reasons for this incompetence, follows from our previous discussion of the nature of conceptual analysis. The method of conceptual analysis cannot make ontological claims. It cannot, so to speak, go from the clarification of the uses of language to the application of that language; conceptual analysis does not, as such, consist in itself using or applying the language it analyzes. The question "Is there a reason-for-the-existence-of-the-world?" is, in one sense, an existential question. We are asking whether *there is* or *there is not* a reason-for-the-existence-of-the-world. If neither the concept "reason-for-the-existence-of-the-world," nor the question in which it makes its appearance, can be condemned as faulty or confused, then the method of conceptual analysis cannot, by itself, give an answer to this question. It cannot determine whether there is anything to which the concept "reason-for-the-existence-of-the-world" can be applied or withheld, in a correct affirmative (or negative) statement.

Just as we should have to resort to more than conceptual analysis, namely, visual experience, to determine whether or not there is something than can be described by the use of a particular color word, e.g., "blue," in a particular region at a particular time; or, just as we should have to resort to appropriate mathematical methods to determine whether there are, or are not, at least 748 prime numbers between 36,579,452,397 and 476,090,789,-

563; or, just as we should have to resort to appropriate evaluative methods to ascertain whether there are (or, are not) any saintly characters of the stature of Buddha in the world at the present time, so, in general, to know that anything does, or does not, exist, cannot be ascertained simply by having done a thorough job in clarifying how a certain term is to be understood—assuming that it can be shown the use of the term is neither self-contradictory or otherwise vacuous.

Another way of putting this point, is to say that the question "Is there a reason-for-the-existence-of-the-world?" is a first-order question, and can be answered, at best, by a first-order statement, either affirmatively or negatively. However, a second-order type of analysis—which is what conceptual analysis is—cannot provide a first-order type of answer. What we are looking for, in order to solve the mystery of existence by some rational method, is some way of obtaining a first-order answer (whether affirmative or negative) to the question "Is there a reason-for-the-existence-of-the-world?" *This*, however, conceptual analysis cannot, by itself, yield. It would be futile, therefore, to look to philosophy in the form of conceptual analysis, as constituting a rational method by which an affirmative (or negative) answer can be found to the question stating the mystery of existence.

It might be asked, however, how I should classify my own discussion in this book. Is it not, too, an exercise in conceptual analysis? And if it is, is not the thesis being defended here, that the question "Is there a reason-for-the-existence-of-the-world?" is unanswerable, a result of conceptual analysis? And is not *this* an answer, too, to the question? I should reply as follows. The discussion of this book is, in part, an exercise in conceptual analysis. It undertakes, among other things, to clarify the use of the phrase "reason-for-the-existence-of-the-world." However, the *statement* "The question 'Is there a reason-for-the-existence-of-the-world?' is unanswerable" is a result that rests upon certain *factual* considerations, viz., considerations about the methods actually used by men to know reasons. In saying "There is no rational method by which the question 'Is there a reason-for-the-existence-of-the-world?' is capable of being answered," I have stated what is, at bottom, a factual conclusion, arrived at by *applying* the fruits of conceptual analysis, i.e., by canvassing the actual facts of human cognitive equipment. The "answer" contained in the statement "The question 'Is there a reason-for-the-existence-of-the-world?' is unanswerable" is *not* an *answer* to the question "Is there a reason-for-the-existence-of-the-world?"; it is, rather a *reply* to anyone who would look for an answer to that question. It consists in the claim—based partly on factual considerations, and partly on conceptual considerations—that no answer to the question is available: the question is unanswerable.

(2) *Metaphysics.*—If philosophy in the form of conceptual analysis cannot establish that there is, or is not, a reason-for-the-existence-of-the-world, it would surely be plausible to expect that philosophy, in the sense of metaphysics, ought to be able to do so. Here, if anywhere, one would expect to find the intellectual interest and rational means by which a resolution to our question can be obtained. For, is it not the purpose of metaphysics to provide a comprehensive world-view? And would it not be a central theme of any comprehensive world-view to deal with this issue? Indeed, do we not find from the earliest development of world-views among the pre-Socratics down to the most recent examples of our own day, that the way in which this, or closely related, questions are answered, is, in fact, one of the means by which we differentiate the variety of metaphysical views defended by different philosophers? Whatever, then, may be the relative failures of common sense, science, religious experience, or conceptual analysis to give us guidance in dealing with our present theme, do we not turn with justifiable confidence to metaphysics to do what none of the others can do? We must now, finally, meet this last hurdle in our inquiry, to see what merit there is in this claim. Only if we can succeed in showing that this resource, too, must fail—as do all the others—in giving us any rational means for solving the mystery of existence, can we uphold the general thesis that the question expressing this mystery is truly unanswerable.

What follows, it needs to be remarked, will not itself be a discussion *in* metaphysics, so much as it will be a consideration of the cognitive status *of* metaphysics, and, in particular, of the power of metaphysics to give us knowledge of the existence or non-existence of a reason-for-the-existence-of-the-world.

In order to proceed with our investigation, it is necessary, first of all, to note that we need not be obliged to furnish some clear-cut definition of the term "metaphysics." The fact is, this term covers a wide variety of examples of philosophic construction and investigation. It will not do, for example, to take some formula such as Aristotle's well-known characterization of metaphysics—he called it "first philosophy"—namely, "a study of being *qua* being," as adequate to comprehend all examples of what can be included under this heading. Nor would Kant's account of metaphysics—as the attempt to establish synthetic a priori truths about what transcends experience (an attempt that Kant regards as incapable of realization)—be any more successful.

The possible objections to the first formula are twofold: In the first place, when taken out of the immediate context of Aristotle's own discussion, the formula is so vague and lacking in specific conceptual content, as to allow for the most diverse interpretations of its meaning. As a result, a survey of the altogether different conceptions of metaphysics that might be comprised under this formula, would be cloaked by only an apparent agreement as to its subject matter and goals. A second objection to Aristotle's formula, is of the opposite character: if its terms are understood to have the particular meanings Aristotle gave them, then, although it expresses what Aristotle understood by "first philosophy," it does not coincide with what others mean by "metaphysics." In short, the formula betrays a particular point of view *in* metaphysics and would, therefore, be as unsatisfactory for the purposes of providing a *neutral* account of metaphysics as, say, the Idealist account of metaphysics as "the study of Reality as contrasted with Appearance."

The difficulty with Kant's conception of metaphysics is that it, also, is too restrictive in its meaning. By confining himself to those types of metaphysical systems that undertake to provide infallible knowledge about some supersensible, or transcendent, reality, Kant substitutes what is, admittedly, an important and influential strand in the history of the subject, for the entire complex of inquiries and intellectual constructions that are equally entitled to be called by the same name.

A more fruitful procedure in determining what metaphysics is about, is to begin simply by identifying a number of clear and unmistakable examples, taken from the writings of philosophers who, in one way or another, are commonly recognized to have constructed metaphysical world-views. Given such a list, it would then be possible to distinguish among them certain lines of comparison and contrast, not only with respect to the actual content of their respective metaphysical views, but with respect, as well, to the way in which the metaphysical enterprise is conceived. In any such minimal list, one would have to include the relevant writings of the following major philosophers: Plato, Aristotle, Thomas Aquinas, Descartes, Spinoza, Leibniz, Hegel, and Whitehead. The list, of course, could be made much longer. However, whether relatively short or much extended, it is possible to discern in the thinkers included, a type of philosophic concern that warrants us in putting them in the same broad category, and in using their writings as the very criterion of what we mean by "metaphysics."

It is not within the province of the present discussion to attempt any full-scale analysis of the particular metaphysical systems or world-views associated with any of the thinkers mentioned, nor, to make point-for-point comparisons and contrasts concerning their individual points of view. Nevertheless, one broad line of division may be noticed that serves to differentiate one group of views from another. It is the distinction sometimes expressed as that between "transcendent" and "immanent" metaphysical schemes.[3] On the one hand, we find systems that are dominantly other-worldly, in the sense of positing some being, reality, or mode of existence that is wholly different from anything encountered in ordinary sense-experience, or in the domain of natural events. Access to this transcendent, and eminently real domain, or entity, will be variously described by different metaphysicians. For Plato, for example, the eternal realm of intelligible Forms can only be discovered by a purified act of intellectual vision, yielding perfect and infallible rational knowledge, as contrasted with the blundering, shifting, and imperfect reliance on sensation and belief that characterize our modes of access to the world of ordinary experience. Similarly,

[3] Cf. W. H. Walsh, *Metaphysics* (London, 1963).

for a theist such as St. Thomas, the being of God wholly transcends the mode of existence belonging to the created world and
all that the latter contains. The classic attacks on metaphysics
by Hume and Kant, as well as the more recent efforts of the
logical positivists to eliminate metaphysics, have taken transcendent metaphsics as the primary target of their criticism.

On the other hand, the metaphysical views of thinkers such
as Aristotle or Spinoza are predominantly immanent or this-
worldly. Their preoccupation is, primarily, to fashion a categoreal scheme, or a systematic and comprehensive view of the
structure of Nature, in which all the variety of levels and modes
of existence that Nature produces, and that experience discerns,
will be seen in their proper relationships. The underlying scheme
of intelligibility that the metaphysician proposes, and that ordinary common sense or scientific experience could fill out, by way
of detail and corroboration, is a scheme that primarily has to
do with the world as open to our inspection, and not with some
transcendent reality.

The distinction between the two types of metaphyics we have
drawn, is at best a rough one, and it would be difficult to find
"pure" cases of either type. There are, for example, important
remnants of Platonism in Aristotle, and of supernaturalism in
Spinoza. Similarly, Descartes, Leibniz, Hegel, and Whitehead
display, in their thought, important "mixed" features which a
more detailed study of their systems would bring out. Finally,
even Plato and St. Thomas, whose thought exemplifies the
emphasis given to a transcendent reality, are, in many ways, also
interested in elaborating a categoreal scheme by which to achieve
some descriptive account of the world of ordinary experience.
Despite these qualifications, the division between "immanent" and
"transcendent" metaphysical schemes is valuable in helping to
discriminate the different types of main drive and interest of the
major metaphysical systems. Among other things, it helps correct any one-sided characterization of metaphysics itself.

Of central importance to any consideration of the scope of
metaphysics, is the question of the cognitive status of the results
it reaches. Despite the wide-ranging differences among metaphysical systems, there is one fairly dominant note of tacit agree-

ment that runs through much of the traditional literature of the subject. It is this: the successful pursuit of metaphysics will issue in a disclosure of the actual structure, or character, of the world—if not in its detail, then at least in its overall features. Most metaphysicians, in short, have been committed to some form of realistic conception of the power of metaphysical inquiry to give us the truth about the world. The form metaphysical knowledge will take, the method proposed to reach and warrant this knowledge, and the domain of entities of which this knowledge will be claimed, will, of course, be variously described by different metaphysical systems. Plato's account of the difference between the world of forms and the ordinary world of sensory experience; Aristotle's doctrine of substance; St. Thomas's distinction between the necessary being of God and the contingent status of the created world; Descartes's account of the world of extended bodily substances capable, in principle, of being rendered intelligible by a universal mathematical physics; Spinoza's doctrine of Nature as constituted of infinite attributes and intelligible in itself; Leibniz's doctrine of monadism; Hegel's doctrine of a dialectically unfolding universal Spirit that, in its absolute totality, is a coherent and rational order—all of these are intended, by their authors, to give us true insight into the actual structure of what exists, and not simply to be, in each case, a way of thinking about the world, with no claim to ultimate truth.

In saying that the authors of these traditional systems of thought are guided by a realistic conception of the power of metaphysical knowledge, I do not mean to assert that they were all "rationalists." Some indeed were. And even among the rationalists, the achievement of infallible knowledge was differently described: for Plato, it was of the realm of Forms that knowledge was to be had, while for Spinoza it was of the entire domain of Nature; and so on. Others, however, who also had a conception of infallible knowledge—for example, St. Thomas—reserved a special role for faith and revelation. On the other hand, many philosophers—of whom Aristotle is a leading example—gave strong emphasis to the role of experience in building up our knowledge of the details of the world of natural substances. However—this is the important point—these "empiricists" were just as strongly dominated by a realistic view of the cognitive status of metaphysical assertions and committments, as the rationalist or fideist views. For some, the model for metaphysical knowledge is found in the rigorous demonstrations of the mathematician, for others, it is the pattern of observationally-supported inductive generalizations of the empirical sciences. Some take the deliverances of unsophisticated common sense as their guide, while others subordinate the claims of metaphysical knowledge to the unquestioned certifications of ultimate truth, already (supposedly) given us in divine revelations. Despite these differences, however, most traditional conceptions of metaphysical knowledge were developed from within the framework of a common presupposition: that metaphysics is a body of discourse whose statements and arguments can be judged in terms of their literal truth and falsity; it is the proper task of metaphysics to give us a uniquely correct picture of the world.

This underlying and virtually unanimously-held presupposition of the character of metaphysics, however, is open to serious doubt. Because the underlying assumption as to the cognitive status of metaphysical assertions and arguments needs to be challenged, both the adherence to this or that positive metaphysical scheme as containing the truth, and the positivist attempt to eradicate metaphysics as a legitimate domain of inquiry altogether, are equally misguided.

One way of bringing out where the principal issue lies, in any consideration of the cognitive status of metaphysics, is to stress that what is involved, is not a question of the degree of *certainty* of metaphysical knowledge, but its *reality*. Traditionally, the controversies among rival metaphysical schools have been over questions of *methods* of achieving certainty, or of the proper *degree* of certainty one might achieve by the use of different methods. There have been many differences among both the proponents and attackers of metaphysical philosophies, as to the degree of certainty available to metaphysics. Some, who took mathematics as their guide, or appealed to the self-warranting acts of revelation, mystical insight, intellectual intuition, or faith, were prepared to claim comparable absolute certainty for their metaphysical systems. Others, of a more empirical temper of mind, would come down on the side of "belief," rather than of "knowledge." Metaphysics, they would say, could only give us probable or conjectural truths, not infallible and final insights into the structure of reality; we can only get, to adapt Plato's well-known phrase, "likely stories" about the ultimate character of reality. Taking elementary empirical science as their guide (rather than mathematics), these "empirical" metaphysicians tend to think of empirical science as primarily a matter of establishing inductive generalizations on the basis of observed individual instances. Such inductive generalizations are literally descriptive of Nature's phenomena, though lacking in certainty. Hence any application to individual instances, for purposes of prediction or explanation, would similarly be lacking in certainty. This conception of empirical science is then used as a model on which to base the claim that the arguments of metaphysics, too, could never give us certainty. The generalizations metaphysics attempts are far less securely supported by the evidence than the generalizations of science; and any claims made in their behalf, therefore, as adequate to interpret all experience and reality, are highly tentative and corrigible. Finally, those philosophers (the positivists, for example) who denied that it is possible for metaphysics to achieve either certainty or probability, would say metaphysics has zero certainty, since its statements lack the possibility of achieving *any* degree of evidential support. Most claims for one degree of certainty or another for metaphysical knowledge—from one extreme to the other, and running the entire gamut of possibilities—have thus been predicated on the assumption that metaphysics is concerned with and claims competence to disclose some real, antecedent structure possessed by the world. It is precisely this realistic assumption or presupposition, however, that needs to be examined. Once we see the possible grounds for challenging it, the question of the degree of certainty of metaphysical knowledge loses its central importance, and takes on a wholly different character.

The inadequacy of the realism inherent in traditional views of the cognitive status and powers of metaphysical systems cannot be proved. One can only hope to build up a case for showing the superiority of what we may call the "conceptualist" (or "instrumentalist") view of the cognitive role of metaphysical theories. Insofar as this can be done, one should not say that the realist view has been demonstrated to be wrong; rather, that it is far less adequate in helping us to understand what is involved in the construction and use of metaphysical theories. To be consistent, it will be necessary to admit, in advance, that the alternative view, here to be sketched, cannot claim any certainty—or even "probability"—for itself. Rather, it is a way of looking at metaphysical theories, and their cognitive status, that seems to make greater sense. However, whether it does make greater sense, or not, is a matter that calls for decision on the part of the reader and the student of metaphysical inquiries, and is not a matter of what "the facts tell us," or of the logical requiredness of some demonstrative proof.

The broad change from the traditional realistic way of thinking of metaphysical systems, to what I have called the "conceptualist" way, is one that has come about, in recent philosophy, as a result of the contributions made by several different lines of thought. Looking at the matter historically, it is possible to single out the following important contributions to its fuller development and clarification:

(1) The appeal to scientific knowledge as the very model and paradigm of what knowledge is, has always exercised a controlling influence over the minds of philosophers, from the days of Plato and Aristotle, down to the present time. The ways in which traditional rationalists and empiricists looked to what they took to be the character of science, as their guide in constructing their own systems, or in criticizing those of others, are familiar stories. Recent development in the philosophy of science, which benefit from the contributions of Henri Poincaré, Pierre Duhem, N. R. Campbell, and others, have been no less decisive in giving us a conception of knowledge that not only makes for a deeper appreciation of science, but has repercussions for metaphysics as well.

One of the major emphases in the philosophy of science that these writers have made familiar, is the role of *theories* in science. Theories need to be distinguished from inductive generalizations, and from reports of observational or experimental findings. They are free intellectual creative constructions. They feed upon models and analogies of various sorts, and are to be judged not in terms of any test of literal correspondence with the facts, but in terms of their general utility and pragmatic fruitfulness. Theories are not proven true nor disproven as false. Nor does it make sense to say that they can be judged with respect to their being successive approximations to some inherent structure of reality, as if they constituted finer and finer keys which one day might, finally, unlock the secrets of Nature; or as if they might allow us, at last, to fit all the parts of a puzzle together in a uniquely correct solution. Theories are ways of looking at phemonena. Some are better than others. And for certain types of problems one may, in fact, use one type of theory, while for other types of problems (in the same broad region of inquiry, for example in mechanics) one may use altogether different, "rival," or "incompatible" theories. All this may be done without any inconsistency whatever, and without having to assume that, some day, one will be able to replace these partially adequate theories by a single, true account.

Some aspects of the foregoing conception of the role and value of theories in science, can be extended to provide a better appreciation of the nature of metaphysical "theories." Instead of using as our model the older conceptions of a deductive scheme of proofs from self-evident first principles, or (as the other chief alternative), the empirically established fund of inductive generalizations of elementary science, we look to the role of scientific theory, as showing what can be accomplished on the most advanced levels of science. Metaphysical theories will be recogized to have much in common with scientific theories. They, too, will be found to result from the exploitation of some fundamental analogy, or way of looking at things. They, too, serve an important role of being devices of conceptual and systematic integration, binding whole ranges of "fact" together, and providing the means for their interpretation. Again, like scientific theories, metaphysical theories cannot be shown to be wrong, in the sense of being literally falsified. They can only be shown to be less consistent, less useful, less rich in conceptual connections, less comprehensive in their range, or founded on key analogies that are less deployable and fertile than those contained in other, rival, metaphysical theories.

At the same time, it would be necessary to guard against any exaggerated claims of similarity between metaphysical theories and scientific ones. There are important differences. One such difference has to do with the range of "facts" encompassed. Whereas scientific theories, however broad, are normally restricted to one type of subject matter, or level of natural phenomena, metaphysical theories are unrestricted in their scope. They would encompass all phases of human experience, and deal with anything that can be said to belong, in some way, to the world or to reality. And there is another, even more obvious difference: scientific theories can be tested. Particularly in the more developed sciences, such as mathematical physics, one can make deductions from the premises of a theory (or, in accordance with the rules of inference which, in one sense, the theory itself is) to determinate conclusions. These conclusions, if offered as predictions, must square with observed fact. Scientific theories, to qualify as acceptable, must lead to predictions that can be confirmed. Should a scientific theory continue to fail in this respect, it will normally be shelved in favor of some alternative theory. Again, along with predictive power, good theories must meet the additional requirements of logical simplicity and comprehensiveness of coverage. The "good sense" of the scientific community of experts, as Duhem puts it, tends to establish certain theories as satisfactory, at a certain stage of inquiry, and to sanction the dropping of others, not because the latter have been definitely disproved, but because they have been found wanting, according to these criteria. In short, there is a fair degree of agreement as to what the facts are that need explaining, before a theory can be seriously accepted by scientists.

In the case of metaphysical theories, however, there is not, clearly, the same interest in providing explanations of specific items of fact, nor in making predictions. Nor, finally, is there even any basic agreement as to what the "facts" are, that need to to be acknowledged in a metaphysical system. What is taken to be a "fact"—of relevance to a metaphysical system—is itself a matter of philosophic decision and point of view. The criteria for choosing among metaphysical systems are thus far less a matter of agreement than are comparable criteria for choice among competing scientific theories. Because there are these important differences, we cannot say that metaphysics is some kind of science, or super-science. It is not a science at all. It is not engaged in yielding explanations or predictions in the same way that science is. Nor, of course, is metaphysics some kind of encyclopedic summary or digest of the results, or findings, of the sciences. Metaphysics is metaphysics and not something else. It is neither science, nor poetry, nor religious discourse. Yet it is to our advantage to try to understand what it is, by seeing it in relation to all these different modes of discourse. That metaphysical theories have something in common with scientific theories, should not blind us to their important differences. The points in which they are alike, are in the use to which they put the creative imagination and the exploitation of analogies for the purposes of systematic conceptual integration. This is a matter which recent ways of thinking have brought to the fore, and in a way that was largely overlooked in treatments of metaphysics in earlier epochs.

(2) Contributions to the understanding of the cognitive status of metaphysical statements and arguments, were made by a number of recent philosophers, among them R. G. Collingwood and Friedrich Waismann. According to Collingwood, metaphysics is the science which investigates and makes explicit what he calls "absolute presuppositions."[4] To see what he means by this term, let us begin with an example he himself uses:

> Thus if you were talking to a pathologist about a certain disease and asked him 'What is the cause of the event E which you say sometimes happens in this disease?' he will reply 'The cause of E is C'; and if he were in a communicative mood he might go on to say 'That was established by So-and-so, in a piece of research that is now regarded as classical.' You might go on to ask: 'I suppose before So-and-so found out what the cause of E was, he was quite sure it had a cause?' The answer would be 'Quite sure, of course.' If you now say 'Why?' he will probably answer 'Because everything that happens has a cause.' If you are importunate enough to ask 'But

[4] R. G. Collingwood, *An Essay on Metaphysics* (Oxford, 1940).

how do you know that everything that happens has a cause?' he will probably blow up right in your face, because you have put your finger on one of his absolute presuppositions. . . But if he keeps his temper and gives you a civil and candid answer, it will be to the following effect. 'That is a thing we take for granted in my job. We don't question it. We don't try to verify it. It isn't a thing anybody has discovered, like microbes or the circulation of the blood. It is a thing we just take for granted.'[5]

According to Collingwood, "absolute presuppositions" have a different logical status from what he calls "relative presuppositions." Thus, if I were to use a tape-measure to answer the question how long a certain object is, I should tacitly presuppose that the tape-measure I am using is sufficiently accurate to give a reliable reading. However, I might question this presupposition, and ask "Is this tape-measure accurate?" I might then proceed to determine, by suitable procedures, whether, indeed, it is accurate, and thus obtain an answer to my question. The proposition about the accuracy of the tape-measure which I assumed, but did not initially question, Collingwood calls a "relative presupposition." It, too, as is the case with ordinary propositions, can be considered an answer to some question. It makes sense to inquire into its truth or falsity, and to undertake to verify it, in order to determine which of these it is.

By contrast, however, with relative presuppositions, absolute presuppositions are not ordinary propositions. They are not answers to questions which can be said to be true or false, and it makes no sense to undertake to verify them. Absolute presuppositions cannot be said to be confirmed or disconfirmed by anything found in experience. Nor can we appeal to ordinary criteria of formal, or logical, consistency by which to judge the acceptability of some particular set of absolute presuppositions. To one whose absolute presuppositions have been unearthed *and challenged*, the reply would be, simply, that to deny them would be absurd. In saying this, the individual shows that his absolute presuppositions serve as the unquestioned, ultimate conceptual framework in terms of which he looks at the world, guides his inquiries, and interprets his experience. Collingwood recognizes, of course,

[5] *Ibid.*, p. 31.

that there are differences among men in the absolute presuppositions they adopt, though there are also cases of overlapping and partial agreement.

Now, it might be thought that to exhibit absolute presuppositions in their operation as interpreting our experience, and to attempt to defend or criticize their relative effectiveness in accomplishing these tasks, would be the proper taks of metaphysics. For Collingwood, however, the proper task of metaphysics is *historical*. According to him, it it *not* the task of metaphysics to advocate some particular scheme of absolute presuppositions, or to show its relative superiority to some other scheme. Rather, what the metaphysician must do, is to survey what in fact have been, or are, the absolute presuppositions made *by others*—to bring these out into the open, and to report on them.

My own principal interest, in the present discussion, is in Collingwood's analysis of the role of absolute presuppositions, as a valuable contribution to our understanding of the nature of metaphysics. I should wish, however, to reject Collingwood's strained and odd theory that metaphysics is simply a second-order historical investigation of the absolute presuppositions prevalent at different epochs. It is not necessary, however, to accept this account of the purely historical character of metaphysics, in order to appreciate the merit of what he has to say about the cognitive role, or logical status, of absolute presuppositions. On the contrary, it would seem to me that the putting forth and detailed working-out of absolute presuppositions, is better described by the term "metaphysics," than the kind of historical study Collingwood has in mind.

(3) As another example of fruitful contributions made by recent philosophers to a theory of the cognitive status of metaphysical theories, I turn next to the views of Friedrich Waismann. Building on the broad framework of ideas contained in Wittgenstein's later writings, Waismann makes some acute observations about the status of metaphysics, in his essay "How I See Philosophy."[6] Waismann stresses the fact that in considering the role of metaphysics, we must avoid the error committed by the posi-

---

[6] F. Waismann, "How I See Philosophy," in *Contemporary British Philosophy* (Third Series), edited by H. D. Lewis (London, 1956), pp. 447-490.

tivists who condemn metaphysics as nonsense. "To say that metaphysics is nonsense *is* nonsense."[7] For, to understand what metaphysics is, we must not assume it is some form of science or
mathematics *manqué*. It is not the task of metaphysics to give us
information or explanations of a factual sort, as in the case of the
empirical sciences. Nor must it be thought as giving demonstrative
proofs in the manner of mathematics. Indeed, not only are there
no proofs or theorems in metaphysics; one can say "there are no
questions which can be decided, Yes or No."[8]

   This is not to deny that there are arguments in philosophy. On
the contrary, it is the task of the metaphysician to try to "build
up a case" for his point of view by offering arguments of all sorts.
These resemble, in many ways, the argument a lawyer might
present. There is no question here of irrefutable proofs from self-
evident premises. Nor is the outcome of such arguments something which can be verified, in any simple or direct way, by
appealing to the facts of experience. What is called for, instead, is
something like a *decision*. However, unlike the decision of guilt
or innocence that the lawyer aims at, what distinguishes the
primary interest of the metaphysician is the advocacy of a certain
way of looking at the world. His concern is to offer us a *vision*
of the world; and when he points to the relative inadequacies of
older, inherited visions, he proposes a re-vision of the world in new
and, he believes, more fruitful terms. Such major conceptual revisions are what the great philosophers accomplished.

   Metaphysicians, like artists, are the antennae of their time: they
   have a flair for feeling which way the spirit is moving. (There is a
   Rilke poem about it.) There is something visionary about great
   metaphysicians as if they had the power to see beyond the horizons
   of their time. Take, for instance, Descartes' work. That it has given
   rise to endless metaphysical quibbles is certainly a thing to hold
   against it. Yet if we attend to the spirit rather than to the words
   I am greatly inclined to say that there is a certain grandeur in it,
   a prophetic aspect of the comprehensibility of nature, a bold antici-
   pation of what has been achieved in science at a much later date.
   The true successors of Descartes were those who translated the

[7] *Ibid.*, p. 489.
[8] *Ibid.*, p. 447.

spirit of this philosophy into deeds, not Spinoza or Malebranche but Newton and the mathematical description of nature.[9]

What Waismann calls attention to, of great importance to our present theme, is that although metaphysics is a rational enterprise and uses arguments to support a point of view, it cannot be said that any metaphysical point of view is true, or that it is false. It cannot be said to have been either proved or refuted by any appeal to logic, or by any appeal to experience. The life of a metaphysical system is the way it has us look at the world, and what we see in looking at the world in one way rather than another. We cannot say that one system, rather than another, gives us a correct, or true, picture of the facts—of the way the world *really is;* we can only value what has been lit up for us by seeing the world through the eyes of the metaphysician. "Though to an outsider he [the metaphysician] appears to advance all sorts of arguments, this is not the decisive point. What is decisive is that he has seen things from a new angle of vision."[10]

In the above sketch, I have singled out just a few of the leading contributions to the overall viewpoint that sees in a metaphysical system the presence of a conceptual scheme that is not to be regarded as being either true or false, that nevertheless offers a rationally elaborated vision of the world, and that rests upon some guiding analogy or "root metaphor."[11] In terms of this approach, we can understand a metaphysical system for what it is, particularly when compared to such diverse modes of intellectual construction as poetic myths, scientific theories, or practical decisions. A metaphysical scheme is not exactly like any one of these, although it bears some resemblances to each of them. When Aristotle developed the concept of substance, at the very heart of his metaphysical vision, he took the kind of thing he was familiar with in his study of biological organisms, and used it as the basic model in terms of which to understand the world in all its diversity. The notions of matter and form, potentiality and actuality, teleology

[9] *Ibid.*, pp. 489-90.

[10] *Ibid.*, p. 483.

[11] For the use of the term "root metaphor" in understanding "world hypotheses," see S. C. Pepper, *World Hypotheses* (Berkeley and Los Angeles, 1948), Chap. 5. Cf. D. M. Emmet, *The Nature of Metaphysical Thinking* (London, 1945), and W. H. Walsh, *op. cit.*

and necessity, etc., (as ramifications of the concept of substance) are offered by him as fundamental conceptual tools in terms of which to interpret all that exists. Similarly, when St. Thomas worked out the details of a theistic metaphysics, he elaborated a view of the world in which the complex images of Father, Judge, and Divine Craftsman were made to serve central roles of description and explanation. One could traverse the history of metaphysical speculation in this fashion, and identify the subtle, complicated, startling, fresh, or shockingly paradoxical visions contained in each of the great metaphysical systems from Parmenides to Whitehead. Whatever the peculiar absolute presuppositions, root-metaphors, or conceptual revisions these systems exhibit, they exemplify—each in its own way—the *sui generis* intellectual contribution that belongs to metaphysics. For each illustrates the fashioning of a conceptual system to fill the perennial human need to obtain some unifying, total vision of the world in which we live.

Our present focal question is whether philosophy, in the sense of metaphysics, has the resources by which to establish either that there is, or is not, a reason-for-the-existence-of-the-world, and, if it answers this question in the affirmative, to say in what such a reason-for-the-existence-of-the-world consists.

Now, to this question it may be said, by way of initial objection, that the possibility of finding an appropriate answer does not even exist. For, it may be argued, the very fact that we have failed to give any specific content to the phrase "reason-for-the-existence-of-the-world," other than by means of contextual definition, makes it impossible, as a matter of logic, for any answer to be given. Unless we know what we are looking for, how can we tell whether we shall succeed or fail in finding it? And is not the phrase "reason-for-the-existence-of-the-world" so completely lacking in any determinate meaning, that without any advance clues as to what to look for, we are asking a senseless question? The reply to this objection is twofold: In the first place, the phrase "reason-for-the-existence-of-the-world" is not wholly devoid of meaning, as the objection alleges, since we can say that *if* it existed, and *if* it were known, it would serve to explain, uniquely, the existence of the world; and this, already—though meager—gives the phrase in question enough meaning for us to be able to operate with it. The phrase is not, as claimed, wholly indeterminate and vacuous, although, by the very nature of the case, it is impossible to give it any more meaning, short of making specific metaphysical claims. These metaphysical claims would either specify further characteristics by which to identify such a reason, or else be of the kind that belong to a metaphysical system which dispenses with such a notion altogether. And this leads to the second difficulty with the above-stated objection. It is that to assert there is no reason-for-the-existence-of-the-world, is already to engage in the metaphysical game, and to make first-order claims about the world. But to do this, is to beg the question, as far as the present phase of our discussion is concerned. We should want to know by what rational method metaphysics can establish either that there is, or is not, a reason-for-the-existence-of-the-world; and it will not do, at the outset to have already settled this issue, without advancing one's reasons for making a particular choice. We should, therefore, need to examine, explicitly, the grounds for saying that metaphysics, by the very nature of the kind of study it is, is (or, is not) able to provide a rational way of knowing that there is, or is not, a reason-for-the-existence-of-the-world. And it is to this task that I turn next. My argument shall be, that metaphysics is *not* able to provide a satisfactory rational means by which to answer the question whether there is, or is not, a reason-for-the-existence-of-the-world. But at least we shall not have settled this question by default, or by begging it in advance.

Let us return, once again, to a point made in an earlier discussion. What we are given—of relevance to metaphysics—is the existence of the world. However, we are not given, among the "facts" from which we must start, either that there is, or is not, a reason-for-the-existence-of-the-world. Neither the presence of such a reason, nor its absence, is a datum of our experience of the world, in the same way, for example, that we can properly say the existence of the world is such a datum. We have also seen that, failing all knowledge of whether there is a reason-for-the-existence-of-the-world, we cannot rule out any possibilities as to what such a reason might be, *if* it exists. Thus, we know of reasons which men assign or give, and we say that until men invent or give such reasons, there is no sense in saying that such reasons exist independently of, or antecedently to, human thought and their expression in discourse. We also know of reasons which we discover as investigators; these reasons are had by other minds (human agents) who act in some way, or make something, purposefully. Let us assume that, if there were a reason-for-the-existence-of-the-world, it would be of one or another of the following kinds: (1) A reason-for-the-existence-of-the-world might be a reason which existed only insofar as men (i.e., metaphysicians) assign such a reason; and, until men assign it, there is no sense in saying there is a reason-for-the-existence-of-the-world; or, (2) there might be a reason-for-the-existence-of-the-world, which, if it existed, would have to exist, somehow, independently and objectively—though *not*, of course, in the mind of some other human being. The question we now have to ask is this. Given these two forms in which a possible reason-for-the-existence-of-the-world might exist (let us call them, for short, "an *assigned* reason-for-the-existence-of-the-world" and "an *objective* reason-for-the-existence-of-the-world "), is it within the province of metaphysics to establish by some rational means, that there is (or is not) either type of reason-for-the-existence-of-the-world? My argument will seek to show that metaphysics cannot provide, by any rational means, the knowledge of the presence, or absence, of a reason-for-the-existence-of-the-world of either sort.

We have seen that a characteristic feature of any metaphysical system (whether immanent or transcendent) is that it is founded on the use of some guiding analogy, root-metaphor, or set of absolute presuppositions. It constitutes a way of regarding the world, and nothing more. Therefore, whether some metaphysical system affirms that there is a reason-for-the-existence-of-the-world, or, on the contrary, denies it and does without this idea altogether, it rests on some set of absolute presuppositions. The difficulty with saying that a metaphysical theory gives us a rational way of knowing there is (or, is not) a reason-for-the-existence-of-the-world is that neither a postulate nor an absolute presupposition can provide this knowledge. To say there is, or is not, a reason-for-the-existence-of-the-world, as a matter of first principle, is to beg the question. It is possible to settle any question merely by postulating the answer. Clearly, this is no ground for saying that we have thereby *rationally* established the answer selected. There is, in fact, no essential difference between this postulation and a declaration of faith. However, a declaration of faith is not a rational way of achieving knowledge. If, moreover, one is willing to settle the issue whether there is, or is not, a reason-for-the-existence-of-the-world merely by declaring one's faith, what is superior to the faith of the theory that rests on the Principle of Sufficient Reason for this purpose, to the faith of the irrationalist or sceptic who declares that whereas all other things may have their reasons, there is no reason-for-the-existence-of-the-world?

One might possibly reply to this, that merely as acts of faith, admittedly, there is no difference between them; however, the differences are consequential upon accepting one or the other absolute presupposition (together with other, related presuppositions, to fill out the premises of an entire metaphysical system), and that we must look to see what can be done with metaphysical systems in interpreting the entire range of our experience. And, for example, the upholder of the Principle of Sufficient Reason, who believes there is a reason-for-the-existence-of-the-world, might say that his system, but not that of his opponent, does greater justice to the facts, and can be shown to be superior to the systems of the sceptic, materialist, or agnostic.

The reply to this last objection, however, is that there is no satisfactory way in which one can show that any one metaphysical scheme is superior to the rest. There are no commonly accepted criteria by which to judge metaphysical systems, and to justify our saying that one system is clearly to be preferred to all the rest. For example, we cannot—as a supposed common criterion for judging all metaphysical theories, say we must compare each metaphysical theory with the world as it really is to see to what extent there is some degree of correspondence between what the metaphysical theory asserts and how the world really is. The very concept of "the world as it really is", or the use of the test of correspondence, betray the presence of some particular metaphysical interpretation, and need not be adopted as working concepts (and *a fortiori*, as parts of a criterion for judging metaphysical theories) by all other metaphysical theories. It follows from all of this, that if the question of the existence or non-existence of a reason-for-the-existence-of-the-world is a matter of the way in which a particular conceptual scheme is constructed, and how the existence of the world is to be regarded from a particular perspective, then we must be prepared to recognize that the question of truth or falsity, as this applies to ordinary descriptive statements of fact, would have no applicability or relevance here. Just as we would not say that one poet or myth-maker gives us the literal truth (either completely, or by way of approximation to some final truth); and just as we would not say that a scientific theory (as distinguished from statements of observed regularities or of individual occurrences) is literally true, or approximates to the final truth; and just as we would not say that some scheme of moral rules or some scheme of esthetic appraisals is literally truer than some other scheme; so, in a general way, we should abstain from saying that this or that metaphysical scheme of looking at the world is truer than some other.

There is another objection to saying that the construction of a metaphysical scheme, could rationally establish that there is, or is not, a reason-for-the-existence-of-the-world. Of the broad possibilities canvassed earlier, according to which a reason-for-the-existence-of-the-world could be either an "assigned" reason or an "objective" reason, it would only be the latter, in the last analysis, that would count. We should want to know, quite apart from any conceptual scheme, whether there is, or is not, a reason-for-the-existence-of-the-world. How could this be done, however? In the first place, we cannot step outside our metaphysical sytems to look at the world "directly." Even if, *per impossible,* this could be done, where should we turn, and how should we proceed? Take the simple and familiar situation in which, as investigators, we *can* establish that *other human beings* had reasons for what they did or made. We establish that they had such reasons, and what they were, by getting evidence of the relevant kind (but not by resorting to a theory, myth, or metaphysical construction.) In the simple, straightforward case, this consists in *asking* the person in question, or in examining some document, or other reliable source, for the necessary information. The relevant evidence is obtained through some channel of sensory experience and by interrogation. These resources, however, are completely lacking in trying to establish that there is a reason-for-the-existence-of-the-world. Where, then, shall we turn? We are completely lacking in any clues. The prospects of getting knowledge by some form of "direct" inspection (without having to resort to faith, postulation, or the analogizing speculations of some metaphysical conceptual system) are simply unavailable. Hence this avenue of establishing knowledge of the existence or absence of a reason-for-the-existence-of-the-world is not open to us. We must admit our total ignorance.

CHAPTER XIII

Some Possible Objections

I HAVE ARGUED that the mystery of existence consists in the fact that we have no rational method by which we can know whether there is a reason-for-the-existence-of-the-world, not merely in the ordinary senses of the term "reason," but in a special sense of the term as used in the expression "reason-for-the-existence-of-the-world." I wish to consider, now, by way of conclusion, a number of possible objections to my general thesis.

(1) Someone might argue as follows. "You say we don't have any rational method by which to obtain an answer to the question you raise. Let us grant there is a mystery, because, as you say, there is no suitable method for reaching an answer. This does not mean there is in fact no answer. It only means that there is no way by which any rational human being can reach it. Since there needs to be an answer—whether or not we have the means of knowing it—let us consider in what this would consist. There are two possibilities. To take your own way of putting the matter, either there is a reason-for-the-existence-of-the-world, or there is no reason-for-the-existence-of-the-world. Let us assume, for the sake of argument, contrary to your supposition, that man were given the correct answer. If the answer he were given were the assurance that there is a reason-for-the-existence-of-the-world (and, perhaps, even some partial or total insight into what this is), then one would have to say there no longer would be, for him, a mystery of existence. Man would know there is a reason-for-the-existence-of-the-world, and this would be sufficient to reduce, or

remove, the mystery you posit. On the other hand, let us suppose that, in some way, the answer were obtainable by man, that there is no reason-for-the-existence-of-the-world. According to the way you have defined the mystery of existence, again, there would no longer be any mystery. For we should now know there is no reason-for-the-existence-of-the-world; and this answer, too, is enough to remove the agnosticism you take as the essence of mystery.

"Let us consider what would be man's reaction to this latter possibility, were he given, in some way or other, this final assurance that there is no reason-for-the-existence-of-the-world. Do you really think that, confronted with the existence of the world, man would still not experience a different, and, perhaps more profound sense of the mystery of existence? For would he still not be astounded that there is a world, even though there is no reason-for-its-existence? And would he not persist in asking a different question, now, which might be put as: 'How could it be that the world exists, even though, as I know, there is no reason-for-the-existence-of-the-world?' And would not such a man, in that situation, after all, be no different from that in which *we* now find ourselves? For, why introduce the idea of a special 'reason-for-the-existence-of-the-world'? Why not take the term 'reason' as we ordinarily understand it, and—since, as your own analysis has shown, there is no warrant in saying there is a reason for the existence of the world—simply let it go at that? In the face of this lack of knowledge of any reason for the existence of the world, what your sense of mystery amounts to, is simply a sense of astonishment, an emotional reaction, and nothing more. It is unnecessary to complicate matters by bringing in a special sense of 'reason,' in the form of a 'reason-for-the-existence-of-the-world,' and to locate the meaning of mystery in a lack of knowledge as to how to answer the question 'Is there a reason-for-the-existence-of-the-world?' "

Such an objection would appear to have much in its favor, yet I think it rests on certain false assumptions. In exposing these, I hope to be able to show the greater merit of the kind of position for which I have been arguing. The basic flaw in the above argument is that it violates one of the conditions on which it is necessary, I believe, to insist. The critic asks us, "for the sake of the argument"—a seemingly harmless phrase—to assume that, since we ask the question "Is there a reason-for-the-existence-of-the-world?", there must be an answer somewhere, for someone, some-how. He asks us "to assume for the sake of argument" that we know which of the answers is correct; and he proceeds to point out the consequences of this knowledge. The flaw in this argu-ment, however, is that it fails to take seriously the character of the question "Is there a reason-for-the-existence-of-the-world?", namely, that it is unanswerable. He asks us to answer it, anyhow, if only "hypothetically." But this is what we cannot do. The mystery is not in the world itself. The mystery, rather, is in man's not having any way of rationally answering this ques-tion which he asks concerning the world. Since there is no rational way of answering this question, the mystery—which is a fact of human experience about the world—persists, and cannot be removed by the device the critic suggests.

Nor, therefore, does his attempt to show that, under one of the alternative "answers" he asks us to examine (that there is no reason-for-the-existence-of-the-world), our sense of mystery would reduce to being nothing more than an emotion of aston-ishment. This reduction has been accomplished only by positing an answer to a question which, in fact, we cannot have. Therefore, the asking of the question, and the fact that we realize it is un-answerable by any rational method, is as essential to what the mystery is, as the feeling that accompanies it. Also, of course, the critic's complaint that, by introducing a special sense of "reason," in the form of "reason-for-the-existence-of-the-world," an unnecessary complication has been made, since it is sufficient to operate with the senses of "reason" we already have, would have to be answered by reviewing the kinds of arguments and considerations previously given to support the need for this use of "reason." If these have any merit at all, the proper way of expressing the mystery of existence is, indeed, by means of the fundamental question "Is there a reason-for-the-existence-of-the-world?", and not simply by asking "Why does the world exist?", or "What reason is there for the existence of the world?" And to this preferred formulation of the question, I have argued, there is no answer. It is in the realization and conviction that there is no answer, that the human experience of the mystery of the existence of the world consists.

(2) Another type of objection that might be offered to the way I have sought to analyze the concept of the mystery of existence, would be to say the analysis fails in at least one respect, namely, in locating the element of mystery in the wrong place. The proper mystery lies, it may be said, in the existence of the world, whereas the analysis that has been given, locates the element of mystery in the lack of a possible answer to the question whether there is a reason-for-the-existence-of-the-world. To stress the latter, is to stress our ignorance about how to obtain an answer to a question. It does not, as it should, stress the fact that it is the existence of the world, not human ignorance, which is the primary fact of importance in any analysis of the mystery of existence.

To this objection, I should reply as follows. Let us grant it is the existence of the world which arouses our sense of mystery, and that if mystery were nothing more than a statement of human ignorance—a fact about us alone—and not, also, about the world, the analysis would be faulty. But can such a charge justly be levelled against the foregoing discussion? For what, after all, is it about the existence of the world that constitutes a mystery? Is it not, as we have seen, that *we* wish to know whether *it* has a reason, and that we are unable to supply an answer to this question? It is not the existence of the world, alone, that is the mystery; it is in the fact that we, who are aware of the existence of the world, ask the kinds of questions we do. The fact that we come to recognize these questions to be unanswerable, tells us, not simply something about ourselves; it tells us something about ourselves responding to the existence of the world in a special way, in terms of an unanswerable question. The mystery, so to speak, is in the relation, or interaction, between the puzzled mind and the existence of the world, not in either one, taken separately.

(3) It is sometimes said that it would be futile to look for any solution to the mystery of existence, since any possible answer would only beget other questions of the same type, and so would merely serve to transfer the locus of mystery, rather than to dispel

it entirely. As an example of such metaphysically unsatisfactory "answers," one may point to theism. By solving the mystery of existence of the world, in terms of the doctrine of creation by a transcendent Deity, it becomes necessary to admit the impenetrable mystery in the very existence and character of God himself. God, being wholly other, cannot be comprehended in any positive way. His being, therefore, is a profound mystery.

Now, without stopping to inquire whether such a complaint against theism is warranted or not, it can be replied that, from the point of view of the agnostic position here being defended, this criticism has no merit. For it is of the essence of an agnostic position not only to disclaim any knowledge of *whether* there is a reason-for-the-existence-of-the-world, but also to decline to speculate about *what* it might be, *if* there were such a reason. Since we are wholly lacking in this knowledge, it makes no sense to anticipate what the situation would be like, if there were a reason-for-the-existence-of-the-world, and we knew it. We simply do not know what the character of such a reason-for-the-existence-of-the-world might be (if there were one); hence, we cannot anticipate that it would only provoke the raising of a further mystery.

There is, moreover, a second point. If there were a reason-for-the-existence-of-the-world, and it were known, this would remove the mystery of the existence of the world. Whether or not it, in turn, led to the posing of further questions about itself, would not in any way diminish the effectiveness of the answer such a reason-for-the-existence-of-the-world would give to the mystery of the existence of the world. And it is with the mystery of the existence of the world, that I have been concerned. I think it would be wholly futile, therefore, to speculate about what further mysteries there may be connected with an altogether hypothetical and speculatively entertained reason-for-the-existence-of-the-world.

(4) Let me turn to another objection, this time to the account given of the mystery of existence as defined in terms of the unanswerability of a question. It may be asked whether by "unanswerability" is meant something absolute or relative. And the objection may be put as follows: "If the question posing the mystery of existence is absolutely unanswerable, does this not presume a form of positive knowledge, namely, that there cannot be

an answer to the question; and is not this claim to final and positive knowledge inconsistent with the general position you have adopted? For if, on the one hand, you stress the need for suspension of judgment, and a withholding of any claim to have an answer to the question expressing the mystery of existence, how can such a suspension of judgment be reconciled with the dogmatic assurance that no answer is possible? On the other hand, if you say that the unanswerability to the question posing the mystery of existence is only relatively unanswerable, does this not, by the same token, allow that the question may also be answerable? If one abstains from making any final, or absolute, judgment about possible answers, should we not leave room in our philosophy for the possibility of answering the question? In this case, if an answer is possible, what becomes of your claim that the mystery of existence is an unanswerable question, one for which no answer is *ever* possible?"

By way of reply, I should remark, in the first place, that if presented with the two alternatives "absolute" and "relative," and asked to make a choice, I should wish to characterize my view as a claim to the *relative* unanswerability of the question expressing the mystery of existence. However, in accepting this label, it is immediately necessary to indicate how this is to be understood, and why the allegedly inconsistent consequence that would follow from this—that unanswerability, if meant only "relatively," also allows for answerability—does not, in fact, follow.

In saying that the mystery of existence is unanswerable, I mean "unanswerable relative to the already known rational methods of achieving knowledge of reasons." If "reason" is understood in its ordinary uses—as "purpose," "scientific explanation," or "evidence"—then it makes no sense to say there is a reason for the existence of the world. To this extent, the question "Is there a reason for the existence of the world?" *can* be "answered," namely, by dissolving the question and showing that the question stems from a misuse and misapplication of the ordinary uses of "reason." On the other hand, if "reason" is allowed to include, as a possible extension of its meaning, the idea of a "reason-for-the-existence-of-the-world," then no use of known rational methods (of common sense, science, or philosophic argument) can possibly establish that there is a reason-for-the-existence-of-the-world. The unanswerability of the question "Is there a reason-for-the-existence-of-the-world?" is relative to the use of these known rational methods.

I should not wish to dogmatize about the possibility that some other "rational method," not hitherto known by man, might be developed in the future course of human evolution, or perhaps is already possessed by some special type of "mind" wholly unknown to us. But we, now, have no knowledge of such a method; nor do we have any rational method within our present resources by which we could undertake to establish the existence or character of this "method." In this respect, the idea of a "possible rational method for determining whether or not there is a reason-for-the-existence-of-the-world" is something that we can only, at best, leave room for in our philosophy (as a gap, or schema that might, or might not, be filled), but on which it is futile to speculate.

If one wishes to say, therefore, that there *may* be an answer to the question posing the mystery of existence, I should ask, first, how this "mystery" is to be expressed, and, secondly, how the term "answer" is being used. These terms cannot be left unanalyzed, or their meanings taken for granted. With respect to the first task—the need to clarify the use of the expression "the mystery of existence"—I have tried to establish why it is best to transform, in a series of steps, the original, crudely formulated question (1) "Why is there something rather than nothing?" first, into (2) "Why does the world exist?", and then into (3) "Is there a reason for the world's existence?", and, finally, into (4) "Is there a reason-for-the-existence-of-the-world?" This last form of the question, I suggest, does adequately express the mystery of existence. (While there may be better ways of formulating this mystery, which do not fall into the pitfalls connected with the use of the questions previously criticised and discarded, I do not know of such alternative formulations. However, I should certainly be prepared to grant that some more adequate account than mine, might be given.)

As to the analysis of the term "answer," since the answerability or unanswerability of the question "Is there a reason-for-the-existence-of-the-world?" has to be examined in connection with a possible method for answering it, I have undertaken to show why none of the actual, known methods suffice to answer this question. It is relatively to these known rational methods that, I have argued, we cannot know whether there is a reason-for-the-existence-of-the-world. However, as to whether there is some other "possible rational method" which would suffice to establish whether there is a reason-for-the-existence-of-the-world, I do not wish to make any claim; for, I do not see how we can obtain any knowledge about this "possible method," given our present human situation and our present resources.

In summary then: (1) By using the already known rational methods, we *can* answer the question "Is there a reason for the existence of the world?"—where "reason" is understood in its ordinary uses (as "purpose," "scientific explanation," or "evidence for a statement"). The answer is "There is no reason for the existence of the world." (2) By using the already known rational methods, the question "Is there a reason-for-the-existence-of-the-world?" is *unanswerable*. The unanswerability of this question is relative to known rational methods. It is this type of unanswerability that I have stressed in my examination of the mystery of existence. (3) If one introduces the idea of a *possible* rational method, uniquely suited to discover whether there is a reason-for-the-existence-of-the-world, then, relative to this possible rational method, the question "Is there a reason-for-the-existence-of-the-world?" is *not* unanswerable. However, since, as human beings, we have no way of knowing that there is, in fact, such a rational method, or how we might achieve it through the use of the methods we now have, the possibility that this question might be answered by such a possible method, is, for us, wholly speculative and gratuitous.

*   *   *   *   *

The mystery of existence occupies a position in our efforts to come to terms, philosophically, with the world at large, that is, in some respects, similar to the fact of death, in our efforts to come to terms with the conditions of our own individual life. Each, in its own way, marks the impenetrable boundary that defeats our deepest longings: the one marks the limit to any hope of understanding the existence of the world; the other marks the limit to our hope of finding endless satisfaction in all that we achieve in life. Out of the refusal to acknowledge the first type of limit are born on the one hand those metaphysical schemes that would—in one way or another—penetrate the abysmal mystery of existence and solve it. Out of the other, are born all those religious schemes that promise eternal salvation or immortality to the person. Such systems of thought betray, all too clearly, the attempt to circumvent the genuine limits to human knowledge and aspiration, by indulging in what is, after all, only a fancied perfection and a false idealism. They cannot inspire confidence in their solutions.

A more responsible and candid philosophy would start by acknowledging the facts of the mystery of existence, and the final defeat that awaits us in our personal death. To do so requires courage, clearheadedness, and resignation in the face of the inevitable. However, just as an awareness of one's own death cannot, for a sane and healthy life, be the sole preoccupation of one's thoughts, or the principal factor in determining the goals of one's life, so, an awareness of the mystery of existence cannot be the sole item in a well-rounded philosophical cosmology. Rather, they set the limits within which man must pursue rationality. In the measure in which, collectively as a race, or individually in our personal lives, we manage to introduce, or find, patches of goodness, truth, and beauty, to that extent we have succeeded in counterbalancing and softening the blows of our ultimate defeat. Science, in its manifold and endless quest for intelligibility, can never remove the mystery of existence; but it can make the world, as found, comprehensible in its details, and in the comings-and-goings of its parts. Moral idealism, similarly— the pursuit of values in all those dimensions of personal and social experience that give life meaning and purpose, and rescue it from futility—cannot overcome the fact of death; but it can cheat it, to some extent, of total victory.

In developing the theme of the mystery of existence, in this book, I can only hope to have pointed to some first (or last) words that need to be said in working out a more complete philosophical cosmology, an outlook on the world at large.

INDEX